THE SMITHSONIAN
ATLAS OF
THE AMAZON

THE SMITHSONIAN
ATLAS OF
THE AMAZON

Michael Goulding   Ronaldo Barthem   Efrem Ferreira

Cartography by Roy Duenas

SMITHSONIAN BOOKS • Washington and London

© 2003 by the Smithsonian Institution

In association with Oakwood Arts

Copy editing: Princeton Editorial Associates, Inc.
Production and design: Frank and Merry Thomasson
Designer: Alexandra Littlehales

Library of Congress Cataloging-in-Publication Data
Goulding, Michael.
  The Smithsonian atlas of the Amazon / Michael Goulding, Ronaldo Barthem,
and Efrem Ferreira ; cartography by Roy Duenas.
      p.   cm.
  Includes bibliographical references (p.   ).
  ISBN 1-58834-135-6 (alk. paper)
  1. Rivers—Brazil—Amazon River Watershed. 2. Geomorphology—Brazil—
Amazon River Watershed. 3. Stream ecology—Brazil—Amazon River Watershed.
4. Amazon River Watershed. I. Barthem, Ronaldo. II. Ferreira, Efrem Jorge
Gondim. III. Title.
  GB1264.A5 G68 20003
  551.48 ' 3 ' 09811—dc21   2002030541

British Library Cataloging-in-Publication Data available

Manufactured in Hong Kong
09 08 07 06 05 04 03 02   5 4 3 2 1

♾ The paper used in this publication meets the minimum requirements of the American National Standard for Information Sciences—Permanence of Paper for Printed
Library Materials ANSI Z39.48-1984.

OAKWOOD
ARTS

PAGE 1: **BLACKWATER RIVER**
The Negro flows through rainforest and over sands to form the world's
largest blackwater river.

PAGE 2-3: **NEGRO HEADWATERS**
Cataract on the Vaupés, the main Colombian headwater of the Negro.

RIGHT: **PARÁ RIVER**
The Pará River south of the island of Marajó receives muddy waters from the Amazon.

CONTENTS

◄ **AMAZON HEADWATERS**
A deep gorge of the Apurimac in Peruvian headwaters of the Amazon.

LIST OF MAPS

PREFACE

A *mazon*. The name conjures images of mystery, magic, and bewildering biodiversity in a land of seemingly endless rivers and rainforests. It is here that abundant rainfall, continual warmth, and a drainage basin nearly the size of the United States have allowed our planet's most diverse and extensive rainforest to evolve.

About one-half of the rain that falls in the Amazon is recycled through the rainforest; the other half gathers in streams and rivers and runs to the ocean. From the Andes to the Atlantic, the rivers slice through the rainforest and in many places invade it with floodwaters to form what is perhaps the most singular feature of the great region—its flooded forests. Fish, birds, mammals, and countless numbers of invertebrates meet in these far-flung habitats and remind us that the rainforest and rivers are indeed tightly connected in the evolution of Amazonian life.

Yet the headwaters of the Amazon's great rivers extend far beyond the rainforest and reach locations ranging from the earthquake-shaken valleys of the high and dry Andes in the west to remnants of ancient uplands in the east, which drifted with South America when it separated from Africa more than 100 million years ago. This book is part of the story of this strange and wonderful land as seen from 14 of its largest rivers, including its longest and largest, the Amazon.

Not only is the Amazon the largest river in the world, but two of its transnational tributaries—the Madeira and the Negro—are themselves among the ten largest rivers in the world. The Amazon Basin is a giant complex: usually the names of even its large rivers are known only by people living close to them and by interested academics. Each of these great rivers, however, has its unique personality, shaped by geography, ecology, and, in recent geologic history, by human culture.

In this book we profile the personality of the Amazon River and its major tributaries. This profile includes discussions of the coastal wetlands associated with the Amazon River mouth region. Each one of the drainage basins of the 13 largest tributaries of the Amazon River encompasses at least 38,600 square miles (100,000 km²)—an area at least twice the

size of Costa Rica. The Amazon Basin as a whole is nearly 140 times the size of Costa Rica. The river's largest tributary basin, the Madeira, is itself 28 times larger than Costa Rica.

When we consider that Costa Rica is probably better understood scientifically than any country in the New World tropics, if not any tropical country in the world, it is easy to appreciate the dimensions and challenges that the giant river valleys of the Amazon present to scientists, developers, and managers alike. North Americans and Europeans learned somewhat belatedly that rivers should be treated as ecosystems for the simple reason that upstream changes can have far-reaching downstream effects on hydrological cycles, water quality, and plant and animal ecology. The current large-scale economic development taking place in the Amazon Basin makes it critical to look upstream and downstream to avoid the mistakes that have been made elsewhere in river-basin management.

Amazon has become a charged word that evokes strong emotions and stereotypes. Even when referring only to the geographic heart of South America, Amazon is a mysterious word that can denote the world's largest river, the planet's most expansive rainforest, or, to some, an environmental tragedy that is cynically ignored by politicians and developers alike. During the past two decades, however, scientists, the media, and politicians have successfully brought the conservation debate on the Amazon both to governments and to the public.

As the twenty-first century begins, we are faced with the next challenge of conservation development: What can be done to reconcile conservation concerns with the currently unfolding realities of economic development? There is no easy answer to this question. One-dimensional approaches are bound to fail. There should be little doubt that South American governments and business entrepreneurs will continue to foster large-scale highway, hydroelectric, agricultural, and mining projects as the best ways to generate wealth and perhaps to alleviate poverty in the Amazon.

There is great mineral wealth in the Amazon, including

▲ RIVER AND RAINFOREST SYNERGY

The Napo, a large tributary of the Amazon, shown here in eastern Ecuador.

the world's largest high-grade iron ore deposits in the Tocantins Valley, bauxite in eastern Amazonia, and petroleum in the western reaches. The hydroelectric potential is unmatched. Timber and fish are the two most valuable biological resources, and they are being exploited throughout the Amazon Basin.

More than any other economic activity, however, livestock ranching is responsible for the startling deforestation and fires that are readily apparent on satellite images. Cattle are now an integral economic and cultural reality in the Amazon Basin. Unless foot-and-mouth or some other disease ravages herds, large-scale pasture development can be expected to continue in the near future as long as national or foreign markets are found for beef. Large-scale crop farming has also entered the Amazon, with soybeans leading the way. Conservation in the Amazon will, of necessity, have to be shaped within the economic framework outlined previously.

Academics and other people concerned about the pace of industrialization and development may envision an Amazon in which local peoples fish, hunt, log, harvest non-timber forest products, and engage in ecotourism. This vision dictates that these activities will be guided by the theoretical rules of economic sustainability that have become widely accepted, but still unproven, in the past two decades. A combination of small- and large-scale perspectives, however, will most likely continue to guide development in the Amazon.

Continued migration to cities and the creation of large urban markets locally will probably set the stage for the next phase of conservation challenges in the Amazon. We believe that urbanization in the Amazon will unfold as a positive development for conservation: in cities with improved formal education, the public and the politicians they elect will develop a consciousness that reconciles economic development with environmental policy. Local urban populations will also be better equipped than their rural counterparts to interact politically at national and international levels and to see beyond their immediate borders. Amazonian cities will continue to emerge mostly along rivers, and peoples' desires to know what is happening upstream and downstream will increase. They will become especially interested in developments that adversely affect important fisheries and water quality.

This book is largely about looking beyond the political borders of rural communities, cities, states, and even countries, when examining the Amazon. The nature of rivers and the meteorological events that shape them teach us that nearly all life is downstream or downwind in some ecological sense. A few fish species migrate from near the Amazon River mouth some 2,500–3,100 miles (4,000–5,000 km) upstream to spawn in tributaries in the Andean foothills.

These amazing migratory fish demonstrate that the Amazon is connected ecologically from the Andes to the Atlantic. We must now start to see as far as these fish swim, to protect them and all of the amazing wildlife that depends on healthy rivers and wetlands in the largest river system on Earth. Keeping these rivers, wetlands, and the biological resources of the great ecosystem healthy will also enhance the well-being of humans in the Amazon.

11

ACKNOWLEDGMENTS

For financial assistance we are indebted to the W. Alton Jones Foundation, the Gordon and Betty Moore Foundation, the John D. and Catherine T. MacArthur Foundation, Oakwood Arts and Sciences Charitable Trust, the Columbus Zoo, the Amazon Conservation Association, Judy Sulzberger, the Museu Paraense Emilio Goeldi, the National Institute of Amazonian Research, the Rainforest Alliance, and the Amazon Conservation Team.

We thank the following people for their support: Pete Myers (formerly of the W. Alton Jones Foundation), Adrian Forsyth (Gordon and Betty Moore Foundation), Enrique Ortiz (Gordon and Betty Moore Foundation), Gordon Moore (Gordon and Betty Moore Foundation), Betty Moore (Gordon and Betty Moore Foundation), Steve Moore (Gordon and Betty Moore Foundation), Renée Grisham (Oakwood Arts and Sciences Charitable Trust), John Grisham (Oakwood Arts and Sciences Charitable Trust), Avecita Chicchón (John D. and Catherine T. MacArthur Foundation), Dan Martin (Gordon and Betty Moore Foundation), Mitch Wallerstein (John D. and Catherine T. MacArthur Foundation), Warwick Kerr (Instituto Nacional de Pesquisas da Amazônia), Peter Mann Toledo (Museu Paraense Emilio Goeldi), José Vieira Querobim (Agência Nacional de Energia Elétrica), Dan Katz (Rainforest Alliance), and Mark Plotkin (Amazon Conservation Team).

We are grateful to the Oakwood Arts and Sciences Charitable Trust for financial assistance for book production and TG Media for design. We thank book designer Alexandra Littlehales for her excellent artistic contribution.

The following institutions kindly supplied data: Museu Paraense Emilio Goeldi (Brazil), Instituto Nacional de Pesquisas da Amazônia (Brazil), Agência Nacional de Energia Elétrica (Brazil), Tropenbos (Colombia), and Instituto Amazónico de Investigaciones Científicas (Peru).

We are especially indebted to Robert Meade for his thorough review of the manuscript and hydrological data.

For editorial assistance or review of the manuscript we thank Frank and Merry Thomasson, Vince Burke (Smithsonian Books), Nigel Smith (University of Florida), the staff of Princeton Editorial Associates, Inc., and two anonymous reviewers.

For digital cartography we are indebted to Roy Duenas (USS, Inc.). We also thank Marilyn Weitzman for use of her base map of South American rivers.

For additional photographs we thank Luiz Claudio Marigo, Loren McIntyre, Nigel Smith, Oliver Coomes, Mario Hiraoka, Francisco Alberto Rodríguez, and Hans Plenge.

For research and field assistance we thank Carlos Nordt, Armando Vargas, Francisco Estremadoyro, Carlos Cañas, Loren McIntyre, Raimundo Aragão Serrão, Francisco Alberto Rodríguez, Michael McClain, Emilio Mayorga, Jerry Leenheer, Paul van Damme, Alejandro Rosselli, Andrew K. Johnston, and Miguel Pinedo-Vasquez.

◄ **LAND OF THE FLOODED FORESTS**
Rivers and rainforests are intimately linked in the evolution of Amazonian life. This aerial view is of Amanã, a blackwater region adjacent to the Amazon River in northwestern Brazil, where the rainforest is inundated for six months each year.

CHAPTER ONE

DIVERSE DIMENSIONS

Like any great land the Amazon has many faces, some ancient and others shaped by relatively recent geologic and geographic events. In addition to water, geology and vegetation have largely molded the nature of Amazonian rivers. Viewed geologically about one-half of the Amazon consists of two ancient upland areas, known to geologists as shields, which now rarely exceed 3,300 ft (1,000 m) in elevation. These uplands are separated by the main river in the east.

The rest of the Amazon is mostly a giant sedimentary basin that lies below 1,000 ft (300 m) in elevation and occupies approximately 35 percent of the entire drainage. There has been so much deposition that the lowland sedimentary region has sunk under its own weight. Sediment depths of more than 16,400 ft (5,000 m) have been recorded. Towering elevations reaching the equatorial snowline are found only in the geologically youthful Andes, which form the western watershed of the Amazon and account for no more than approximately 15 percent of the area of the basin.

Scientists now generally agree that the Amazon River reversed its course in recent geologic history. The ancient eastern uplands, known as the Brazilian and Guiana Shields, were contiguous at the surface until approximately 12 million years ago, when the formation of the present Amazon River and its floodplain separated them. Previous to this time the Amazon River appears to have run east to west until turning sharply northward toward the Orinoco Basin.

One can only imagine the immensity of a river basin that included both the Amazon and Orinoco Rivers and spanned nearly all of northern South America. Today shared species of channel catfish and freshwater turtles remind us of this former connection, along with other widely distributed animal and plant groups that predate the reversal of flow of the Amazon River.

River courses in the Amazon have not been static through geologic time, and this explains why the entire lowland region was subject to heavy deposition. Within the lowland sedimentary region, there have been major marine transgressions when sea levels were higher than they are today. The

◁ **THE RAINFOREST CANOPY**

Most of the Amazon's biodiversity is found in or depends on the shade of the rainforest canopy. Floodplain and upland rainforest canopies are usually connected. Under natural conditions rainforest usually grows along most Amazonian rivers and generally covers at least one-third to one-half of the floodplains. Consequently, at least one-third to one-half of the total floodplain area would be shaded where large-scale deforestation has not taken place.

▲ THE AMAZON BASIN AND CONTIGUOUS TOCANTINS BASIN

The Amazon Basin drainage stretches from within 60 miles (100 km) of the Pacific Ocean to the Atlantic Ocean more than 3,100 miles (5,000 km) by air to the east. The Tocantins is sometimes not considered a tributary of the Amazon River because its waters discharge into the Pará River south of the island of Marajó. A small percentage of Amazon River water, however, flows south of the island of Marajó and mixes with discharge from the Tocantins. It is only a matter of preference to exclude the Tocantins Basin from the Amazon Basin. Ecologically and geographically the Tocantins is undoubtedly a part of the Amazon Basin.

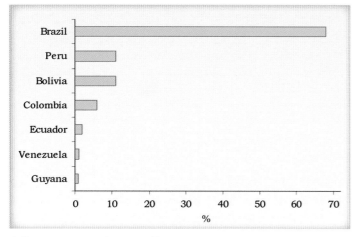

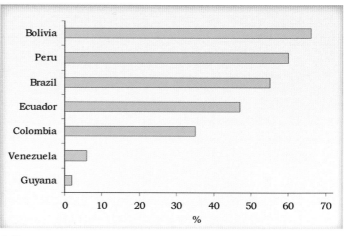

▲ PERCENTAGE OF AMAZON BASIN IN EACH COUNTRY

Brazil alone accounts for slightly more than two-thirds of the Amazon Basin's total area. Venezuela and Guyana each claim less than 1 percent of the Amazon Basin.

▲ PERCENTAGE OF EACH COUNTRY IN THE AMAZON BASIN

Relative to country size, Bolivia is the most Amazonian country. Nearly 70 percent of Bolivia is in the Amazon Basin. Nevertheless both Brazil and Peru have larger absolute areas of the Amazon Basin.

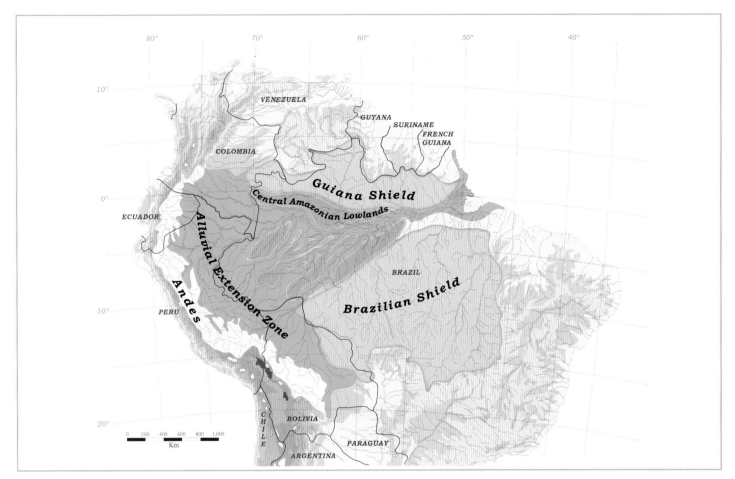

▲ PRINCIPAL ECOLOGICAL-GEOLOGIC ZONES OF THE AMAZON BASIN

The Amazon drainage encompasses high mountains (the Andes), ancient uplands (the Brazilian and Guiana Shields), and vast lowlands (the Alluvial Extension Zone and the Central Amazonian Lowlands). These major zones largely determine the chemical nature of Amazonian rivers and were the main stages for the evolution of plants and animals. Because the Andes are still rising, that principal ecological-geological zone has been the most active of the three during recent geologic time. The huge sediment loads carried by Amazonian rivers with headwaters in the Andes functionally extend the deposition zone of the high mountains to the western shores of the Atlantic near the Amazon River mouth. The Alluvial Extension Zone is technically not a geologic unit because most of it is within the lowlands of the Amazon. Nevertheless recognizing this zone provides a convenient reminder of the far-flung influence of Andean sediments on the ecology of rivers.

Brazilian and Guiana Shields predate the rise of the Andes. In fact the high Andean cordilleras are newborn in comparison, and the ancient highland shields supplied most of the lowland sediments in the central and eastern Amazon Basin.

The clash of the Nazca and South American geologic plates led to the birth and rise of the Andes, beginning approximately 15 million years ago. Today the Andes tower 13,100–16,400 ft (4,000–5,000 m) above the Amazon Basin. The steep slopes of the Andes, in conjunction with unstable and unconsolidated geology and heavy rainfall on the eastern slopes, have resulted in at least ten million years of heavy erosion.

As the Andes rose they continued to supply new materials for erosion. The rivers have carried enormous quantities of sediments eastward. The soils of Amazonian floodplains with headwaters in the Andes are dominated by Andean alluvium deposited annually with the seasonal floods. The zone of Andean deposition is very broad in the west, because headwaters have constantly meandered across the deep sediments in the cordilleran forelands. It is not unusual for rivers in this region to deviate laterally by several kilometers from their courses of the previous year.

The Andean cordilleras cast a long geologic shadow over the Amazon. Massive erosion stuffs Andean headwater tributaries with huge quantities of sediments that are transported across northern South America to be

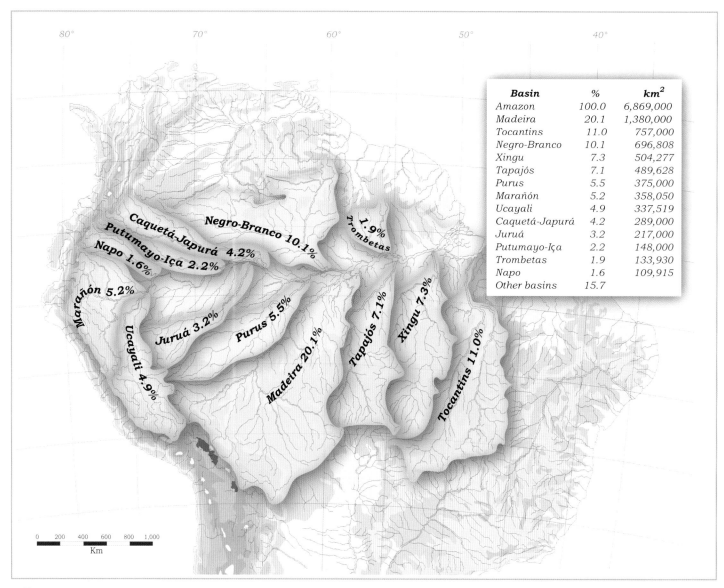

Basin	%	km²
Amazon	100.0	6,869,000
Madeira	20.1	1,380,000
Tocantins	11.0	757,000
Negro-Branco	10.1	696,808
Xingu	7.3	504,277
Tapajós	7.1	489,628
Purus	5.5	375,000
Marañón	5.2	358,050
Ucayali	4.9	337,519
Caquetá-Japurá	4.2	289,000
Juruá	3.2	217,000
Putumayo-Içá	2.2	148,000
Trombetas	1.9	133,930
Napo	1.6	109,915
Other basins	15.7	

▲ TRIBUTARY AREAS

Occupying more than 2.6 million square miles (6.8 million km²), the Amazon is the largest river basin in the world. We include the Tocantins Basin as part of the Amazon Basin because it is geographically and ecologically connected to it and the Tocantins River flows into Amazon River waters via Marajó Bay. The Amazon Basin is nearly twice the size of the second largest river basin in the world, that of the Congo with approximately 1.4 million square miles (3.7 million km²). The Amazon Basin is the size of the continental United States, less California and Texas, or approximately 80 percent of the size of Brazil, South America's largest country.

The Madeira Basin is the largest tributary area of the Amazon drainage and is nearly twice the size of any other tributary basin. Encompassing 540,000 square miles (1.4 million km²), the Madeira Basin is slightly larger than Peru and nearly three times the size of France. The Madeira Basin covers 20 percent of the Amazon Basin and lies within Brazil, Bolivia, and Peru.

Based on area, seven of the eight largest tributaries of the Amazon River are in the southern Amazon Basin. Ninety to 100 percent of the area encompassed by each of the six largest basins lies in Brazil. Approximately 40 percent of the Madeira Basin lies within Brazil. Only the Negro and Putumayo-Içá Basins have areas that lie within four Amazonian countries. Ninety percent of the Negro Basin, however, is within Brazil.

deposited in and along rivers or in the Atlantic Ocean. Andean sediments, throughout time, have been deposited on the floodplains and in the river channels by an annual cycle of deposition and erosion.

At least 30 percent of the Amazon River flows across floodplains; thus it is easy to understand how so much sediment gets deposited. In river channels, Andean sediments are most evident as islands or, during the low-water period, as beaches and sandbars. When one steps on an Amazon River beach or floodplain, even near the mouth region, the footprints are cast in Andean sediments.

Within the Amazon Basin the Andes form an arc stretching 2,800 miles (4,500 km) from Bolivia to Colombia. As a whole the Andes are still rising, and parts of the cordilleras are highly unstable and subject to regular tectonic activity, including earthquakes. There are at least five active volcanoes in Amazonian headwater regions. They are all in Ecuador in the upper Napo and Pastaza headwaters. These volcanoes include Reventador, Antisana, Cotopaxi, Tungurahua, and Sangay. Sangay and Reventador were the last to erupt, both spewing volcanic materials in the 1970s. Material from volcanic deposits can darken some rivers, such as headwater tributaries of the Napo.

During the past 2.4 million years, there have been periods when average temperatures at the Earth's surface have increased. During these periods, sea levels rose due to increased polar ice melting. Scientists assume that large areas of the Amazon lowlands were submerged when sea levels were any-

where from a few to tens of meters higher than they are at present. Ancient floodplains no longer inundated can be found above areas presently subject to flooding. The present configuration of the Amazon floodplain was formed over the past 7,000 years. Most of the floodplain has been filled with Andean sediments.

Amazon River tributaries that carry relatively few sediments, such as the Negro and the Tapajós, have characteristic wide and deep lower courses that are referred to as mouth-lakes. During the Ice Ages, when sea levels were lower than they are now, fast currents excavated the deep mouth-lakes. The mouth-bays have not had time to fill with river sediments; the archipelagoes above the mouth-bays represent their main deposition zones.

The Amazon Basin contains the most extensive rainforest in the world, which is at least four times larger than either of the next two largest tropical forest regions, Indonesia and the Congo Basin. Approximately one-sixth of all broadleaf forest in the world lies within the Amazon. The South American rainforest is not confined to the Amazon Basin, but is also found in the Orinoco Basin and along the Atlantic coast of Brazil and the Pacific coasts of Colombia and Ecuador. Approximately 85 percent of the South American rainforest, however, is found in the Amazon Basin.

Until the 1970s, rainforest covered about two-thirds, or 1.5 million square miles (4 million km²), of the Amazon. Since then approximately 10–15 percent of the rainforest has been heavily modified, although some of it has returned to secondary forest. Brazil alone has at least three times more Amazonian rain-

forest than do all other South American countries. Peru is second with approximately one-fifth the rainforest area of Brazil, but has at least three times more than any other Andean country. Relative to its size Bolivia has less rainforest than other Amazonian countries because most of its eastern plains are savannas.

Deforestation in the Amazon Basin has attracted international attention since the early 1980s. The three principal international concerns, at least in the media, have been planetary depletion of oxygen, release of carbon dioxide that might lead to global warming, and destruction of biodiversity. The idea that the Amazon rainforest can be considered the "lungs of the Earth" is a fallacy. The Earth's oxygen supply was built up over hundreds of millions of years because the rate of photosynthesis (an oxygen producer) has been greater than the rate of decomposition of dead material (an oxygen consumer). The decomposition of Amazonian leaf litter consumes just about as much oxygen as the living vegetation produces. Marine phytoplankton also play a larger role in oxygen production than do tropical rainforests.

Global warming is now being hotly debated, although most scientists generally accept that human activities have significantly increased the amount of greenhouse gases in the atmosphere, most notably carbon dioxide and sulfuric acid, causing average temperatures at the Earth's surface to rise. The global contribution to greenhouse gases from rainforest burning, however, appears to be minimal compared with the amount released from fossil fuel combustion. The entire Amazonian rainforest would

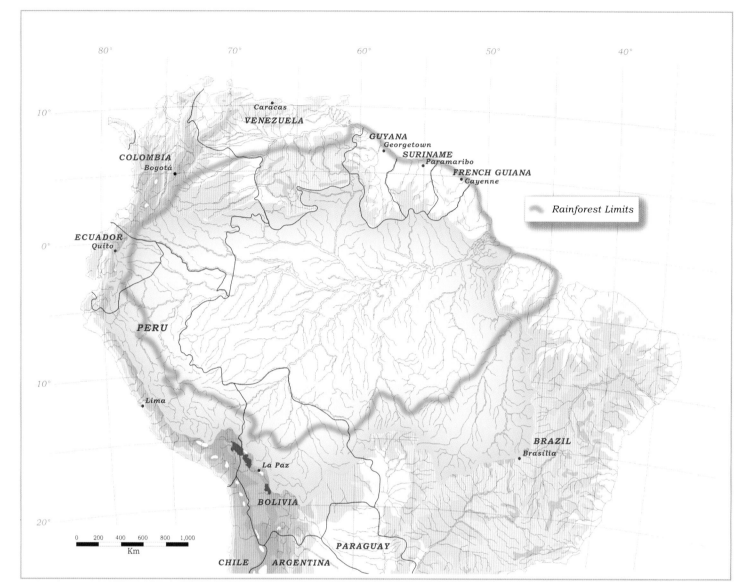

▲ THE AMAZON RAINFOREST

Rainforest occupies most of the Amazon Basin and extends northward and eastward beyond it. Biologists and geographers often refer to this entire rainforest region as the Amazon rainforest. Within the Amazon rainforest, however, there are large savannas, and 10–15 percent of the rainforest has been deforested. Rainforest is disappearing the fastest along its southern limits in Brazil, where there has been large-scale deforestation in the past three decades.

have to be burned in less than a decade to sound an alarm for global warming. This does not mean that burning in the Amazon is unimportant, just that it is of less concern than other sources of greenhouse gases. And deforestation releases more than just greenhouse gases: mercury is one example of a toxic element released by deforestation that has been of concern in the Amazon.

Rainforests are the richest ecosystems our planet has ever known. Because there is a close correlation between total ecosystem size and number of species, the Amazon Basin is generally accepted to be the biological frontrunner in terms of species richness. No one knows how many species there might be in the Amazon Basin. The most accurate counts are for flowering plants (25,000 species) and vertebrates (more than 5,000 species). These figures, however, represent only a small percentage of the number of invertebrate species present in the Amazon.

Most of the species living in the rainforest are insects whose life histories are intimately linked to rainforest trees and to the bromeliads, orchids, and other epiphytes that grow on the trees. One large tree might have several hundred species of insects associated with it. It is nearly impossible to say how much biodiversity has been lost in the 10 percent of the Amazon rainforest that has been cleared, because so little is known about the rainforest. Unless there is a massive effort to catalog invertebrate species and their distribution—which seems unlikely, considering the costs involved—it is doubtful that estimates of rainforest biodiversity losses will accurately represent the number of species of insects, spiders, and other arthropods lost.

From a functional point of view, the rainforest might be thought of as a parasol, pump, and recycler. The vast rainforest canopy provides shade 66–165 ft (20–50 m) below it, thus providing a giant cooling and humidifying system for a myriad of life forms. Remove the rainforest, and temperature increases and humidity decreases—changes that endanger biodiversity.

The rainforest controls a large part of the hydrological cycle because trees transpire (pump) water drawn from the soils back into the atmosphere and decrease runoff. Runoff is decreased both because of pumping and the braking effect the rainforest has on rainfall and flowing surface waters. In general, water levels in rivers in forested watersheds rise and fall more slowly compared with water levels in rivers in deforested watersheds. And the rainforest is the great recycler, because the roots of its vegetation have fungi specially adapted to increase the uptake of phosphorus, potassium, and other limited nutrients. Through this recycling mechanism the rainforest is able to flourish on the poor soils that are characteristic of most of the Amazon Basin.

In addition to the rainforest and the geologic foundations, individual tributary basins also shape the face of the Amazon. Several of the Amazon's tributary basins, such as the Madeira and the Tocantins, are larger than most European countries. The Madeira Basin, for example, is nearly three times as large as France. The Amazon's tributaries are not ecological replicates of one another. Each tributary is distinct, based on the diverse lands it encompasses and on the human activities that are changing the nature of the landscape.

Beginning in the east, the Tocantins Basin might well be characterized as the industrial gateway to the Amazon. This is because industry in this region has been spurred by dams, large-scale deforestation for cattle ranching, logging, and road building, all of which have significantly altered the basin in the past few decades. The Xingu and Tapajós Basins immediately to the west drain a naturally eroded landscape with clearwater rivers. Together these two basins can be characterized as the great clearwater lands of the Amazon.

The Madeira Basin, bridging the Andes, Amazon lowlands, and Brazilian Shield, is not only the core of the Amazon Basin, but of South America as well. The Madeira Basin is geologically and geographically complex because, in addition to its enormous size, its headwaters arise in the Andes and on the Brazilian Shield.

Farther west, the Purus and Juruá Basins represent a land of meanders, where the main rivers serpentine more than 1,850 miles (3,000 km). The Ucayali and Marañón Basins of Peru have headwaters in high Andean deserts but mouth regions in the Amazon rainforest and a bewildering number of habitats in between. Ecologically these giant tributaries are in the shadows of the Andes. The Napo, Putumayo-Içá, and Caquetá-Japurá Basins tap the equator in the northwestern Amazon. The Negro Basin is most characterized by its white sands and black waters. Its drainage, however, as with the Trombetas Basin to the east, also includes the ancient Guiana Shield. This entire region might be thought of as a land of black waters and ancient lands.

CHAPTER TWO

FLOW OF THE RIVERS

The headwaters of the Amazon's largest rivers range from approximately 1,550 to 4,200 miles (2,500–6,800 km) from the Amazon River mouth. There has been much debate about what exactly constitutes the headwaters of the Amazon River, although all serious observers accept the Ucayali of Peru to be the hydrographical equivalent of the upper Amazon River. Most debate centers on what stream in the Ucayali headwaters is farthest from the Amazon River mouth and on the exact location of the mouth of the Amazon River.

Using modern global positioning systems (GPS), recent expeditions have tried to pinpoint the Ucayali headwaters in the department of Arequipa, just south of the department of Cuzco, to within tens of meters. The problem, however, is that expedition members did not remeasure distances to the Atlantic Ocean but instead appended their new findings to downstream figures already published but not necessarily verified independently. The aim of these exercises is usually to determine if the Amazon River is longer than the Nile, and usually that is what expedition leaders would like to prove. There are plenty of estimates of the length of the Amazon River, ranging from 3,700 to 4,850 miles (6,000–7,800 km). If the higher estimates are accepted, then one can conclude that the Amazon is indeed longer than the Nile.

River lengths have traditionally been measured with map wheels that trace channels on aerial photographs or large-scale maps. Yet there is uncertainty in this method because investigators usually do not state whether they ran the map wheel around the outside or the inside of a river bend or in the middle of the river channel. To a certain extent the accuracy of river length measurements made with a map wheel also depends on the skill of the person using the device. New estimates are now being made on computers by using digitized satellite imagery and counting pixel lengths. Again, however, there can be variability in such estimates, depending on exactly where within river channels pixels are measured to calculate distances.

The best estimate we have is that the Amazon River is approximately 4,000–4,200 miles (6,500–6,800 km) long if the mouth is taken to be near Balique, just east of 50° W. The length of the Nile is usually stated to be 4,100 miles (6,650 km).

◀ MANU NATIONAL PARK

Manu River in Manu National Park, Peru, meanders through the Amazon lowlands.

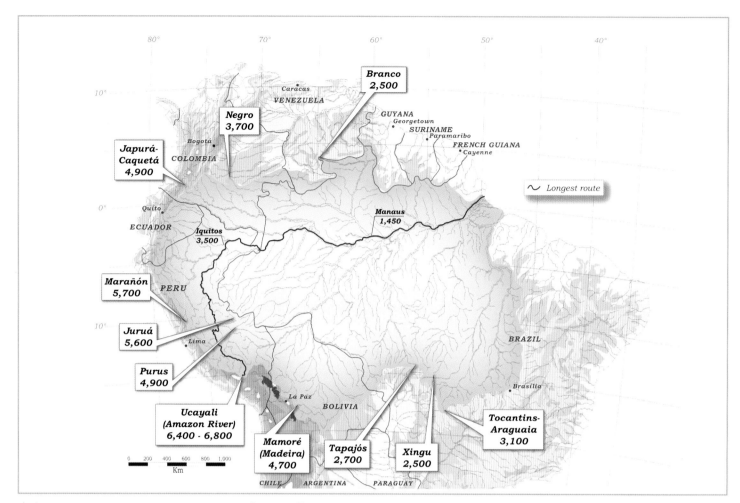

△ APPROXIMATE HEADWATER DISTANCES FROM AMAZON RIVER MOUTH

The Amazon and Nile Rivers are approximately the same length and both have been cited as the longest river in the world. Based on current data one cannot justifiably claim that one river is longer than the other. Measuring exact river distances is extremely difficult. The most scientifically accurate estimate of the length of the Amazon River is 3,950–4,200 miles (6,400–6,800 km). The length of the River changes yearly because of the constantly shifting channels.

Needless to say, the "longest river" debate will continue to ping-pong until both rivers are measured in exactly the same way and at about the same time, preferably by the same team of investigators—one that includes partisans of both the Amazon and the Nile as the world's longest river.

River channels constantly change, especially in highly meandering tributaries such as the Ucayali, and thus river lengths are never constant. Considering that using map wheels or digital images would result in a 5-percent error (220–240 miles [350–390 km])

for the Amazon River, it is absurd to state an exact length. Finding new headwater streams or determining the GPS coordinates of previously described headwaters will not resolve the debate.

South Americans divide the Amazon River into four main stretches, with the Amazonas appearing twice. Beginning upriver in Peru is the Ucayali, followed downstream by the Amazonas in Peru and Colombia. After entering Brazil the Amazon River is called the Solimões until its confluence with the Negro, where it is again called

the Amazonas. Amazon River headwaters of the Ucayali, in downstream order, are the Apurimac, the Ene, and the Tambo.

The Amazon is the only river basin in the world that has three tributaries (the Purus, the Juruá, and the Madeira) longer than 1,850 miles (3,000 km). The Madeira, at 2,078 miles (3,352 km), is the longest, but it is still second to the Missouri River, which at 2,310 miles (3,726 km) is the longest tributary in the world. The longest meandering rivers in the Amazon—the Purus, the Juruá, and the Ucayali—are all southern tributaries. This serpentine trio is found in an enormous alluvial zone, where soft sediments have allowed the tributaries to meander wildly across their broad floodplains. The length of the Purus, for example, is more than twice the aerial distance from its mouth to its headwaters.

Rainfall is not distributed evenly either spatially or temporally in the Amazon Basin. In general it rains intensely (> 8 in. [200 mm]/month) for about six months each year, although there are exceptions where rainfall is high throughout the year. March and April are the rainiest months in the southern Amazon Basin, whereas near the equator in the north they are June and July. The heaviest rains fall during the summer months of the Southern Hemisphere. Most of the Amazon Basin is subject to a fairly intense dry season for at least two to three months, in which there may be several weeks without heavy precipitation.

More than 90 percent of the atmospheric water vapor that reaches the Amazon Basin comes from the Atlantic. The Andes form a natural barrier to westward vapor flow and also prevent major input from the Pacific. Approximately 60 percent of the precipitation that falls in the Amazon Basin is recycled directly to the atmosphere by transpiration through the rainforest and evaporation at the upper level of the canopy. This dual return of water to the atmosphere is called evapotranspiration. The other 40 percent makes its way to the Atlantic through the giant network of rivers. Water vapor is returned to the Amazon Basin by moisture-laden

▲ **FARTHEST HEADWATERS OF THE AMAZON RIVER**

The farthest headwaters of the Amazon River are above 13,100 ft (4,000 m) in the upper Ucayali Valley of Peru and approximately 3,950–4,200 miles (6,400–6,800 km) from the Atlantic.

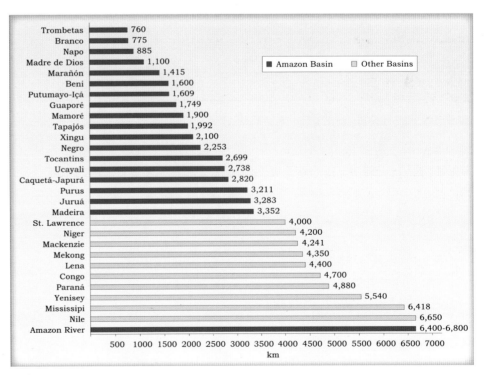

▲ **COMPARATIVE RIVER LENGTHS**

The Amazon River has three tributaries more than 1,850 miles (3,000 km) long and eight more than 1,250 miles (2,000 km) long. The Amazon's longest tributary, the Madeira, is about one-half the length of the main river.

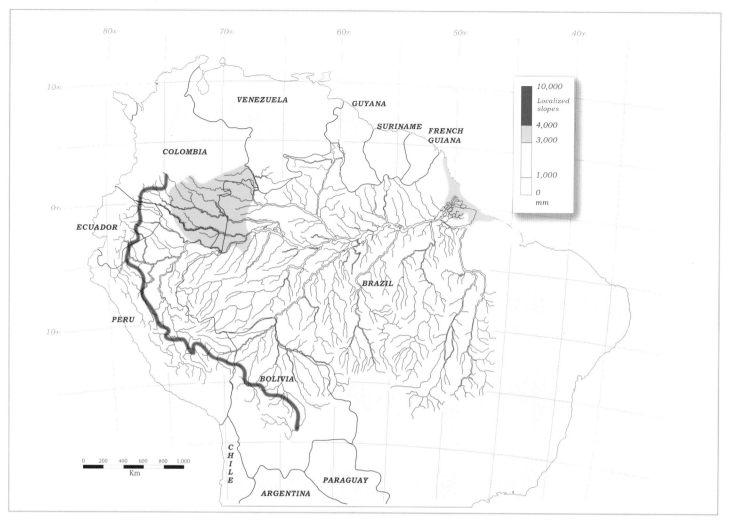

	10,000
	Localized slopes
	4,000
	3,000
	1,000
	0
	mm

▲ AVERAGE ANNUAL PRECIPITATION

Most of the Amazon Basin receives 60–100 in. (1,500–2,500 mm) of annual precipitation. Extremely heavy but localized rain falls along parts of the eastern Andes, where annual totals can exceed 200 in. (5,000 mm). No more than about one-third to one-half of the eastern Andes, however, receives more than 155 in. (4,000 mm) of rain annually. The Northwestern Amazon and the coastal region near the Amazon River mouth have annual totals exceeding 120 in. (3,000 mm).

Atmospheric Water Vapor
2,400 km³

Evapotranspiration
9,600 km³/year

Rain
16,300 km³/year

59%

Discharge of Amazon River
6,700 km³/year

41%

◀ THE RECYCLING OF WATER

Most of the rain that falls annually in the Amazon Basin does not make it to sea but is recycled back into the atmosphere. The amount of annual rainfall in the Basin is approximately six times greater than the average volume of atmospheric water vapor at any given time. Approximately 40 percent of the total annual rainfall makes it to the sea.

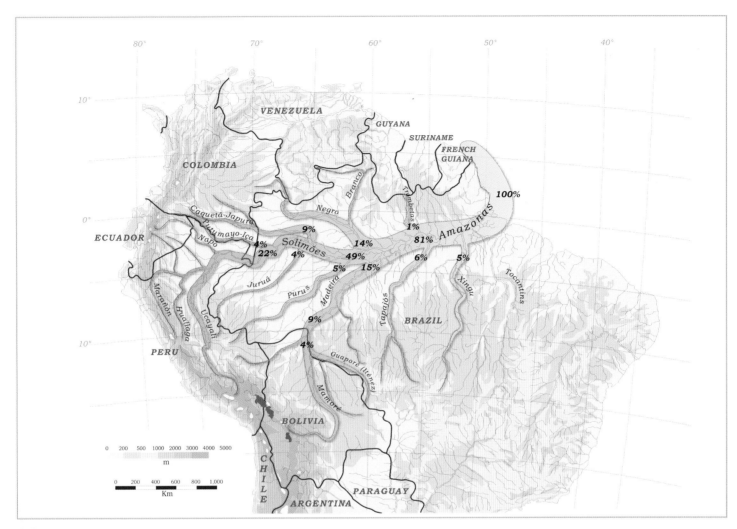

▲ RIVER DISCHARGE

The Amazon River accounts for approximately 15–16 percent of the freshwater delivered to all of the oceans annually. The Negro was long considered the Amazon River's largest tributary in terms of average annual discharge. Recent data indicate that annual discharge of the Madeira River exceeds that of the Negro.

northeasterly and southeasterly winds.

The most rainfall in the Amazon Basin occurs in some Andean foothill regions up to approximately 4,900 ft (1,500 m) that are in the direct path of moisture-laden winds. Annual totals exceeding 470 in. (12,000 mm) have been recorded. Most of the Amazon Basin, however, receives 60–120 in. (1,500–3,000 mm) annually. Two major exceptions are the equatorial region in the northwestern Amazon Basin and a coastal belt 30–125 miles (50–200 km) long running northward from just

south of the Amazon River estuary. The northwestern high-rainfall region is near the equator and thus is subject to prolonged summer heating and therefore increased convective precipitation. The coastal belt receives daily moisture-laden winds that increase total annual precipitation. Intense afternoon heating of moisture-heavy coastal air results in highly predictable daily showers by which Belém residents claim they can set their watches.

In general the farther south one goes in the Amazon Basin, the drier the

▲ THE RIVER SEA

The Amazon River's discharge is so large that tidal saltwater never flows into its mouth. An ocean freighter is shown here entering the Amazon River mouth.

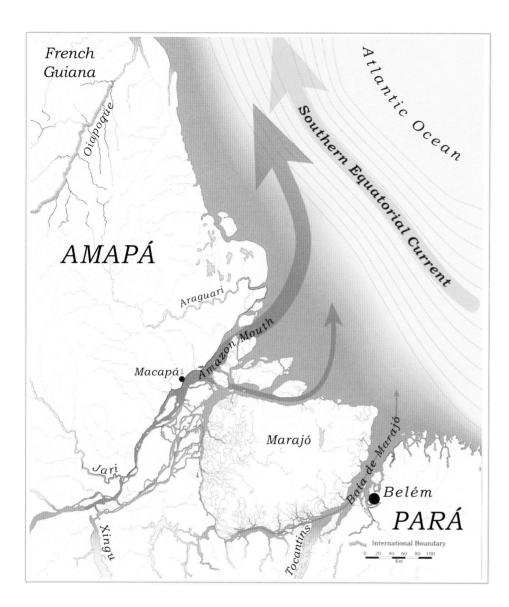

◁ THE AMAZON'S FLOW TO THE
ATLANTIC OCEAN
After entering the Atlantic Ocean, water from
the Amazon River is deflected northward
along the coast by the Southern Equatorial
Current. A small amount of water from the
Amazon also flows south around the large
island of Marajó and past Belém.

climate. Northward the pattern is different because of the prolonged summer heating and increased convective precipitation mentioned previously. To the east of the northwestern deluge, precipitation decreases in the Guiana Shield region.

The Amazon River drains approximately 38 percent of continental South America and accounts for 15–16 percent of the total river water reaching the world's oceans. The Amazon River's discharge is five times that of the Congo and 12 times that of the Mississippi. Based on discharge the world's first (the Amazon), fifth (the Madeira), and sixth (the Negro) largest rivers are in the Amazon Basin. The second, third, and fourth are, respectively, the Congo, the Orinoco, and the Yangtze.

Estimates of Amazon River discharge have gradually increased in the past two decades as more measurements were made. Brazilian hydrologists now calculate that the average discharge of the Amazon River is approximately 57 million gallons (214 million liters) per second, an estimate that admittedly means very little to most readers. To get a better perspective on this quantity, consider that New York City consumes approximately 1.1 billion gallons (4.2 billion liters) of water per day, or approximately 4 trillion gallons (15 trillion liters) per year. In approximately 2 hours the Amazon River would supply all the water New York City's 7.5 million residents use in one year. The annual discharge of the Amazon River would cover all of France with 43 ft (13 m) of water.

Although the Negro Basin is about only one-half the size of that of the Madeira, it contributes nearly as much water to the Amazon River. The western Negro headwaters center on the equatorial high-rainfall region that

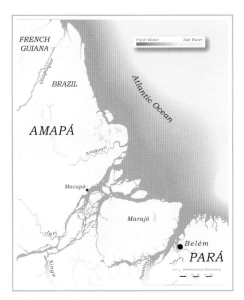

▲ **AMAZON RIVER DISCHARGE DURING THE HIGH-WATER PERIOD**

Between May and July every year, at the height of Amazon River floods, freshwater can be found 100 miles (160 km) out to sea.

▶ **AMAZON RIVER WATER MOVES INLAND DURING THE LOW-WATER PERIOD**

During the annual low-water period (August to December) of the Amazon River, marine waters invade Marajó Bay northeast of Belém.

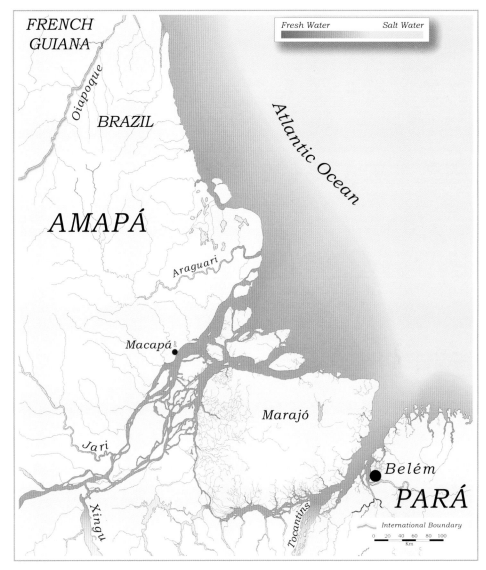

receives more than 120 in. (3,000 mm) of rain per year. In comparison, a large part of the southern Madeira Basin, especially in Bolivia, receives less than 80 in. (2,000 mm) per year.

At the Brazilian-Peruvian-Colombian border, the Amazon River is carrying approximately 20 percent of its average discharge at the mouth. The Madeira and the Negro between them contribute nearly one-third of the Amazon's water, at 15 percent and 14 percent, respectively. Below the mouth of the Madeira, 560 miles (900 km) from the Atlantic, the Amazon River is swollen with 80 percent of its average discharge.

The Amazon bifurcates around the world's largest river island, Marajó. Only a small percentage of its discharge, however, flows south and east through Marajó Bay to the Atlantic. The main southern channel of the Amazon—the Estreito de Breves—is considered a strait rather than a river or fork. Although no accurate measurements are available, it seems safe to assume that less than 1 percent of the Amazon's water discharges through Marajó Bay. Nevertheless, the flow is sufficient to muddy Marajó Bay during most of the year.

The Amazon River discharges

enough water every month to prevent saltwater from invading the main channel. Southeast of Marajó Bay, however, between September and November, brackish water penetrates as far inland as Belém during the low-water period of the Amazon and Tocantins Rivers.

The water the Amazon discharges into the Atlantic is deflected northward by the Southern Equatorial Current. The water along the entire coast of the state of Amapá is brackish, often with a freshwater layer on top, because of the huge quantity of water that works its way to sea. Saltwater never invades the

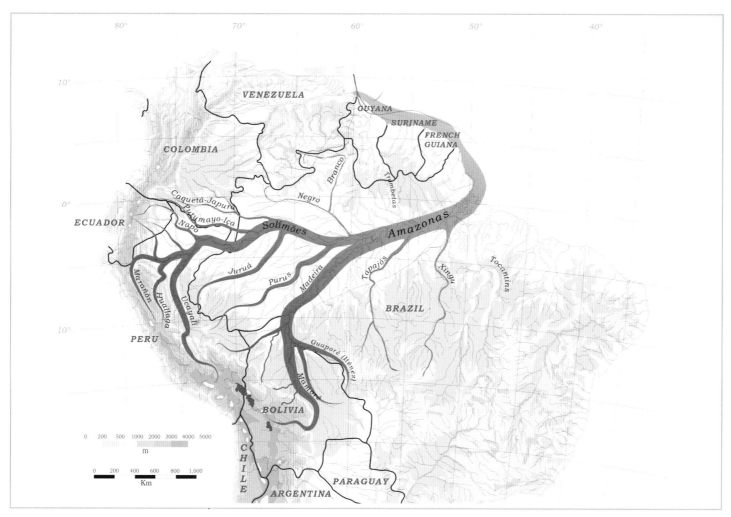

▲ AMAZON SEDIMENT TRANSPORT

This schematic map shows the relative flow of sediments, in the form of sand, clay, and loam, from the Andes to the Atlantic. Non-Andean tributaries contribute relatively little of the Amazon River's suspended sediment load. The Madeira and Ucayali Rivers are the main contributors to the Amazon River's heavy sediment load.

Amazon River mouth north of Marajó. An obvious testament to this observation is the vast tidal forest consisting almost entirely of rainforest species. Once water discharged by the Amazon is deflected northward, saltwater and brackish water underlie it.

The mouth region of the Amazon River is relatively shallow; depths are usually less than 33 ft (10 m). Channel depths average approximately 66 ft (20 m) near Macapá. The mouth region is subject to a tidal bore—large waves that move up the main river and coastal streams. The bore is caused by a combination of shallow waters and submerged sand dunes that force incoming waves to rise higher than normal. The *pororoca*, as the tidal bore is called, averages less than 6.5 ft (2 m) and is strongest in March.

During its flooding season, the Amazon River discharges so much water into the Atlantic that this water travels approximately 100 miles (160 km) out to sea. The seaward freshwater, however, is no deeper than approximately 16.5 ft (5 m) and, because fresh water is lighter than saltwater, it is literally riding on top of the heavier water. Oceanic water is also slightly cooler, which also contributes to making it heavier than the Amazon River water.

Based on productivity, Amazon and Atlantic waters form a perfect marriage. Amazon River water is muddy but relatively rich in nutrients. Atlantic water, however, is highly transparent, allowing light to penetrate, but relatively poor in nutrients. Relatively high nutrient concentrations combined with good transparency leads to increased production of phytoplankton and thus also of organisms higher in the food chain.

Along with the Yellow River in China and the Ganges-Brahmaputra River in India and Bangladesh, the Amazon ranks among the three largest contributors of fluvial sediments to the oceans. Compared with most other large river basins in the world, however, the Amazon has a relatively low sediment yield. This is because the main erosion zone of the Amazon is restricted to approximately one-seventh of the basin that includes the Andes and contiguous Amazonian lowlands in the far west. This zone contributes perhaps 85–90 percent of all sediments discharged through the Amazon River mouth. Most of the sediments transported annually come from elevations below approximately 1,600 ft (500 m), although their origins may have been higher during Andean uplift.

The Amazon annually transports an estimated 1.2 billion tons of sediments past Óbidos, where the narrowest downstream stretch of the river is found. Approximately 75 percent of the sediments transported past Óbidos reach the Atlantic in any given year. The other 25 percent are deposited in the lower 500 miles (800 km) of the river. Shore currents transport approximately 30 percent of the sediments that reach the Atlantic along the French Guiana, Suriname, and Guyana coasts. Some of the sediments are deposited as far north as the Orinoco Delta.

Total sediment concentrations in the Amazon River decrease from west to east because large amounts of low-sediment water, especially from the Negro, the Tapajós, and the Xingu, enter the main river in Brazil. Nearly 90 percent of the Amazon River's

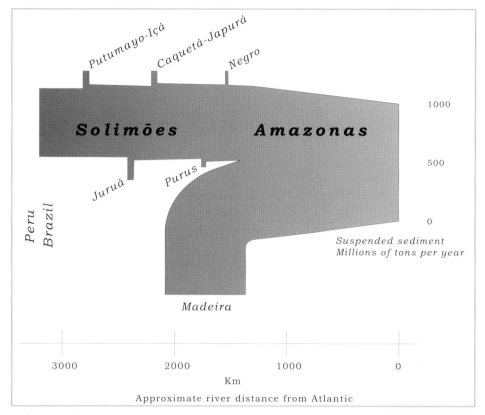

▲ **AMAZON RIVER SEDIMENTS**

This chart by hydrologist Robert Meade shows the distribution of sediment contributions from the Amazon's main stem and tributaries in Brazil.

▲ **ALLUVIAL FLOODPLAIN OF AMAZON RIVER**

The rich soils of the Amazon River floodplain are derived from Andean alluvium transported annually downstream and deposited during the floods. Some of the alluvium has collapsed and will be carried farther downstream and redeposited when the river rises. This site along the Amazonas in Brazil is a new alluvial island that appeared during the low-water period.

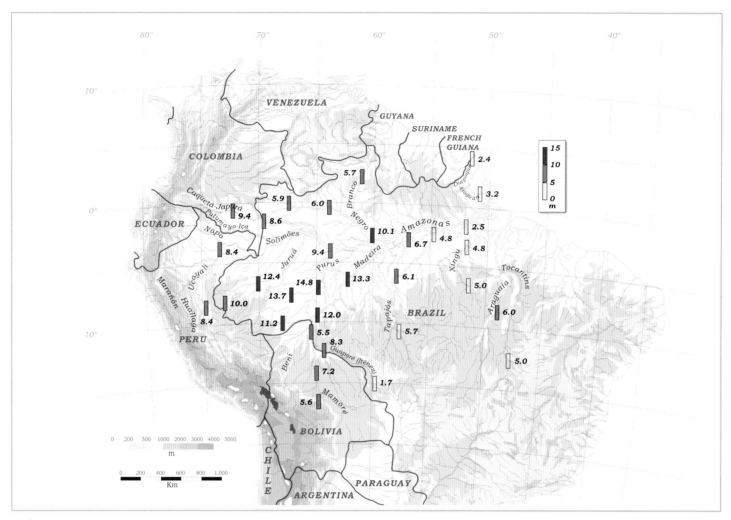

▲ **AVERAGE ANNUAL RIVER-LEVEL FLUCTUATION**

Average annual river-level fluctuation in the lowland Amazon Basin ranges from approximately 13 to 42.5 ft (4–13 m). The greatest fluctuations are in southwestern Brazilian rivers, especially the Madeira, the Purus, and the Juruá.

sediment load comes from the Madeira, the Ucayali, and the Marañón Basins.

Sediment transport is highly dynamic in the Amazon River because of fluctuating river levels and vast floodplains. The highest sediment concentrations occur during the rising-water period. Because it takes river water at least one month to flow from the Andes to the Atlantic, sediment loads in much of the River are relatively high for a few weeks after the main rainy season in the west. Scientists estimate that at least 30 percent of Amazon River water flows through the

floodplains before reentering the main channel and that floodwaters deposit 80 percent of all the sediments transported over floodplains. Annual floodplain deposition at any given place depends mostly on river-level fluctuation and duration of flooding. It is not unusual, however, for 8–12 in. (20–30 cm) of sediments to be deposited annually.

As floodplains are being built up they are also being eroded. Erosion takes place mostly on riverbanks, where currents remove soft sediments annually and deposit them elsewhere. Riverbank cave-ins are a well-known

phenomenon along muddy rivers in the Amazon. When river levels begin to fall rapidly, soft riverbanks 16.5–33 ft (5–10 m) high become unstable after the wall of floodwater that was supporting them is gone. When these cave-ins plunge into the water, they often carry enormous trees and other vegetation with them. It is not unusual for floodplain farmers to lose their banana, manioc, cacao, and other crops to these cave-ins.

Hydrologist Robert Meade estimated that the Amazon River floodplain between the Purus and the Negro might be recycled every 2,500

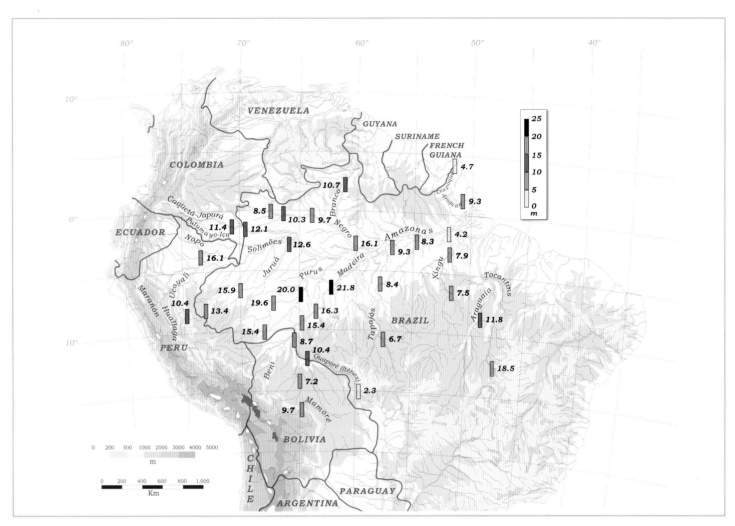

⚠ **RANGES BETWEEN HIGHEST AND LOWEST KNOWN RIVER LEVELS**

Floodplains are usually defined by their extreme flood levels, and these might only appear every few decades. Several places in the Amazon Basin have absolute ranges exceeding 66 ft (20 m) between the highest and lowest known river levels. In general the highest extremes are in the same areas with the highest average annual river-level fluctuations.

years by the annual deposition and erosion process. Recycling times are probably greater for the entire Amazon River floodplain. Where erosion is intense near the Andes, floodplains might be recycled in a matter of centuries or perhaps even decades for smaller streams.

The most striking telltale of Amazonian seasonality is river-level fluctuation. Average annual river-level fluctuations ranging from approximately 13 to 49 ft (4–15 m) have been measured. River-level data have been collected in some parts of the Brazilian

Amazon for nearly a century. Because the Andean countries (Bolivia, Peru, Ecuador, and Colombia) have been slow to invest in hydrological data, we have a relatively poor understanding of river-level fluctuation near and in the Andes. Andean headwaters can fluctuate radically on even a daily basis because of heavy rainfall and narrow river valleys. It is not unusual, for example, for water levels in rivers in the Andean foothills to rise 13–19.5 ft (4–6 m) in a single day and then to drop again in a day or two.

In the Amazon Basin, average

annual river-level fluctuations are most extreme in an area stretching from the middle Madeira River in the east to the middle Juruá River in the west. Average annual river-level fluctuations in this area range from approximately 33 to 49 ft (10–15 m).

West of the mouth of the Madeira, average annual river-level fluctuations in the Amazon River range from approximately 26 to 33 ft (8–10 m). Downstream of the Madeira, averages decrease progressively: in the estuary, daily tides reduce river-level fluctuation to less than 6 ft (2 m). At Manaus,

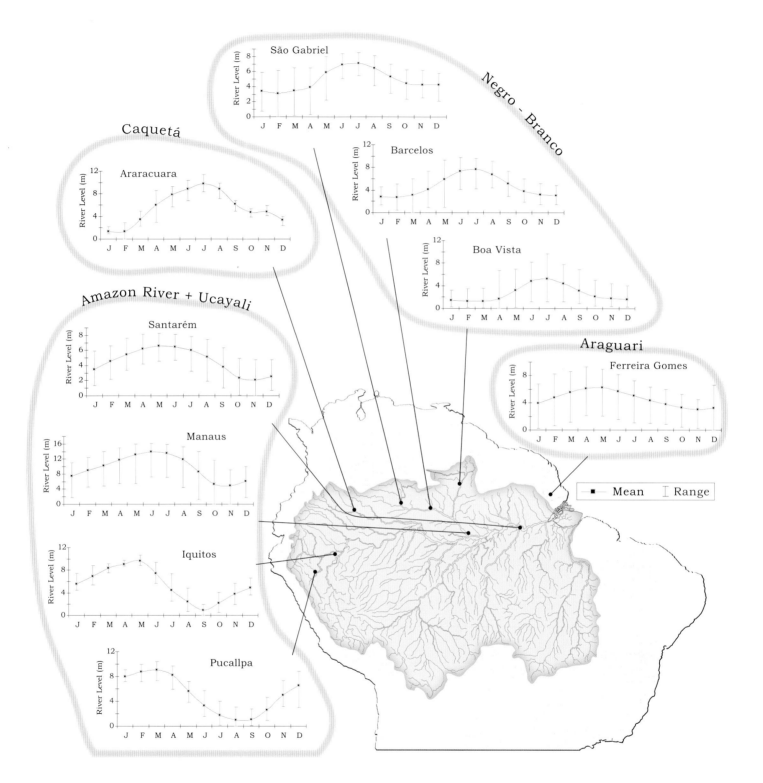

▲ **RIVER-LEVEL FLUCTUATION OF AMAZON RIVER, UCAYALI, AND NORTHERN TRIBUTARIES**

The Amazon River usually floods first in its western reaches, with peaks reached between March and May. In the central Amazon near Manaus, Amazon River levels are controlled by contributions from northern and southern tributaries, and peaks are usually reached in June. Northern headwaters are near the equator and their water levels can be falling between October and February while the Amazon River is rising because of the contributions from large southern tributaries. River-level fluctuation of the coastal Araguari is not influenced by the Amazon River, although ocean tides significantly influence water levels in its lower reaches.

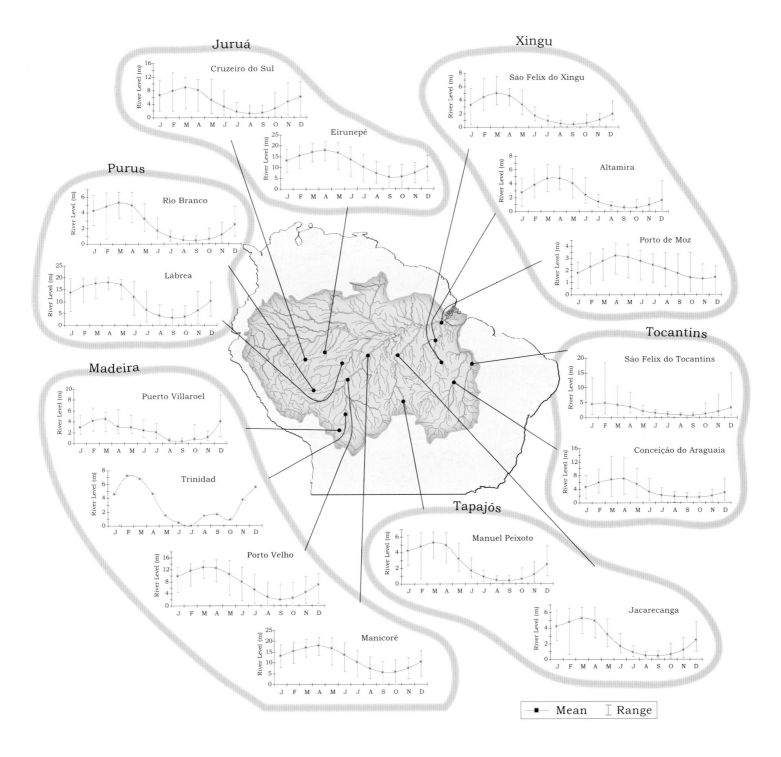

▲ RIVER-LEVEL FLUCTUATION OF SOUTHERN TRIBUTARIES

Most of the Amazon River's southern tributaries at points approximately 185 miles (300 km) or more upriver from their mouths reach their peak flood levels in March or April. Water levels are lowest usually between August and October. Lower sections of the southern tributaries are heavily influenced by the backwater effect of the Amazon River and rise and fall under the influence of the main stem.

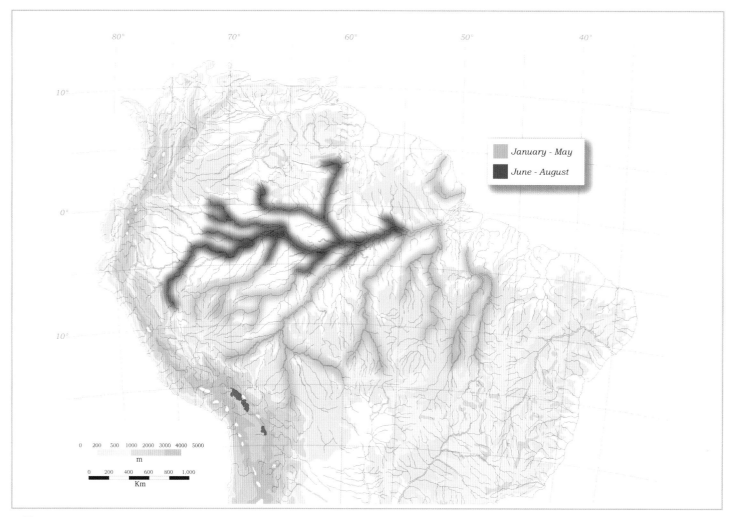

January - May
June - August

▲ **THE FLOODING SEASON**

On average the lowland rivers of the Amazon are in flood six to seven months annually. In a calendar year the southern tributaries are the first to flood. Flooding near the Andes is more sporadic, but few data have been collected in this region.

in the center of the Amazon, the average is approximately 33 ft (10 m). Headwaters and the middle stretches of Brazilian and Guiana Shield tributaries fluctuate from approximately 13 to 16.5 ft (4–5 m) annually.

When considering floods humans seem to think more about averages than extremes. This is evident throughout the world, where people live on floodplains and take into account only average flood levels. Whenever the periodic extreme floods come, they are considered natural disasters, often causing loss of life and billions of dollars in property damage.

Flood levels tend to deviate more than low-water levels. The range between high and low extremes of Amazonian river levels is approximately 1.5–2.0 times greater than the average annual fluctuation. The greatest extremes recorded are from the Madeira, the Purus, and the Tocantins in their middle stretches and exceed 66 ft (20 m). All of the large rivers appear to have years when floods are minimal and years when there is no pronounced low-water period. On average, however, floods in most of the Amazon Basin are fairly predictable.

The Amazon River flood is com-

plex—there is no simple upstream-to-downstream seasonal wave. In a calendar year, the first peak-flood levels are reached in April and May near the mouth of the Xingu, approximately 125 miles (200 km) from the Atlantic. The next peak floods are in May in the Amazonas stretch near Iquitos, Peru. The final peak floods are in the central Amazon near Manaus in June and July, about two months after the highest rainfall months. Robert Meade identified the reason for this flooding anomaly as a backwater effect caused by seasonal differences in the arrival times of floods from the tributaries.

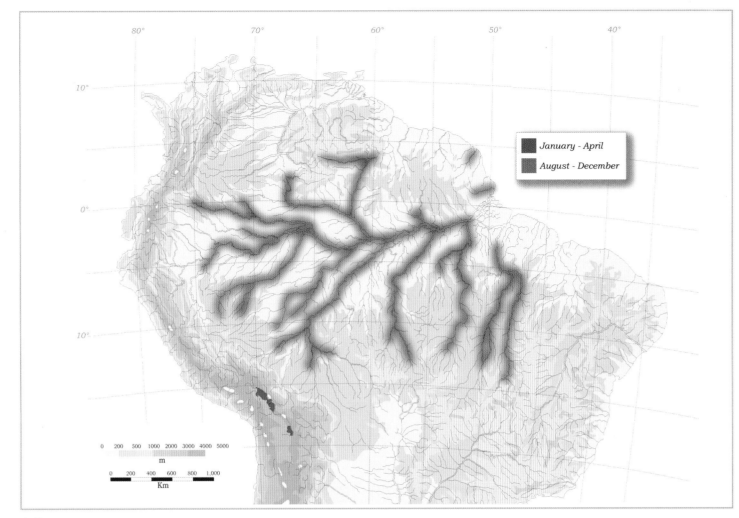

January - April

August - December

▲ THE LOW-WATER SEASON

Most of the Amazon Basin undergoes a fairly intense dry season between August and December, and this is generally the low-water period. An exception is the equatorial region in the north, where the floods can last until September.

The backwater impact may be viewed functionally as a natural dam caused by higher river levels in the Amazon than in some of its southern tributaries. The southern tributaries reach their peak discharges at least two months earlier than the main stem. The Amazon River does not fluctuate with its southern tributaries alone, however, because northern tributaries, especially the Negro, empty significant amounts of water into the Amazon. In addition, peak contributions of water from northern tributaries are two to three months later in the year than contributions from the southern tributaries.

The backwater effect is felt some 500 miles (800 km) up the Madeira and the Purus and causes falling river stages as much as 7–10 ft (2–3 m) higher than rising stages at any given discharge. A similar but less extensive backwater effect occurs in the Tapajós and the Xingu. The lower Amazon River floods first because the backwater impact is decreased. On the northern side the backwater reaches approximately 180–250 miles (300–400 km) up the Negro.

Although the water levels in the upper and middle Negro begin to fall in November and December, water levels in the Amazon River are already rising by this time. The Amazon River's backwater affect causes the lower Negro to rise two to three months before the rainy season of the upper and middle Negro. Likewise, the later flooding season of the middle and upper Negro, and of several other northern tributaries, causes the Amazon River to remain in flood two to three months longer than might be expected if the southern tributaries alone controlled the main river's fluctuation.

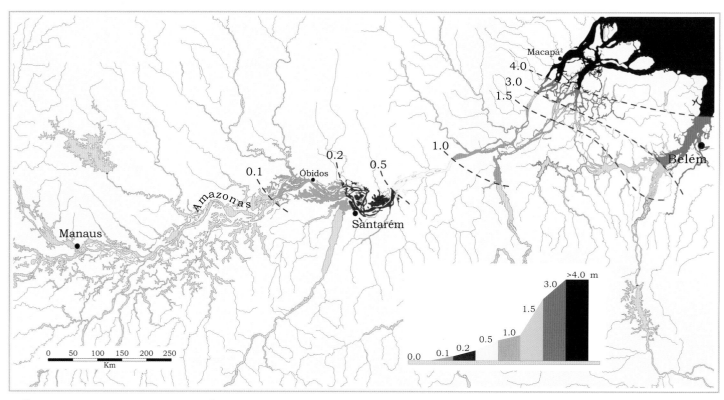

▲ OCEANIC TIDAL LEVELS IN THE LOWER AMAZON RIVER REGION

Even at the highest river stages, the surface of the lowermost 625 miles (1,000 km) of the Amazon River is less than 100 ft. (30 m) above sea level. The bottom on the channel near Óbidos is 130–165 ft (40–50 m) below sea level. Oceanic tides are noticeable as far as the city of Óbidos, some 500 miles (800 km) upstream. Near the mouth of the Amazon River, the maximum tidal range is approximately 13 ft (4 m). Changes in Amazon River levels are not perceivable outside of the mouth. River-level variation of the Amazon within 125 miles (200 km) of the Atlantic is largely controlled by the tides although there is a slight increase of 1.6 ft (<0.5 m) in absolute river level during the high-water period. Near the mouth of the Xingu River, 125 miles (200 km) upstream, maximum tidal range is approximately 6.2 ft (1.9 m); during the low-water period it averages 4.3 ft (1.3 m).

The Amazon River has a strong tidal bore—called *pororoca* locally—which is most evident near the mouth region. The bore, or uplifted solitary wave, is caused when spring tides overcome the river's current in shallow waters that are usually less than 10–13 ft (3–4 m) deep. The bore is noticeable only during low tides, when it can reach 6.5 ft (2 m) in height as it rolls 6–9 miles (10–15 km) per hour upstream. The bore's force is sufficient to demolish riverbanks and cause huge trees to crash into the water. Local mariners consider the Amazon River pororoca to be dangerous and give it due respect.

◄ LOW-WATER PERIOD OF NEGRO

The Negro has about a six month low-water period and six month high-water period. This photograph shows the same village pictured at right, but now during the low-water period

MIDDLE RIO NEGRO

▼ **HIGH-WATER PERIOD OF NEGRO**

River levels fluctuate approximately
16.5–33 ft (5–10 m) along the Negro. The
greatest fluctuations are in the lowest
reaches. This photograph shows the same
village pictured at left, but now during the
height of an annual flood.

CHAPTER THREE

COLORFUL RIVERS AND WETLANDS

The river landscapes of the Amazon are beautifully colored by distinct water types. Amazonian whitewater, blackwater, and clearwater rivers have been widely recognized in writings since at least 1865, when Alfred Russel Wallace's *Narrative of Travels on the Amazon and Rio Negro* brought them to the world's attention. "White water" as an English term to describe Amazonian rivers was borrowed from the Portuguese *água branca,* which was and still is used in Brazil. The Spanish equivalent, *agua blanca,* which is less common, is used in Bolivia, Peru, Ecuador, and Colombia to describe muddy rivers.

In English, "whitewater" usually refers to frothy water flowing over rapids, as in the term "whitewater rafting." To avoid confusion, the term "muddy river" is used when referring to a turbid Amazonian river, with the proviso that in Brazil, such rivers are usually referred to as whitewater rivers. The other two major color types of Amazonian rivers are black water and clear water. They share the characteristic of having minimal sediment loads.

Muddy rivers are café au lait in color. Near the Andes, however, after intense rainstorms, which can cause significant local erosion, the color of some tributaries might best be described as reddish brown. Most of the muddy rivers of the Amazon have tributaries in the Andes. The tributaries of the Purus and the Juruá, however, are in the Alluvial Extension Zone, where sediments from the west have been deposited within and along the downstream channels and on floodplains.

Several rivers draining the Guiana Shield—most notably the Branco, as its name suggests—are relatively muddy. Their average sediment concentrations, however, are only one-tenth that of the Amazon and Madeira Rivers, and they often become somewhat clear during the low-water period. The turbid Guiana Shield tributaries are herein referred to as "semi-muddy rivers."

In general muddy rivers with headwaters in the Andes have a higher nutrient content than the blackwater and clearwater rivers. The pH of water in muddy rivers is often near or above neutral (7.0). At elevations higher than approximately 6,550 ft (2,000 m) in the Andes, the pH of river water can be above 8.0. Water in rivers at these elevations in the Andes is also often extremely hard.

The Andes are essentially the main nutrient bank for the Amazon River, as well as for seven of its

◀ **NEGRO SANDS AND BLACK WATER**
The Negro might be described as a giant teapot. Its acidic waters are the result of plant compounds that have been incompletely decomposed in upland soils, in streams, and in the main river.

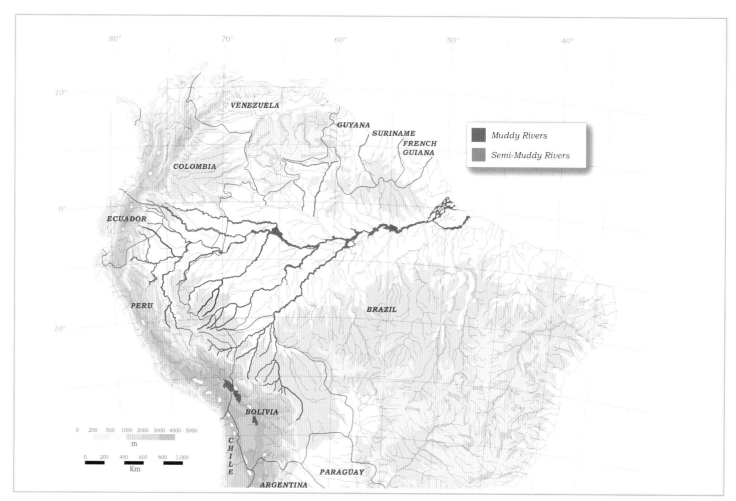

▲ MUDDY RIVERS

The muddiest rivers in the Amazon have headwaters in the Andes. The quantity of sediments discharged by Andean tributaries is sufficient to muddy the Amazon River from the foothills to the Atlantic. Several tributaries of the Guiana Shield are also turbid. The largest of these turbid tributaries is the Branco. Determining to what degree they might be considered muddy is somewhat subjective. Perhaps "semi-muddy rivers" is the most accurate term for these turbid rivers. Andean and Guiana Shield sediments have different chemical and mineral compositions of the transported materials. The mineral assemblages coming from the Guiana Shield are very mature, having been exposed to millions of years of mostly chemical erosion within the ancient soils of a tectonically quiescent landscape. The mature minerals result in less turbidity. Andean soil material, in contrast, is mostly immature and contains large quantities of minerals that muddy river water. Rapid tectonic uplift of Andean mountain chains and consequent accelerated erosion leave little opportunity for the transformation of rock debris into more mature mineral species.

◀ THE MUDDY AMAZON RIVER

The Amazon River near Santarém, some 1,850 miles (3,000 km) from the Andes and 500 miles (800 km) from the Atlantic, carries most of the sediment load that is eventually delivered to the Atlantic. Muddy water is often called "whitewater" in the Amazon, but the term is confusing in English because it refers to rapids or frothy water.

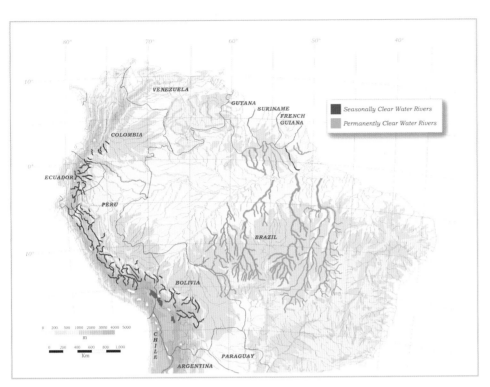

CLEARWATER RIVERS

Small clearwater rivers are found throughout the Amazon Basin. Most of the large clearwater rivers, however, drain the Brazilian Shield, and to a much lesser extent the Guiana Shield, ancient upland regions where erosion for hundreds of million of years has left relatively small amounts of unconsolidated materials that can be washed into the streams, especially where there is vegetation cover. Andean headwaters above approximately 130 ft (400 m) are seasonally clear and some might even be described as nearly crystalline.

MEETING OF THE AMAZON AND TAPAJÓS RIVERS

The clear, almost bluish water of the Tapajós contrasts strikingly with the muddy Amazon River on the right. The Tapajós drains a large part of the ancient Brazilian Shield. The Tapajós and other clearwater rivers have no visible impact on the transparency of the Amazon River beyond approximately 6 miles (10 km) downstream of their confluences with the main stem.

13 largest tributaries. The soils of the lowland Amazon are generally poor in nutrients, especially phosphorus, potassium, and nitrogen. In contrast, the soil muddy rivers flow through is derived from nutrient-rich volcanic material in the Andes.

Muddy water blocks sunlight and inhibits the production of phytoplankton and other algae. Most of the large rivers of the western Amazon, however, are flanked by large floodplains. Dissolved nutrients carried in suspended sediments reach the floodplains annually when floodwaters invade the inundated zone. On the floodplains the sediments settle to the bottom, and transparency improves enough to allow relatively high phytoplankton

production in the open waters usually referred to as lakes.

Where current does not impede growth, in addition to phytoplankton, a rich flora of floating plants with suspended roots also takes advantage of nutrient-rich floodplain waters. Water hyacinth is a good example of such floating plants. In shallower waters along the riverbanks and on the floodplains, rooted plants, such as cane grass, tap alluvial nutrients and form the famous floating meadows of the Amazon. When water levels rise, floating-meadow grasses can grow several centimeters per day and stay afloat. If water depths exceed 16–19.5 ft (5–6 m), the grasses become uprooted, and meadows can become free floating.

CLEARWATER STREAMS

There are tens of thousands of small clearwater streams in the Amazon Basin. The type shown here is characteristic of much of the central Amazon region where rainforest grows on clay soils. Rainforest streams become more turbid during the rainy season, when there is increased local erosion.

▲ MEETING OF THE NEGRO AND AMAZON (SOLIMÕES) RIVERS

The confluence of the Negro and the Solimões is one of the great wonders of the Amazon Basin and attracts thousands of tourists each year. Negro water is dark and thus absorbs more heat than the muddy water in the Amazon River. The warmer water in the Negro is lighter and literally rides on top of the cooler, heavier water in the Amazon for a short distance. The waters quickly mix due to the turbulence of the main river.

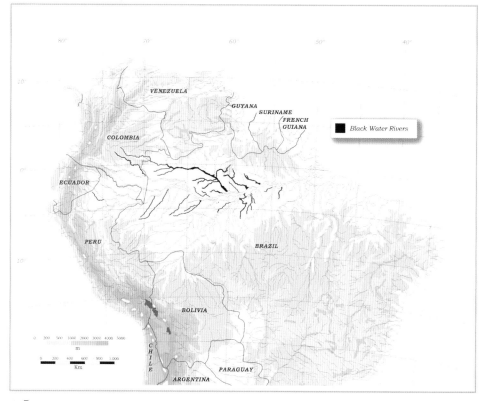

▲ BLACKWATER RIVERS

Small blackwater rivers or streams are found throughout the Amazon Basin. Most, however, are concentrated in the central Amazon and Negro region, where sandy soils predominate. The Negro River is not only the largest blackwater river in the world but also the world's second largest tributary in terms of annual discharge.

Amazonian clear water is a relative term. Limnologists—scientists who study bodies of fresh water—have rightly pointed out that there are many gradations of water color in the Amazon, especially within the clearwater and blackwater types. Clearwater rivers might range seasonally from crystalline to fairly murky, where visibility is less than 3 ft (1 m). Some clearwater rivers can also be slightly tinted by organic compounds. For simplicity the clearwater rivers of the Amazon Basin can be divided into three main groups: the large Brazilian and Guiana Shield tributaries; the Andean headwaters above approximately 1,300 ft (400 m); and clearwater streams and small rivers originating in the lowlands below approximately 1,000 ft (300 m).

Compared with muddy rivers, all clearwater rivers and streams of the Amazon Basin have minimal suspended sediment loads. For example, the average sediment concentration per a particular volume of water in the Tapajós can be 1 percent of that for the same volume in the Amazon River. When there is no gold mining in headwaters, the average sediment concentration in the Tapajós is less than one-tenth of that in the Amazon. Seasonally clearwater rivers and streams of the Andes can have very high sediment loads during intense rainstorms. River and stream gradients, however, are steep enough that sediments are soon washed downriver or downstream once the rains stop. The rivers and streams then begin to clear again.

Clearwater rivers and streams show considerable chemical variability. In general concentrations of major nutrients in Amazonian waters are much lower than the world average for fresh water. The rivers of the central Amazon region have the lowest concentrations, followed by those of the Brazilian and Guiana Shields. The chemistry of lowland rainforest streams is often very similar to that of rain water: concentrations of major nutrients are low and sodium can be a relatively dominant chemical in the water. In comparison, concentrations of major nutrients in muddy rivers are high and calcium is the predominant chemical in the water.

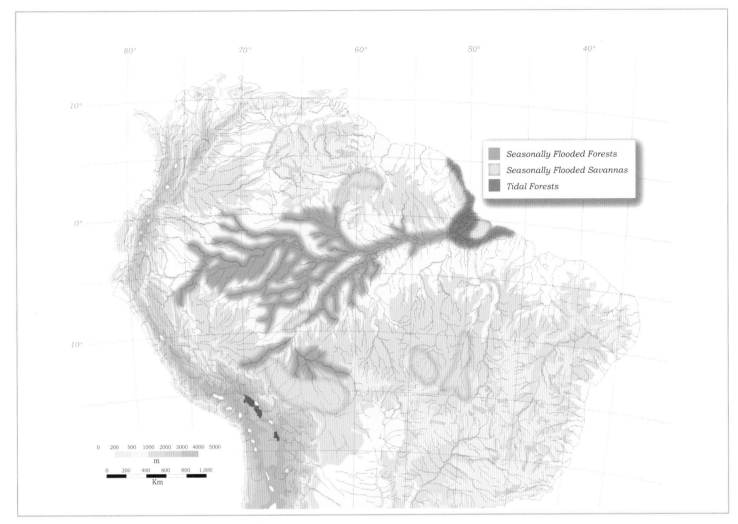

▲ MAJOR FLOODABLE HABITATS IN THE AMAZON BASIN

Perhaps 6–8 percent of the Amazon Basin is subject to some degree of flooding. The prevailing vegetation in floodable areas is forest and savanna. All of the large rivers have floodplains that are seasonally inundated. There are also extensive areas of flooded forest along small streams, which cannot be shown on this map.

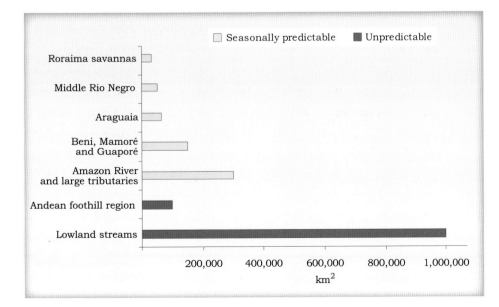

◀ FLOODING REGIMES OF AMAZONIAN RIVERS AND STREAMS

Most of the floodplain area in the Amazon Basin is along small streams where flooding is ephemeral, unpredictable, and regulated by local rains. These areas may only be flooded for a few hours or days at a time. The Amazon River and its larger tributaries have fairly predictable flooding regimes and are inundated much longer than small streams. Wolfgang Junk of the Max Planck Institute estimated that there may be 386,100 square miles (1 million km²) of floodable area in the Amazon Basin along lowland streams.

▲ FLOODPLAIN WATERS AND VEGETATION

The Solimões floodplain has a rich mixture of water types and vegetation. The Amazon River supplies floodplains with muddy water rich in nutrients. The vitality of floating meadows is dependent on an annual injection of sediment- and nutrient-rich Amazon River water.

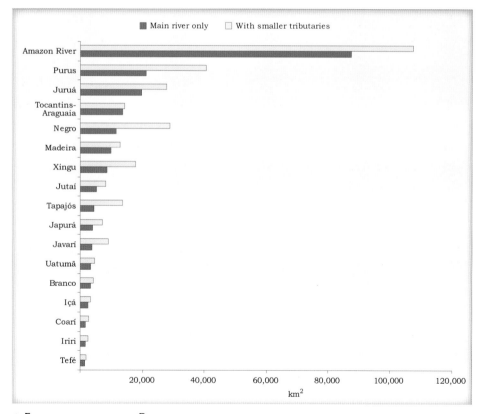

▲ FLOODPLAIN AREAS OF BRAZILIAN RIVERS

More than one-third of all the floodplain area in the Amazon Basin is found along the Amazon River. The highly meandering Purus and Juruá Rivers have large floodplains compared with their annual discharge. The meandering Ucayali River of Peru also has a large floodplain. Wolfgang Junk of the Max Planck Institute calculated the floodplain areas shown here.

Interestingly, rainforest streams often have even lower sodium values than rain water, indicating how efficient the rainforest is at removing nutrients. Most clearwater rivers and streams in the central and eastern Amazon Basin are slightly acidic, with pH values ranging between approximately 6.0 and 6.8. In the western Amazon Basin, pH values increase and can be above neutral (7.0) in areas dominated by Andean sediments.

Although many clearwater streams and rivers have floating plants, nowhere are they as exuberant and extensive as the great floating meadows in muddy rivers. In general clearwater rivers do not have enough nutrients to support vast herbaceous plant communities. Because of better light conditions, however, phytoplankton production can be considerably greater in clearwater channels than in muddy-river channels. The large mouth-bays of the Tapajós and the Xingu, for example, collect nutrients that, along with relatively good light penetration, support seasonal phytoplankton explosions, called blooms. When they appear, the term "green soup" is used to describe mouth-bay waters.

Seasonally clearwater rivers are most evident in the Andes above approximately 1,300 ft (400 m). Most of the suspended sediments transported down Amazonian rivers are derived annually below this elevation. Many Andean headwaters are turbid only during local rainstorms, although these storms may last anywhere from a few days to weeks.

Deforestation within the headwater regions of many of the rivers of the Brazilian and Guiana Shields will likely

▲ ISOLATED RIPARIAN FOREST
Riparian forest in the Llanos de Mojos of eastern Bolivia was extensively modified by indigenous peoples even before the arrival of Europeans in the sixteenth century. The isolated patch of floodable forest shown here on an island resembles what much of the present savanna might have looked like before human activities.

▲ PALM SAVANNAS OF MARAJÓ ISLAND
Most of the savannas of the Amazon Basin are inundated directly by rain water rather than overflowing rivers. Little is yet know about the aquatic ecology of these habitats. Most of them have been radically modified by agricultural development since the sixteenth century.

cause these rivers to become seasonally clearwater rivers. Increased erosion associated with large-scale agricultural development will also help bring about this change. Agricultural and mining activities have significantly altered the watersheds of many of the smaller tributaries of the Tocantins, the Xingu, and the Tapajós, and their waters have become more turbid.

Blackwater rivers are not confined to the Amazon Basin, but they attain their greatest proportions there. The aptly named Negro (Spanish and Portuguese for the color black) is the sixth largest river in the world, based on annual discharge; the second largest tributary in the world; and the largest blackwater river in the world. The Negro probably discharges more water than all the other blackwater rivers of the world combined.

The great blackwater region of the Amazon Basin centers on the Negro but also extends westward and eastward to include many of the small tributaries whose headwaters rise in the lowlands dominated by sandy soils. Small blackwater rivers and rainforest streams are found in all Amazonian countries, but Brazil can easily claim to be the blackwater capital of the world.

Black water is essentially tea that is brewed in areas where plant compounds are not completely decomposed. Black water can be formed wherever the rate of carbon fixation (photosynthesis) and its partial decay to soluble organic acids exceeds its rate of complete decay to carbon dioxide (oxidation). This phenomenon can take place on land, in groundwater, or in streams, rivers, and lakes.

All the medium and large blackwater rivers of the Amazon Basin have drainage basins dominated by sandy soils. The exact physical and biological processes leading to blackwater formation are complex and probably vary, depending on the local circumstances.

In the case of the Negro and other central Amazonian blackwater rivers, however, podsolic soils are the key.

Podsolic soils in the central Amazon are characterized by a sandy upper horizon over clay, but most of the rainforest grows on soils where clay dominates the upper horizon. The huge quantities of sand found in the central Amazon Basin—which centers on the Negro—were transported there over hundreds of millions of years from the Guiana Shield as it eroded. The sandy regions are characterized by stunted vegetation, called *campinas* and *capinaranas,* caused by a paucity of nutrients.

Litter decomposes slower on and in sandy soils than in rainforest clay soils. Sandy-soil plant communities appear to have special fungi (ectomycorrhizae) that inhibit other fungi species that are associated with litter decomposition. Furthermore, clay, unlike sand, filters or binds organic compounds. Its absence or burial

▶ SEASONALLY FLOODED FOREST

The Amazon River has more than 38,600 square miles (100,000 km²) of floodplain forest that is seasonally inundated for two to eight months each year. Most floodplain forest along the Amazon River is inundated for about six months annually. The maximum water depth in inundated floodplain forests along the Amazon River ranges from 13 to 26 ft (4–8 m).

▲ TIDAL FOREST

Most of the Amazon River mouth region is covered by tidal forest that is dominated by freshwater tree species. These forests are inundated twice daily compared with forests in the central Amazon that are flooded seasonally.

beneath sand means that little filtering takes place.

The darkest waters appear to be produced in areas where the upper sandy horizon is less than approximately 10 ft (3 m) deep, and tree roots can therefore reach the underlying clay horizon. Sandy-soil forests where roots are able to reach the underlying clay horizon produce more leaves than counterparts growing in areas where the sandy horizon is deeper than 10 ft. With more leaf production and thus increased leaf litter, more organic compounds are decomposed, which results in darker water.

Although dark in color, black water is so poor in nutrients that it is nearly equivalent chemically to distilled water.

The high concentrations of organic compounds in black water, renders it highly acidic. The pH of water in the Negro ranges from approximately 3.8 to 5.4. Measurements vary with location and time of year. The pH values of water in smaller blackwater rivers of the central Amazon appears to be higher than pH values of water in the Negro.

The total area (>154,000 square miles [400,000 km²]) subject to heavy seasonal flooding in the Amazon Basin is probably larger than the size of either the British Isles or California. Approximately 6–8 percent of the Amazon Basin can be considered wetlands. The lengths of small streams that are inundated laterally during rainstorms have never been measured accurately. One

estimate of their combined length indicates that at least 386,000 square miles (1 million km²) of floodable areas exist along small streams. If this estimate is accurate, then approximately one-sixth of the Amazon Basin is subject to some type of flooding. Floodplains of the Amazon River and its large tributaries, however, account for the most extensive areas that are inundated for long periods of time. The area of these floodplains exceeds 135,000 square miles (350,000 km²)—an area three times the size of Florida.

Floodable forest, open waters, and floating meadows characterize the huge floodplains of the central Amazon Basin. Depending on the exact floodplain configuration, these three habitats

can vary considerably in proportion to
one another. A reasonable estimate,
however, is that each covers about one-
third of the total floodplain area.

The central Amazon region has
only one flooding season, and it can last
six to seven months. During flooding
season, water depths on floodplains
rarely exceed 66 ft (20 m); greater
depths are found only in some of the
deeper lakes. Flooded forest can be
inundated to depths greater than 33 ft
(10 m) in some areas of the Madeira and
the Purus. Average water depths, however, are probably 13–16.5 ft (4–5 m) in
most of the central Amazon.

The higher parts of the floodplains,
such as levees, might be inundated for
only one to three months. Lower areas,
in comparison, can be inundated for
eight to nine months and, in exception-
able years, can be inundated for the
entire year. Floodplain forests can toler-
ate two to three years of nonintermit-
tent flooding. If the flooding lasts
longer, trees and shrubs begin to die, as
happened in the early 1970s when there
were extended floods.

Flooding near the Andes and in its
foothills is less predictable than in the
central Amazon. Floodplains, such as
those in Manu National Park in Peru,
are higher and often are inundated for
only a few weeks each year. Water depth
on inundated floodplains near the
Andes averages less than 3 ft (1 m).

The Amazon Basin has four large
floodable savanna regions: (1) the eastern Bolivian plains, which center on the
Llanos de Mojos between the Guaporé
(Iténez) and the Beni; (2) the Bananal
Island region of the Araguaia; (3) the
Roraima savannas along the Branco in
the upper Negro Basin; and (4) the
eastern savannas of the giant island of
Marajó and coastal areas north of the
mouth of the Amazon River. These
low-lying areas are inundated mostly by
local rain water, although there is also
considerable river spillover in all but the
Marajó Island region. The area of savannas in the Amazon Basin will continue
to increase with deforestation. Most of
the wetland savannas will become bordered by upland savanna, which will
increase in area at the expense of rainforest because of deforestation.

▲ Floodplain forest- and meadow-lakes

The Amazon River floodplain has thousands of open water bodies that are usually referred to as "lakes." During the floods the various smaller water bodies can be joined to form larger floodplain lakes. At this site in the Mamirauá Sustainable Development Reserve of the middle Solimões region, the lakes are largely surrounded by forest. The open water bodies are bordered by herbaceous vegetation, which floats during the annual floods.

◀ Wild rice

Wild rice often dominates the lower parts of floodplains. The wild species (*Oryza* spp.) are edible but seldom harvested. A wide variety of birds and fishes feed on rice seeds. These species of wild rice could have genetic importance in the future.

▲ LIFE AFLOAT

Floating meadows consist of both rooted and free-floating plants. The flowering water hyacinth shown in the foreground can become rooted if left stranded on the ground. Otherwise it floats with its nutrient-absorbing roots dangling in the water. Grasses and arums seen in the background stay rooted for most if not all of the year. Floating meadows provide important nursery habitats for fish and other aquatic animals.

◀ THE GREAT GRASSES

Two grass species dominate the floating meadows of central Amazon River flood-plains. Each is dominant in its preferred depth zone. In the deepest areas, *Paspalum repens*, the darker grass in the foreground, grows. Immediately behind it is *Echinochloa polystachya*. Various grass, sedge, and other herbaceous species can be seen in the lighter areas in front of the forest.

CHAPTER FOUR

HUMAN FOOTPRINTS

Nearly the size of the continental United States, the Amazon Basin is one of the most sparsely populated areas on Earth. With a population of approximately 20 million people, the Amazon has less than four people per 0.4 square mile (1 km²). In comparison, population densities in Brazil are five times greater, in the United States over 6 times greater, in China over 32 times greater and 75 times greater in India.

Admittedly densities alone mean very little. Densities are more meaningful when compared with the availability of arable land and other resources. How much arable land there is in the Amazon Basin is debatable. Arable land is usually considered land that is capable of producing crops. If pastureland is considered a crop, then perhaps 80 percent of all the Amazon Basin is arable. There is no evidence, however, that the Amazon Basin could economically sustain 2.5 million square miles (4 million km²) of pasture, because there would not be a market for the meat produced. The Amazon region must compete with central and southern Brazil, where beef productivity is much higher. The closing of international export markets because of

mad-cow and foot-and-mouth disease has also put a damper on Brazil's beef export expectations. Improved livestock health, however, could change this scenario.

The Amazon region is a net importer of foodstuffs. This is a good indication of the relatively small amount of land that can be considered arable from an economic perspective. Viewed in this light, the population density in the Amazon is high relative to the area's level of food production. Some argue that the Amazon could be self-sufficient in food production. The argument, however, fails to consider that productivity and quality for many if not most crops will continue to be higher elsewhere. Thus there are economic incentives for importing cheaper and better foods. This trend will continue with increased urbanization and improved air, water, and highway transportation.

Since about 1950 the Amazon region has rapidly urbanized. Perhaps 75 percent of the lowland population is now in cities with at least 5,000 people. Three cities—Belém, Manaus, and Iquitos—have populations of more than 1 million. Manaus, with a population of 1.4 million, appears to be the largest

◀ ENTRY INTO THE AMAZON
Early explorers viewed the Amazon as a "river-sea" because of its giant size. Today nearly the entire giant river system has been impacted to some extent by human activities.

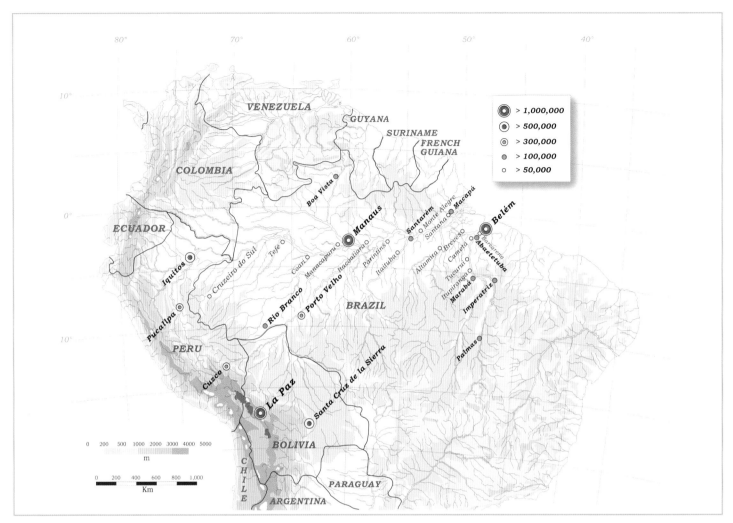

▲ URBANIZATION

La Paz is the largest city in the Amazon drainage, although it is located near a small headwater stream within the upper Beni (Madeira) Basin in Bolivia. Three cities with populations of more than one million—Manaus and Belém in Brazil and Iquitos in Peru—lie along the Amazon River. Pucallpa in Peru and Santa Cruz de la Sierra in Bolivia are fast-growing cities and will probably surpass the one million mark within the next few decades.

◀ ROADS AND STREAMS

Humans settle near small streams in the uplands of Brazil because a reliable water supply exists for people and livestock. In addition to impoundments, deforestation and subsequent sediment runoff extensively modify streams along roads.

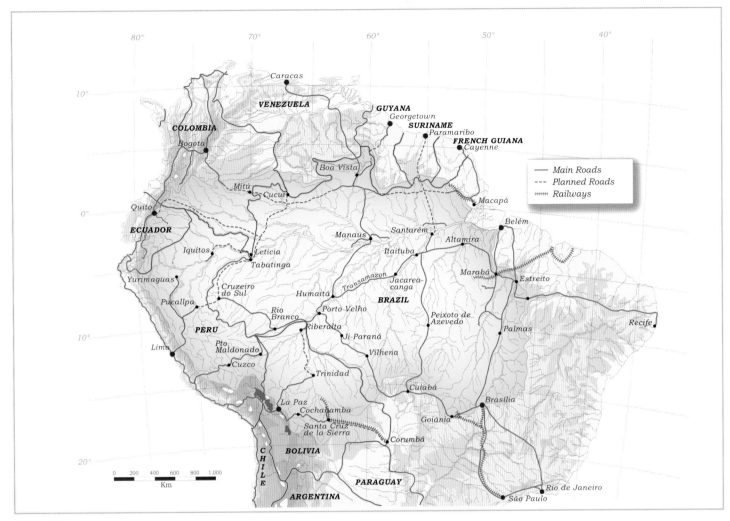

▲ THE AMAZON HIGHWAY NETWORK

The Amazon Basin now has more than 12,400 miles (20,000 km) of mostly unpaved highways connecting many of the region's main cities. There are perhaps another 62,000 miles (100,000 km) of feeder roads. Amazonian highways now provide connections from Brazil to Bolivia, Peru, Venezuela, and the Guyana border. The highways have been the main corridors for rural settlement, agricultural development, and deforestation.

city in the lowland region of the Amazon Basin. La Paz, Bolivia, with a population of 1.5 million, is technically the most populated city in the Amazon drainage. In the Mamoré headwaters, Santa Cruz de la Sierra, Bolivia's second most populated city, is rapidly becoming the country's economic hub. Pucallpa, on the Ucayali in Peru, is also growing rapidly and its population will soon pass the one-half million mark.

Agricultural colonization in the Amazon Basin has been steady since the 1970s. In Brazil most colonists in the 1970s migrated to Rondônia and Acre, but now they are gravitating to Pará, Roraima, and Amazonas. Colonized areas are nearly always heavily deforested. In Bolivia and Peru agricultural colonists (*andinos*) from the highlands have migrated to the Andean foothills and contiguous Amazonian lowlands. The five most heavily colonized areas in Andean headwaters of the Amazon Basin are (1) the Chapare region in the upper Mamoré Basin of Bolivia; (2) the region near Puerto Maldonado in the upper Madre de Dios in Peru; (3) the region along the Ucayali and its tributary, the Urubamba, in Peru; (4) the Oriente region of Ecuador in the upper Napo Basin; and (5) the foothill regions of the upper Putumayo and Caquetá Valleys in Colombia.

The media and many academics still have a strong bias against Amazonian cities. There is a tendency to portray Amazonian populations as rural and scattered along the rivers or new highways. This is ironic because most people in the Amazon, as elsewhere in the world, would prefer to live in cities.

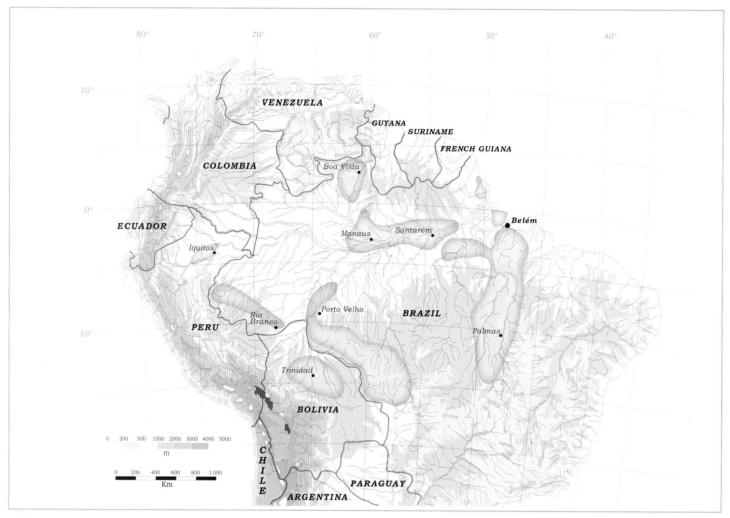

▲ MAIN CATTLE RANCHING AREAS

Cattle ranching may be seen ecologically as the "Africanization"of the Amazon. African grasses and a few species of grazing mammals largely replace the rainforest and its rich arboreal fauna. Although Amazonian cattle ranching has been heavily criticized, it now appears to be profitable and can be expected to continue to expand and lead to more deforestation.

The Amazon will continue to urbanize, and it is in cities that birth rates will fall and education and health will improve.

Until the 1970s the Amazon Basin had relatively few roads. Even now most of the major cities are not connected by a reliable highway network. Nevertheless, highways and roads have been the main focus of most large-scale development projects. The Belém-Brasília highway, completed in 1965, was the first great highway into the Brazilian Amazon and spearheaded agricultural settlement, logging,

and mining in the Tocantins Valley.

In 1970 the Brazilian military government made a commitment to integrate the Amazon Basin with the rest of the country by building 9,300 miles (15,000 km) of pioneer roads. The 2,050-mile-long (3,300 km) Transamazon highway, slicing across the southern drainage from Marabá on the Tocantins to Humaitá on the Madeira, was to be the main east-west artery. The government planned to settle one million families there by 1980. International concern was expressed at the grandiose

scheme and, in many ways, the Transamazon ignited the debates that continue to this day on the rationality of large-scale development in rainforest ecosystems before understanding how they function.

Based on the Brazilian government's goals, scientists have generally considered the Transamazon a failure. Today there are fewer than 50,000 rural families living along the highway. Only small portions of the Transamazon highway are paved, and the stretch between Itaituba on the Tapajós and

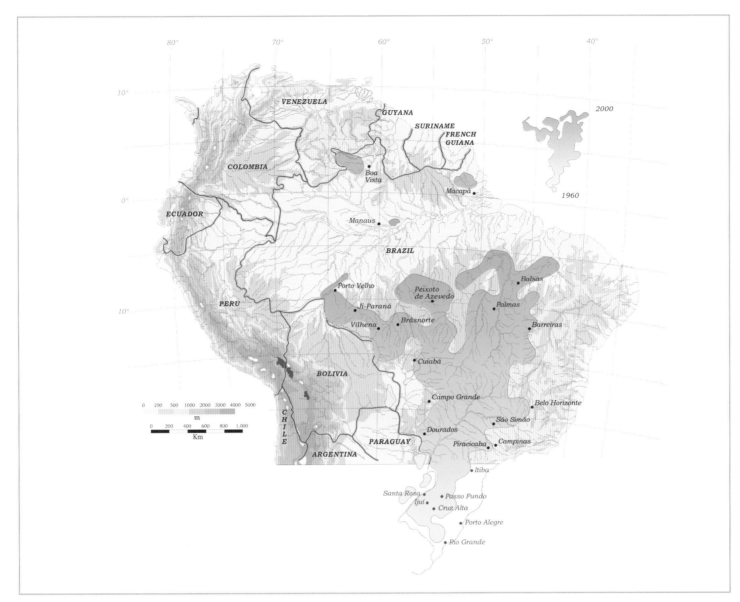

▲ Soybean frontier

The Brazilian soybean frontier is pushing into the Amazon Basin. This map shows the approximate limits of soybean expansion since the 1960s. At present soybeans are planted in less than 5 percent of the area within the limits shown here. Plans for major soybean farms in Brazil will continue the expansion of this frontier.

▶ Roads from the Andes

Farmers from the Andean highlands are colonizing the foothills and lowlands in Bolivia, Peru, Ecuador, and Colombia. Roads, such as the one shown here in the upper Madre de Dios Basin in Peru, invariably lead to increased human populations and accelerated deforestation associated with expansion of agricultural frontiers.

⬛ STREAM DESTRUCTION

Deforestation for cattle ranching in the Amazon has led to the destruction of thousands, if not tens of thousands, of rainforest streams. Once the rainforest is cleared, water in the streams literally evaporates away during the dry season. Small reservoirs are needed to retain stream water for cattle, such as shown here in the state of Acre.

⬛ LOW PRODUCTIVITY

Beef production per hectare on Amazonian upland soils is less than 20 percent of the levels elsewhere in the world. No more than one to two head of cattle can be grazed on Amazonian upland pastures. Soils are rapidly depleted of major nutrients, and during the dry season there is little growth of grasses. Cheap land and labor and few taxes, however, make cattle ranching profitable for large landowners.

⬛ THE SOYBEAN FRONTIER

The soybean frontier has expanded from southern and central Brazil into the Amazon Basin, especially in the upper and middle Tocantins, Xingu, and Tapajós Valleys. The large-scale sophisticated technology of soybean farms stands in sharp contrast to traditional slash-and-burn agriculture practiced in the Amazon.

Humaitá on the Madeira is often impassable during the rainy season. The Transamazon's main impact has been large-scale deforestation for cattle ranching, especially between the Tocantins and Tapajós Rivers. In the 1980s the Transamazon also facilitated access to gold-rich regions in the middle Tapajós and Xingu Basins.

The Brasília-Manaus corridor, via Cuiabá, was completed in the mid-1970s and paved by the 1990s. The 550-mile-long (900 km) stretch between Porto Velho and Manaus, however, proved too expensive to maintain and has nearly been abandoned. In the 1990s pioneer road building shifted to the north, and the Manaus-Boa Vista highway was paved. This highway continues to the Venezuelan border, and it is now possible to drive from Manaus to Caracas in approximately 36 hours. A paved highway was also built between Boa Vista and the Guyana border in anticipation of an Atlantic link through Georgetown.

There are few roads connecting Brazil with Bolivia, Peru, Ecuador, and Colombia. The only dependable route currently goes from Rio Branco to Acre and then to Puerto Maldonado on the Madre de Dios River in Peru. There are plans to finish a highway between Cruzeiro do Sul on the Juruá in Brazil and Pucallpa on the Ucayali in Peru.

Bolivia, Peru, Ecuador, and Colombia now have highways across the cordilleras and into the Amazon Basin. None of the trans-Andean highways are fully paved; most have only a few kilometers of asphalt near department capitals in the Andes. Passage is often difficult if not impossible during the rainy season because of

FORESTED LANDSCAPES IN SOYBEAN REGION
Forests of the southern Amazon Basin in the middle and upper Tocantins, Xingu, and Tapajós Valleys are generally drier and shorter than their central Amazonian counterparts. Drier forests are easily removed to provide land for large-scale agriculture. Previously shaded streams often dry completely up once the trees are removed.

frequent rock and mud slides in areas of unstable geology.

The Lima-Pucallpa highway, completed in the 1940s, is now the main artery serving development of the middle Ucayali region in Peru. The Cochabamba-Santa Cruz de la Sierra highway, which runs through the famous coca-growing Chapare region of Bolivia, has become a major artery to Bolivia's agricultural and petroleum frontier in the upper Mamoré Basin. In Ecuador the Oriente, as Ecuadorians call the Napo rainforest region, has roads from Quito to various oil-producing areas in the eastern lowlands. Colombian roads now penetrate the upper Putumayo and Caquetá Basins.

Environmentalists and the mainstream media have severely criticized Amazon cattle ranching, to the extent of creating myths about McDonald's turning the South American rainforest into hamburgers. (McDonald's, in fact, does not purchase beef from the Amazon.) Nevertheless, cattle ranching is now so extensive in the Amazon Basin that giant conflagrations are detected on satellite images during the dry season when pastures and forests are burned to clear them of vegetation. Almost one-third of the area of the state of Roraima, for example, has been burned by both small-scale and large-scale landowners for pasture development.

Large-scale cattle ranching will continue in the Amazon Basin, and it will be driven by both cultural and economic factors. Cattle and a preference for wide-open landscapes are integral parts of South American cultural history. A lack of large-scale economic alternatives has also guaranteed that cattle ranching will remain popular with investors and government agencies.

Most of the attention given to cattle ranching focuses on upland areas in pioneer zones, such as along the Transamazon highway in the southern drainage and in the western frontiers of Rondônia and Acre in Brazil. Cattle ranching, however, has possibly had

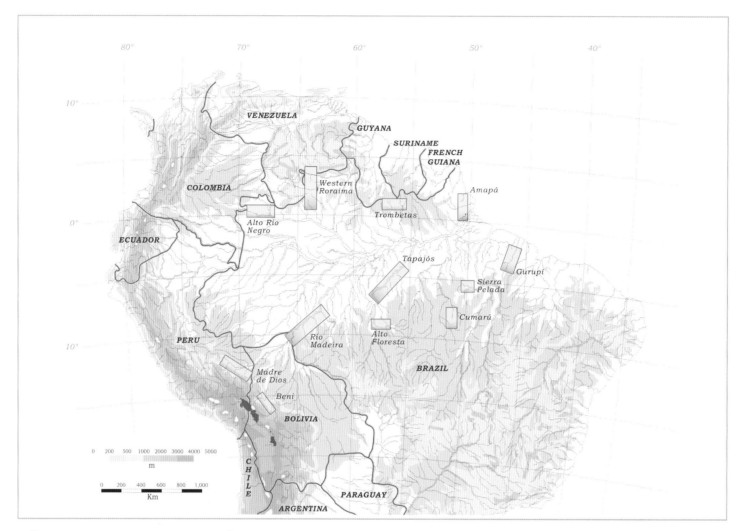

▲ PRINCIPAL GOLD MINING AREAS OF THE AMAZON

The Brazilian and Guiana Shields and the Andes are the gold-bearing regions of the Amazon Basin. Most gold has been mined from alluvial deposits in large rivers and streams. The gold rush in the Brazilian Amazon has declined since the early 1990s. At present gold mining is most extensive within the upper Madre de Dios region in Peru and the upper Beni region in Bolivia.

greater impacts on aquatic than on terrestrial habitats. Neither environmentalists nor developers and their government backers seem to take its effects on aquatic ecosystems into account when discussing cattle ranching. As the map on p. 54 shows, most cattle ranching in the Amazon Basin is concentrated in the middle and upper reaches of the main river systems. Downstream impacts can be far-reaching.

As deforested areas increase in size, larger parts of the watersheds will also be impacted. The effect on streams has been immense. This is because lack of forest shade causes these waterways to wither away during the dry season, thus also destroying the aquatic animals as well. One dried-up stream on a particular ranch may seem trivial, but when one considers that there are thousands of kilometers of such streams in a watershed, then the potential for large-scale impacts on watersheds becomes apparent. Stream destruction is perhaps the most overlooked threat from cattle ranching in the Amazon Basin.

Cattle ranching has also had major impacts along the Amazon River, especially between the Negro and the estuary. In this region deforestation takes place both on floodplains and in uplands. During the dry season cattle can graze on floodplain pastures. During the floods livestock are moved to upland pastures. Cattle ranching along the Amazon River is creating large corridors between the main channels and the upland rainforest. Also of concern is the destruction of streams that drain into floodplain lakes. Floodplain fish and other aquatic animals use these

▲ SLUICING FOR GOLD

There are several thousand gold miners with small-scale operations in the upper Madre de Dios River and its tributaries. Teams of three to five people use small sluices to strain alluvial gold from the thick gravel. An average gold miner makes less than $5 a day and work is limited to six months during the low-water period.

▶ WATERS WITH AND WITHOUT GOLD MINING

The turbid water in the foreground is from a stream in the upper Madre de Dios foothills that is being placer mined. The clearwater Noshiniskato River in the middle of the photograph is what its tributary was like before gold mining turned it turbid. Most of the foothill streams, however, are turbid during the rainy season; thus it is difficult to know to what extent increased turbidity during the low-water period might impact fish and other aquatic organisms.

▶ GUTTED STREAMS

The riverbeds of thousands of Brazilian and Guiana Shield streams have been churned for gold since the early 1970s. Streambeds were usually mined to a depth of 10–13 ft (3–4 m), and the impact of this on fish is not known.

▲ WASHING THE RIVERBANKS AWAY

Hundreds of kilometers of riverbanks in the upper Madre de Dios drainage have been blasted away by hydraulic mining. The fine silt and clay is discharged into the river after being channeled through a sluice. It appears that gold miners have increased the turbidity of the Madre de Dios River, at least during the low-water period. How far downstream from gold mining sites on the Madre de Dios impacts may reach is unknown.

⚠ MERCURY AND CITRUS JUICE

Citrus juice is often used in conjunction with mercury to amalgamate gold. The acidic juice removes oxidants (rust) and thus allow mercury to bind more easily to gold.

⚠ MECHANIZED GOLD MINING

Floodplains of the upper Madre de Dios in Peru have literally been turned over for alluvial gold. Mechanized operations using tractors and large sluices have devastated floodplains along the Inabari, Colorado, and other tributaries of the upper Madre de Dios Basin.

VENEZUELA

COLOMBIA

ECUADOR

PERU

RIO MADRE DE
DIOS, PERU

BOLIVIA

BRAZIL

streams seasonally for shelter and breeding.

It is unclear how much cattle ranching can expand in the Amazon Basin. If economics alone dictated its expansion, then the horizon might be in sight. Political and cultural factors, however, such as land ownership, are often the principal factors behind cattle ranching. Most cattle ranch owners live in cities, and their *fazendas* in Brazil or *haciendas* in the Spanish-speaking countries are part of their perception of wealth. Cattle ranching is likely to continue to expand near large urban centers.

Chicken farming in the Amazon is actually more productive and economical than cattle ranching. Although poultry rations are imported, the price of chicken is about one-half the price of beef. It is possible that chicken ranching will eventually slow the expansion of cattle ranching. Another scenario is that diseases, such as foot-and-mouth, will destroy export markets for beef

and thus the viability of cattle ranch expansion.

Although cattle ranching still dominates the agricultural frontiers in the Amazon Basin, large-scale crop farming has made major advances. Such tree crops as coffee, oranges, coconuts, and African oil palm have proven economically viable, although they appear to have a limited market. Rice farming is advancing in Brazil and Peru and, in some cases, is taking place on floodplains. Brazil is investing heavily in soybeans, a crop that grows relatively well on poor soils and has an international market. Soybean production has expanded greatly from southern and central Brazil and is now advancing rapidly into the Amazon Basin. Soybeans are being viewed as the next wonder crop that will complement cattle ranching in the conquest of the Amazon rainforest. Unlike cattle ranching, at least as practiced in most of the Amazon, soybean farming entails the heavy use of pesticides, often in areas near rivers.

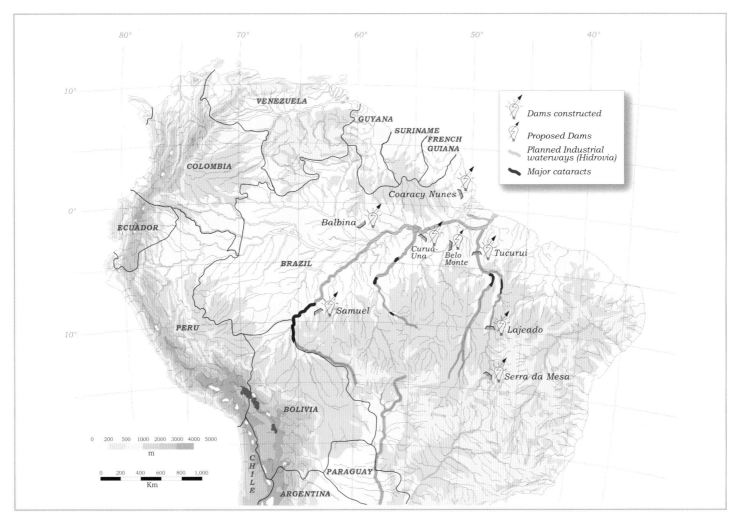

▲ DAMS AND INDUSTRIAL WATERWAYS

Brazil has ambitious plans for an industrial waterway network that will connect the Amazon Basin with the country's central and southern states. The "Hidrovia," as the industrial waterway is called, will facilitate export of soybeans from central Brazil, including the southern Amazon drainage, to international markets. Six large dams have been built or are near completion in the Brazilian Amazon. None of the Andean countries have dammed a large Amazonian river, although Bolivia has considered impounding the Beni where it leaves the Andes. Plans are now underway in Brazil to construct the largest dam in the Amazon Basin at Belo Monte on the lower Xingu.

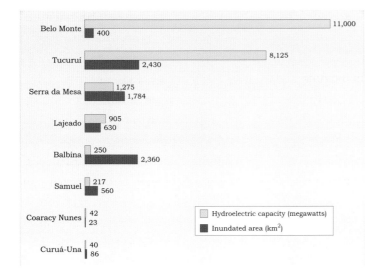

◄ AMAZON DAMS AND RESERVOIRS

Brazil is the only Amazonian country that has constructed large dams. The Belo Monte Dam on the Xingu will be the largest dam in the Amazon Basin and is planned for completion before 2010. The Balbina Dam near Manaus produces relatively little energy, but its reservoir inundates an area nearly as large as that of Tucuruí Reservoir. Despite similar reservoir sizes, the energy output of the Tucuruí Dam is more than 30 times that of the Balbina Dam.

▲ **DEAD RAINFOREST**
The area Balbina Reservoir submerged was not cleared and dead trees are standing nearly 20 years later.

▲ **BALBINA DAM**
Balbina Dam on the blackwater Uatumã near Manaus is considered a financial and environmental disaster. Although the Balbina Reservoir covers nearly 1,500 square miles (2,400 km²), the dam produces only 30 percent of the energy used in nearby Manaus.

Little attention has been given to the implications of heavy pesticide use on aquatic ecosystems in the Amazon Basin.

Gold mining in the Amazon drainage dates to pre-Columbian times, especially in the Andes. Miners began to exploit the lowlands for gold in the seventeenth century, but a gold rush of any significance did not happen until about 1980. The construction of the Transamazon and other highways in the southern drainage, in conjunction with higher gold prices in the 1980s, led to a scouring of the Brazilian Shield region, where large deposits of alluvial and vein gold were known to exist. A ready labor supply was available in drought-tormented northeastern Brazil and, as happened during the rubber boom eight decades to a century earlier, people living in northeastern Brazil migrated to the Amazon Basin wishing to find a better livelihood. Gold mining in the Amazon Basin in the mid-1980s provided work for perhaps as many as 500,000 people.

The 1980s gold rush centered on the Tocantins, Tapajós, and Madeira Valleys. In the Tocantins Valley most gold was extracted from veins at the famous Serra Pelada site in the Carajás region. In the Tapajós and Madeira Valleys nearly all gold was taken from alluvial deposits. Alluvial gold mining expanded to the Guiana Shield in the 1980s, where it took place in headwater areas of coastal rivers in the state of Amapá, in western Roraima, and, sporadically, in the upper Negro region.

Brazilian gold miners also spilled into Venezuela, Bolivia, and Peru. Outside of Brazil the major gold mining regions in the Amazon Basin have been the upper Beni of Bolivia and the Madre de Dios upriver of Puerto Maldonado in Peru. The gold rush burst in the mid-1990s as discovery of new deposits became scarcer and international prices fell. Gold mining continues today at perhaps 20 percent of the level of the 1980s.

Gold mining has been a major environmental concern in the Amazon Basin, principally because of mercury pollution and streambed destruction. Mercury pollution has received the most attention, although the issue is by no means clear-cut: scientists disagree on the ecological impact of mercury in the Amazon Basin. Most studies have focused on direct mercury contamination of resident human populations near mining sites and on the effects of mercury pollution on fish-eating riparian dwellers.

Inorganic mercury is relatively harmless, and miners are in direct contact with it daily. Mercury fumes inhaled or absorbed by the skin lead to direct contamination, but a wider concern is its entrance into food chains. Mercury from gold mining enters the aquatic environment either from precipitated particles that reached the atmosphere in fumes or from tailings. Naturally high levels of mercury may also add to the problem.

Mercury becomes dangerous in food chains when its inorganic form is transformed into an organic form called methyl mercury. Mercury can be methylated, that is, transformed into organic mercury, by microorganisms, in fish guts, and by other biological pathways. The degree of methylation, also called biomethylation, of mercury depends on alkalinity, temperature, anoxia (lacking oxygen), sulfur sources, dissolved organic material, and other factors within the aquatic environment. Methyl mercury, for example, usually accounts for more than 95 percent of the mercury present in fish flesh. Mercury concentrations increase as one moves up the food chain, a process called "bioaccumulation."

Studies have shown that some fish species, or at least populations of them, in the Madeira and Tapajós Valleys have relatively high levels of mercury, as do some fish-eating riparian dwellers. To date, however, no solid evidence has been presented that mercury contamination in the Amazon Basin is more than a local problem. One reason might be that most gold mining in the Amazon Basin has been in places where fish production is minimal or in tributaries characterized by heavy sediment loads. Mercury binds to sediments, and it is possible that sediments have carried most of the mercury downstream, where it was either buried or discharged into the Atlantic. It is possible that there are significant amounts of buried mercury in Madeira, Tapajós, and Amazon River sediments, especially on the floodplains.

The Amazon Basin has the greatest hydroelectric potential in the world. Most of the potential is found in Brazil on the Brazilian Shield. Although there have been suggestions that the Amazon River could be dammed, the Brazilian government has never seriously considered doing so. The Amazon River carries a heavy sediment load, and a reservoir created by a dam would have a short life. The Brazilian government has published various plans to harness the hydroelectric potential in the

BALBINA DAM

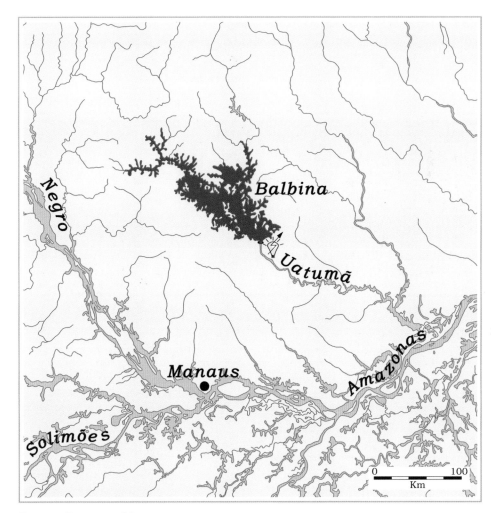

BALBINA DAM NEAR MANAUS

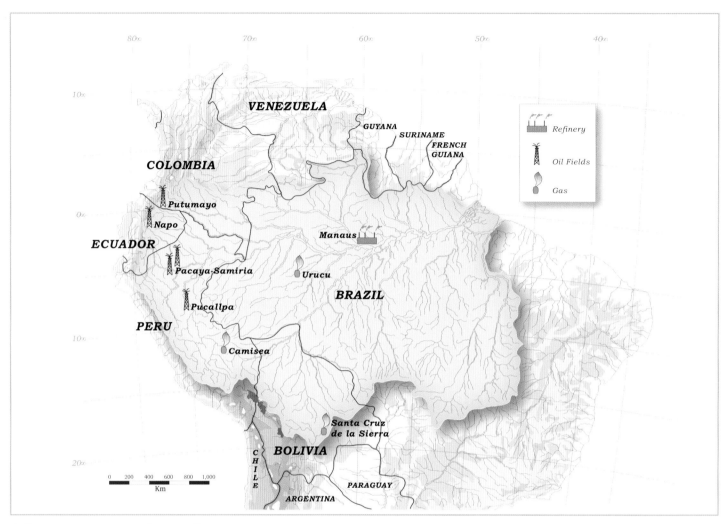

PETROLEUM SITES IN THE AMAZON BASIN

Petroleum companies have explored most of the Amazon Basin for oil and gas. Although petroleum is found throughout the basin, a large part of its known exploitable deposits are in the western Amazon only. The easternmost oil fields are the Urucu gas fields south of the Solimões (Amazon River) between the Purus and Juruá Rivers. The largest oil and gas fields are near the Andes in Peru, Ecuador, Bolivia, and Colombia. There have been oil spills in Peru, Ecuador, and Colombia. Petroleum companies in Amazonian headwaters in Ecuador have been sued in international courts for leaving huge amounts of petroleum wastes after fields were abandoned. Guerrillas in Colombia are of special concern because they have repeatedly blown up oil pipelines, which resulted in local pollution. Peru, Colombia, and Ecuador have pipelines from Amazonian oil fields that cross the Andes to refineries on the Pacific coast. The only large oil refinery in the Amazon Basin is near the confluence of the Amazon and Negro Rivers at Manaus. The Manaus refinery is supplied by tankers transporting oil from Nigeria, the Middle East, and southern Brazil.

THE PETROLEUM PARADOX

The Yanayacu terminal on the Marañón River north of the Pacaya-Samiria Reserve is the start of the North Peruvian pipeline that transports crude oil from the Amazon across the Andes. There is only one oil well in the Pacaya-Samiria Reserve, and the government retains rights to exploit two areas within the reserve.

MARAÑÓN NEAR
PACAYA-SAMIRIA

▲ OIL SPILL ON THE MARAÑÓN

In October 2000 a barge carrying the oil to the Yanayacu terminal (above) went aground and approximately 5,500 barrels of crude oil spilled into the Marañón. The spill, however, was contained, and a disaster was averted. The oil pipeline in the foreground is in the Pacaya-Samiria National Reserve.

Amazon. One of the more ambitious proposals—Plan 2010—called for construction of more than 50 dams on all of the country's major rivers of the Brazilian and Guiana Shields. To date five dams have been completed, and two more will be ready by 2003. Belo Monte Dam, on the Xingu near Altamira, is planned for 2005. It will surpass the Tucurí Dam on the Tocantins in energy output.

Environmentalists usually target the World Bank as the proponent behind Amazonian dams. Most dams, however, have been financed by other means. Government bonds financed the most recent dams. Brazil will continue to find creative ways to finance hydroelectric development despite environmental threats and problems with indigenous groups. Hydroelectric energy now accounts for approximately 50 percent of all the electric energy consumed in the Amazon, although for Brazil it accounts for more than 90 percent.

Dams radically alter rivers both upstream and downstream of impoundments. Upland areas that are inundated are obviously transformed into aquatic environments. Except for the Tocantins, all the Amazonian rivers dammed thus far have been relatively small tributaries, and the environmental impact has been localized. Only in the Tocantins have major fisheries been destroyed or radically altered. No measures were taken to protect migratory species in the Tocantins. Some of the migratory species, however, appear to have adapted to the new situation. Most changes have occurred downstream of Tucuruí Dam, where catfish and shrimp fisheries have declined.

When Belo Monte is completed on the Xingu, large dams in the Amazon Basin will have created at least 3,100 square miles (8,000 km²) of reservoirs—an area about the size of Lake Titicaca, South America's largest lake. The Balbina Dam, on the blackwater Uatumã,

has been the most heavily criticized dam in the Amazon. It is generally considered an economic fiasco and an environmental waste. Balbina's hydroelectric capacity is only 3 percent of that produced by the Tucuruí Dam. Despite great differences in hydroelectric capacity, each dam's reservoir covers approximately 930 square miles (2,400 km²). Balbina can produce no more than about one-half the energy consumed in Manaus, its main market.

There are active plans for at least six more dams on the Tocantins-Araguaia. In the Andean region, only Bolivia has considered building a dam on a large Amazonian tributary. The Beni leaves the Andean foothills through the Cerros de Bala Gorge near Rurrenabaque. The reservoir created by a dam on the Beni, however, would flood a large part of Madidi National Park. Consequently, environmental groups would fiercely oppose plans to construct a dam on this river. The Beni also has a heavy

▲ **MAHOGANY FROM HEADWATERS**

Most floodplain mahogany is harvested in the western Amazon, especially in the Madre de Dios and Ucayali Basins. Harvestable mahogany has been depleted along the main rivers, and loggers are moving into smaller tributaries in search of new sources. Only in protected areas, such as Manu National Park in Peru, is it still possible to see large mahogany trees on the floodplains. In tributaries of the Madre de Dios, timber rafts are floated downstream, and loggers often subsist on wild game, such as the peccary shown here.

sediment load, and it is questionable whether reservoir silting could be controlled.

Small canals have been built in the Amazon Basin since before the European Conquest. Most were designed as shortcuts to avoid huge meanders or to allow access to floodplain lakes. Indigenous groups of the Llanos de Mojos region in Bolivia and Incas in the Andes built relatively sophisticated canals for agriculture. These will be discussed in more detail in following chapters.

More recently Brazil has developed plans to build an extensive industrial waterway, called Hidrovia, to facilitate water transport in the Tocantins, Tapajós, and Madeira Valleys. The expansion of the soybean frontier in the states of Tocantins and Mato Grosso has created a demand for better transportation routes to maritime ports. The Hidrovia system is intended to satisfy this need. When fully functional the Hidrovia system will connect the Amazon Basin with the Paraná Basin in the south. The

Tocantins-Araguaia, the Tapajós, and the Madeira have cataracts. Dams need to be negotiated on the Tocantins-Araguaia. Locks are being installed at Tucuruí Dam. Locks and cataract excavation have been studied as possibilities to negotiate the Madeira rapids between Porto Velho and Guajará-Mirim at the Brazilian-Bolivian border. At present soybeans are transported by truck around the Madeira rapids and then barged to Itacoatiara on the Amazon River, east of Manaus, for further distribution downstream or by road to Venezuela.

Before about 1970, because few roads existed, most logging in the Amazon was on floodplains near urban centers. In addition, the heavy trucks and other equipment necessary to penetrate deep into the rainforest were not available. Timber was harvested mostly during the floods, when logs could be floated off the floodplains to the rivers, where they were then rafted to urban sawmills. With the proliferation of

VENEZUELA

COLOMBIA

ECUADOR

PERU

BOLIVIA

BRAZIL

SOLIMÕES,
MAMIRAUÁ SUSTAINABLE
DEVELOPMENT RESERVE

⚠ THE FLOODPLAIN IS LOGGED

When Manaus, the largest city in the center of the Amazon, began to grow rapidly after the creation of a free trade zone, the floodplains within 300 miles (500 km) of the city were extensively logged to support the booming construction business. By 1980 there were few harvestable trees left on the floodplains near Manaus, and the uplands began to be logged as new roads were built.

▷ THE LOGGING CHALLENGE TO PROTECTED AREAS

Most tropical foresters now believe that floodplain logging is not sustainable. Harvestable timber from natural forests takes decades to reach satisfactory commercial size. Timber is a relatively high-priced resource, and riparian communities have been unable or unwilling to control loggers, many if not most of who live in the local area. In some cases loggers desist once harvestable trees of high-priced species have been depleted. In this scenario logging will only have impacted a few species and not the general structure and diversity of the floodplain forest. Loggers have other impacts, however, such as excessive hunting. Shown here is a site in the Mamirauá Sustainable Development Reserve of the middle Solimões region where there has been some attempt to control logging.

▲ Lonely reminder of deforested levees

Many if not most scientists have assumed that the large grasslands on the Amazon River floodplain downriver of the Negro were natural and not the artifact of deforestation. Large trees and stumps, however, can be found on relic levees, strongly indicating that these areas were once forested.

◀ Uncontrolled floodplain logging

The kapok tree once graced Amazon River levees, and giants towering above the canopy could be seen every few hundred meters. Loggers have largely destroyed the giant along most of the Amazon River floodplain for plywood mills or relatively cheap construction timber.

chainsaws after about 1970, floodplain timber was often cut on site into large planks, and trees could be harvested all year. Throughout the year planks could be either hand carried or floated off the floodplains for transport to urban centers.

This process accelerated the destruction of riverside timber because logging was almost totally unregulated. By the 1980s harvestable floodplain trees were largely gone in the central Amazon, where the construction-hungry market of Manaus provided a ready market. Although the floodplain forest is rich in tree species, fewer than 20 are highly sought for commercial

timber. The species most valued for timber, such as virola, are usually cut first. Once these are depleted, a variety of less valuable species are harvested. Some nontimber species, such as rubber trees of the genus *Hevea*, were also largely depleted because they were used as floats to buoy heavy species that would otherwise sink.

With continued urbanization elsewhere, the floodplain logging scenario that first unfolded in the central Amazon to supply the Manaus market has largely been repeated throughout Amazonia since the early 1980s. In Brazil floodplain loggers are now exploiting the middle and upper Solimões, the

Purus, the Juruá, and the Japurá. Floodplain logging also takes place in the Mamirauá Sustainable Development Reserve at the confluence of the Solimões (Amazon) and Caquetá-Japurá Rivers.

Efforts are underway to control floodplain logging in Mamirauá. Managing this activity, however, has proven difficult in other protected areas, such as Pacaya-Samiria National Park in Peru, where harvestable timber is nearly gone. Of the protected areas with large floodplains, only Manu National Park in Peru has effectively prohibited large-scale commercial logging. River basins contiguous to it, however, are being heavily exploited for both upland and riparian timber. Peruvian loggers have removed most of the mahogany from the Madre de Dios and Ucayali floodplains. Lumberjacks are now heavily exploiting smaller tributaries for mahogany and other species.

Certainly the most symbolic and perhaps the most obvious impact caused by floodplain logging has been the destruction of the giant kapok tree (*Ceiba pentandra*). The kapok was common on the floodplains of all muddy rivers, especially on the high levees, where it stood as the tallest emergent. The kapok's enormous and sprawling crown was unmatched in the floodplain rainforest. Ironically the kapok was not generally considered a first-class timber species, although it was used to some extent for plywood. The emergent giants that were destroyed were at least 100–150 years old.

Tidal forests are also being heavily logged in the Amazon, especially in western Marajó Island. There are several hundred small sawmills operating in the Amazon estuary as well as larger enterprises near Belém. Virola, used for plywood, has been the species most exploited. Harvestable virola trees are scarce, and other timber species are being cut.

Recent studies demonstrate that, compared with other tropical forests, primary production (total photosynthesis) in Amazon River floodplain forests is relatively high but net primary production (production of usable wood) in such forests is relatively low. In other words, trees in floodplain forests grow relatively fast but lack the woody material required for human construction needs. This lack of usable wood is due

to structural components in the trees that are adaptations to floodplain habitats. Therefore logging species that grow in wild floodplain forests do not appear to be sustainable. The few commercially valuable species are logged too quickly to allow for successful natural replacement. Reforesting floodplain or tidal forests for timber species is almost nonexistent in the Amazon, even in areas where highly valued mahogany has been overharvested.

Fish have been an important protein source in the Amazon for both subsistence and urban populations. Nearly all of the major urban centers are located near a large river, which initially facilitated not only transportation but also proximity to fisheries. The fishing industry continues to be one of the main part- and full-time employers in the Amazon, a region that suffers from serious unemployment. In general commercial fisheries are most important in the lowland areas below approximately 820 ft (250 m) in elevation where there are large rivers and floodplains. The mouth region of the Amazon River, including the Marajó Bay area, is also important to freshwater fisheries.

With urbanization, per capita fish consumption has decreased in most Amazonian cities since the 1970s, when fish often accounted for nearly 75 percent of the animal protein consumed. Per capita consumption within cities, however, varies greatly. Supplies of relatively inexpensive fish are still available for people in the lower economic classes. Consumption of fish among subsistence populations in rural areas along rivers remains high.

More than 200 fish species are

▲ **THE LEVEE GIANT**
The kapok tree reaches more than 180 ft (55 m) in height and was the most characteristic emergent tree of the Amazon River floodplain. The kapok tree shown here was about the only tree left in a heavily deforested floodplain area near Santarém.

▲ **THE BUTTRESSED FOREST**
The kapok (*Ceiba pentandra*, Bombacaceae) is the largest tree of the Amazon River floodplain and is usually found on the high levees. The kapok also has the largest buttresses. The flood line can easily be seen above the boy's hand.

▲ A FRUIT- AND SEED-EATING
MIGRATORY FISH

The fruit- and seed-eating tambaqui of
Brazil, or gamitana in Spanish-speaking
countries, is one of the most important food
fish in the Amazon. The tambaqui feeds
heavily in flooded forests during the high-
water season, as shown here, but under-
takes long migrations in river channels
during the low-water period and at the
beginning of the annual floods to reach suit-
able spawning habitats.

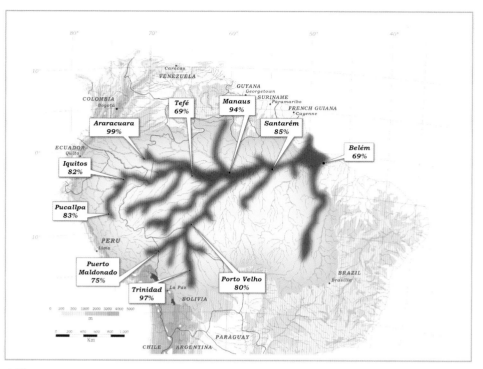

▲ THE IMPORTANCE OF MIGRATORY FISH

Migratory fish account for 69–99 percent of the total catch sold in the large fish markets in the
Amazon Basin. The area in blue includes the main areas fished for migratory species to supply
large urban markets in the lowland Amazon. The high percentages strongly suggest that migratory fish and their habitats need to be protected to maintain a sustainable fisheries.

targeted by the commercial fishing
industry in the Amazon, although only
about 20 species are sold in cities. The
fishing industry in Brazil accounts for
approximately 80 percent of the annual
fish harvested in the Amazon Basin, followed by Peru with approximately 15
percent. The other 5 percent is divided
among Bolivia, Colombia, and Ecuador.

Biologists estimate that subsistence
and commercial fisheries harvest
approximately 150,000–200,000 tons of
fish annually in the Amazon Basin. If
fishermen soon begin to target underex-
ploited instead of overexploited species,
this annual catch level is sustainable.
The first-class species have been heavily
exploited for at least four decades due to
growing urban markets and the proliferation of gillnets and seines since the
1960s. However, fewer than five species

appear to have been seriously overexploited, at least in some rivers.

The most striking characteristic of
Amazonian fisheries is that migratory
species account for most of the commercial catch. The enormous size of the
Amazon Basin, in conjunction with relatively few physical barriers, has provided one of the world's great theaters
for the evolution of long-distance
migratory fish species. The longest
freshwater migrations in the world
appear to be made in the Amazon Basin
by perhaps as many as a dozen species.

Throughout the Amazon, people
living in rural areas along rivers and
commercial fishing fleets target migratory fish. Migratory species account for
approximately 69–99 percent of total
annual catches in major Amazon fish
markets, and many of these species are

among the most prized food fishes.

Some Amazon fish species, such as
the dorado catfish (*Brachyplatystoma flavi-
cans*), use the estuary as a nursery for
their young but migrate 2,500–3,100
miles (4,000–5,000 km) upstream to
spawn in Andean foothills. From the
estuary to the Andes, the dorado is an
important food fish. Other species,
such as the fruit- and seed-eating tambaqui (*Colossoma macropomum*), under-
take long seasonal migrations that often
include muddy, clearwater, and blackwater rivers.

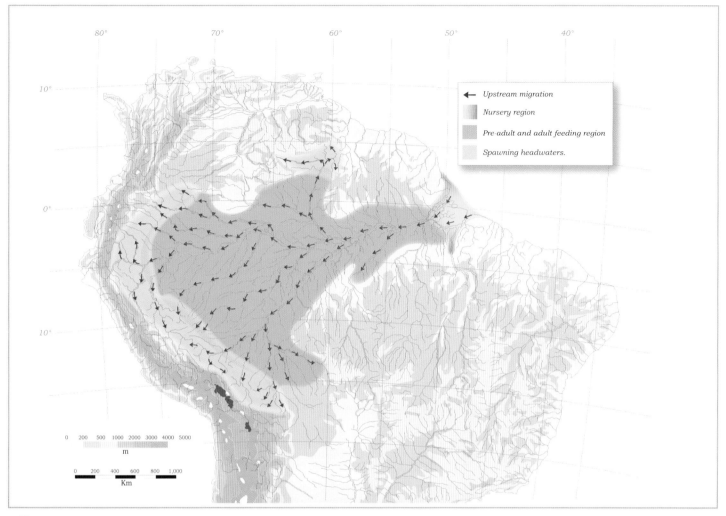

Legend:
← Upstream migration
Nursery region
Pre-adult and adult feeding region
Spawning headwaters.

0 200 500 1000 2000 3000 4000 5000
m

0 200 400 600 800 1,000
Km

▲ THE LONGEST MIGRATION

The migration of the dorado illustrates the extent to which migratory fish species in the Amazon have evolved to use enormous areas for their life histories. This map shows the upstream migration of dorado to reach spawning habitats in headwaters. The dorado is fished commercially from the Amazon River mouth to the Andes.

▶ THE DORADO CATFISH

The dorado is one of the largest catfish in the Amazon and an important food fish. The fish shown here is an adult caught in the Amazonas near Iquitos, Peru.

CHAPTER FIVE

EASTERN WETLANDS
The Amazon Meets the Atlantic

The eastern wetlands near the Amazon River mouth region consist of a complex maze of archipelagoes, a giant island, an enormous and largely freshwater bay, and tidal forests; they are the meeting area of Amazon and Atlantic waters. In the battle between fresh water and saltwater, the fresh water largely dominates the ecology of the eastern region. Amazon River discharge forms a bulwark against marine water, and the coastal wetland savannas are dominated by rain water. The marine influence is most easily detected by the presence of mangroves near the ocean. The giant island of Marajó adds nearly 625 miles (1,000 km) of additional coastline to the eastern wetlands. An internal delta forms a labyrinth of river and forest landscapes.

The Amazon coastal region stretches from the Oiapoque River at the Brazilian-French Guiana border to just southeast of Marajó Bay. Most of this area is not hydrographically in the Amazon Basin. From the viewpoint of Amazon wetlands management, however, it should be considered as ecologically connected. The presence of migratory freshwater catfish attests to its ecological connection with the main river system.

The dominant geographical features north of Marajó Island are the huge quantities of mud that are strewn along the Amapá coast and extensive mangroves. The muddy coast receives most of its sediments from Amazon River discharge. There has been little development along the Amapá coast, and most of the mangrove forests are relatively undisturbed. Amapá's mangroves are used for crabbing, but little commercial fishing is done in the muddy habitats. Most commercial fishing takes place offshore. Cattle ranching activities are moving eastward from the Amapá savannas and beginning to encroach on some of the tidal streams.

Environmental planners have ignored the Amazon River mouth region because very little is known about it. There are still extensive and very impressive tidal forests on some of the islands and along the coast. In contrast to mangroves along the Amapá coast, the forests near the Amazon River mouth are floodplain rainforest. Inland deforestation and savanna burning are encroaching on these coastal freshwater forests. Few people have settled in the mouth region, probably because the huge quantity

◀ **MARAJÓ BAY FISHING**

Fishing is the main economic activity along most of the coast of Marajó Bay. Tidal forests are still relatively undisturbed, and fishermen use these habitats for commercial and subsistence fishing.

▶ **THE COASTAL REGION**

The Atlantic coastal region influenced by the Amazon River is approximately 550 miles (900 km) long. It stretches from northern Pará to at least French Guiana. Amazon River sediments travel even farther northward and reach the Orinoco Delta. Brackish water dominates most of the coastal region except near the mouth of the Amazon River, which is fresh water. Mangrove is the dominant vegetation along the coast. Despite being designated a state conservation unit, the Amazon River estuary region has no functional parks or reserves, and none of the coastal region is protected. There are three protected coastal areas in the state of Amapá. The Piratuba Reserve and the Cabo Orange Reserve occupy more than one-half of the coastal region north of the Araguari. The island of Maracá is swampy and dominated by mangroves.

of mud makes navigation difficult. The mouth region would be an ideal place for a small reserve to protect the easternmost extension of floodplain forest, none of which is protected at present.

The Atlantic side of Marajó Island includes only about one-third of the northern coast of the giant island. Sand dunes and extensive bamboo thickets characterize the northeastern coast, although there are also areas of extensive mangroves. The sand dunes contrast sharply with the mud flats at the mouth of the Amazon River. Annual fires set by cattle ranchers have radically modified Marajó's northeast coast. The extensive bamboo thickets are probably artifacts of fire. The nearshore coastal waters of northeastern Marajó are important nursery habitats for commercial catfish.

Compared with the Amazon River, Marajó Bay discharges relatively little water and sediments. Marajó Bay waters are nevertheless always turbid. Numerous peninsulas and islands characterize the eastern coastal area near the mouth of the Bay. Coastal waters in this region are largely brackish and somewhat turbid because Amazon River sediments, via the Bay, are flushed eastward. Mangroves dominate the coastal vegetation, and the littoral aquatic fauna is largely oceanic. Fresh water, however, does penetrate eastward along the mainland northeast of Marajó Bay during the high-water period (May–July) of the Amazon River. Also, small coastal rivers contribute freshwater locally.

Covering approximately 1,700 square miles (4,500 km²), Marajó Bay is ecologically a part of the Amazon Basin. Although some might question whether this is true, the discharge of the Amazon

▲ TIDAL STREAMS

The headwaters of tidal streams along the Amapá coast are in nearby savannas. Mangrove forest accompanies tidal streams for several kilometers inland, at which point freshwater species dominate. The mangroves along Amapá coastal streams are still relatively undisturbed.

▲ AMAPÁ COAST

The discharge of the Amazon River is sufficient to dilute saltwater along the entire coast of the state of Amapá. Mangroves dominate the tidal, brackish-water forests as shown here near the mouth of the Araguari River.

▼ MUD FLATS OF AMAZON RIVER MOUTH

The mouth of the Amazon River is choked with sediments that get deposited when current speed is reduced by the Atlantic. During low tides, mud flats can extend more than 0.6 miles (1 km) from the forested shore zone.

VENEZUELA

COLOMBIA

ECUADOR

PERU

BOLIVIA

BRAZIL

AMAPÁ COAST

▲ **Fire and nursery habitats**
Tidal streams and their forests are important nursery habitats for fish and crustaceans. Fires on Marajó are uncontrolled and each year invade tidal forests. The extent to which destruction of tidal forests might impact fish and crustacean populations has not been studied.

Marajó Island Coast

River water into the bay should dismiss that doubt. Marajó Bay is bordered on the west by the island of Marajó and on the east by the mainland. Its southern limit is usually taken to be near Belém where the Guamá meets the Pará. Other than transportation, Marajó Bay's main commercial value is fishing. Experimental drilling for petroleum in Marajó Bay has not revealed economically viable deposits of fossil fuels.

Marajó Bay receives large quantities of sediments from the Amazon River via the Breves Channel and the Pará River. Only a small percentage of Amazon River water flows through the Breves Channel, but this discharge is sufficient to muddy Marajó Bay throughout the year. Heavy deforestation in the state of Pará has also increased erosion in the Guamá Basin, which may increase the sediment input into Marajó Bay.

The deepest waters of Marajó Bay are less than 100 ft (30 m) deep. River discharge through Marajó Bay is sufficient to ensure a largely freshwater environment. During the low-water period of the Amazon River, however, the water becomes brackish for approximately 50 miles (80 km) inland from the Atlantic. Near Belém salt concentrations are less than approximately 1 ppt (oceanic water averages 35 ppt).

Brackish water causes sediments to flocculate, that is, bind together and become heavier, which causes them to settle to the bottom. Water transparency is improved, and phytoplankton production increases. Both freshwater and marine species of fish and shrimp use the phytoplankton-rich waters of Marajó Bay as nurseries.

The mainland coastal vegetation of Marajó Bay subject to tidal flooding ranges from mangroves near the Atlantic to freshwater forests farther inland. Occasionally mangrove species are found just beyond Belém, but they are not dominant. Mangrove species so far inland usually appear on new sandbars or mud flats that will eventually be overtaken by freshwater shrub and tree species.

The tidal forests southwest of Belém are an excellent example of the eastern Amazon's richness in palms. Buriti (*Mauritia* spp.) and assaí (*Euterpe* spp.) palms dominate. The assaí palm is exploited for palm hearts and fruit used in juices and ice creams. Local communities have managed the palm-dominated tidal forests relatively well. They leave most of the native forest intact but plant assaí, which can be harvested. Few floodplain communities in the Amazon have managed their flooded forests as well as these communities have in the estuarine region.

Although the mainland of Marajó Bay, with Belém in the center, is heavily populated, the natural tidal zone is still relatively intact. Some mangroves were killed when roads without culverts were built across them. However, these tidal

▲ TIDAL STREAMS OF NORTHERN MARAJÓ
Mangroves and freshwater tree species often grow in the tidal streams of northern Marajó. Boggy soils have protected some of them from the annual fires that ranchers set to burn the savannas. At present, however, there are no programs aimed at protecting the tidal forests of Marajó.

▲ COASTAL SAND DUNES
The contact zone between Amazon River and Marajó Bay discharge is along the northeastern coast near Cape Maguari on the island of Marajó. Unlike at the Amazon River mouth and along coastal Amapá, sand dunes are characteristic of this region. The dunes also contain considerable quantities of silica remains from algae called diatoms. The forests behind the coastal dunes have largely been destroyed by fire.

forests have not been extensively cleared for crop or shrimp farming. There have been some rice- and pasture-farming experiments in the relatively rich soils of some tidal areas. Large-scale farming could one day threaten these habitats. The benefits of any large-scale farming projects in tidal forest areas should be weighed against their impacts on fisheries.

Marajó Bay is polluted to some extent by industrial and urban effluents from Belém and smaller coastal cities. The largest industrial facility on Marajó Bay is an aluminum-processing plant located on the island of Barcarena southwest of Belém. The Barcarena plant is modern, however, and slurry and tailings appear to collect in holding ponds.

Encompassing approximately 19,000 square miles (49,000 km²), Marajó is the largest river island in the world. Marajó is larger than all Caribbean islands except Cuba and Hispaniola (the Dominican Republic and Haiti)—it is more than four times the size of Jamaica and five times that of Puerto Rico. A few European countries, such as Belgium and Switzerland, are smaller than Marajó.

Geographically Marajó Island is naturally divided into its eastern half, with vast savannas, and its western, largely forest-covered half. Most of the giant island is subject to seasonal or tidal flooding. Numerous tidal rivers less than approximately 60 miles (100 km) long slice through the western, forested

region. The eastern interior of Marajó forms an enormous inland basin that collects rain water, which inundates the area for about six to eight months annually. The huge flooded forests of Marajó are related floristically to the Amazon River floodplain forest. Mangroves, which probably account for less than 10 percent of all floodable forest on Marajó, are found mostly along the northern coast and inland along Marajó Bay.

Indigenous peoples, Portuguese colonists, and Brazilian ranchers have all had major impacts on the landscapes of Marajó, especially in the eastern savannas. Marajó's savannas have been burned for centuries, if not thousands of years. The Portuguese reported

▲ THE MEETING OF MARAJÓ BAY AND THE
ATLANTIC OCEAN
Amazon River sediments muddy Marajó Bay
as far as the Atlantic during the entire year.
Near São Caetano at the mouth of Marajó
Bay, the water does not become clear and is
there no invasion of pure saltwater.

ATLANTIC COAST,
SOUTHEAST OF
MARAJÓ BAY

indigenous peoples using fire to corral turtles during the dry season, and this practice continues. It is possible that most of the savannas of eastern Marajó have expanded because of burning. The forests that have survived, such as those dominated by swamp-loving palms, have perhaps been lucky enough to escape fire. With the expansion of modern ranching, however, cattle and water buffalo now trample through these swamp forests, destroying seeds, seedlings, and saplings.

Arari is the largest lake on Marajó and the center of livestock ranching and fishing. The Arari River, whose mouth is just opposite Belém, connects the shallow lake to Marajó Bay.

A canal on the northern part of Marajó, Canal da Tartaruga, was excavated in the 1950s to expedite shipping between Belém and Macapá near the Amazon River mouth. The canal, however, began to drain Arari Lake, and it became necessary to build an earthen dam on the Arari River to save local

fisheries. The Arari Lake region has been almost completely deforested. Savanna grasses are maintained by fire. During the flooding season, the Arari River is joined to one vast sheet of water that inundates the eastern interior of Marajó Island.

A species of bottom-feeding armored catfish called *tamoatá* (*Hoplosternum littorale*) dominates the Arari Lake fishery. The high production of these catfish might be partly related to livestock feces washing into and fertilizing the Lake.

North of the savannas on the eastern half of Marajó Island are immense palm forests that remain swampy for most of the year. The buriti (*Mauritia flexuosa*) and assaí (*Euterpe oleracea*) palms dominate these forests. Assaí is exploited for palm hearts, and helicopters have been used to transport it from otherwise inaccessible areas. Livestock invade the palm forests during the dry season and during the rainy season when water depth is less than approxi-

mately 20 in. (50 cm).

Marajó Island's western tidal forests have been heavily logged for select species. More than 200 sawmills are operating in the Breves region of western Marajó. Clear-cutting is not commonly practiced. Instead individual logs are floated out of forests during high tides or during the rainy season. Valuable species are usually logged until no harvestable trees are left, at which point the next most valuable species is targeted. Harvestable virola (*Virola surinamensis*) trees, for example, have largely been cut, and other species, such as assacu (*Hura crepitans*), are being logged. In the long run the extent to which logging will impact western Marajó will depend on how many commercially valuable species are left. Heavy logging will likely continue for at least another decade or two, at which point most trees of commercial value will have been cut.

Although the state of Pará considers Marajó Island a conservation unit, no protected parks or reserves exist on the Island or surrounding area. Ecotourism has been touted as a management strategy for Marajó. The Island was a major breeding region for wading birds—always a tourist attraction. The rookeries, however, have largely been destroyed, and little is being done to protect those that are left. Unless tourists are attracted to cattle ranches, conservation planners will need to formulate a more aggressive management strategy for Marajó than ecotourism.

North of the Amazon River mouth is Amapá, one of Brazil's great wetland states. The Amazon River borders Amapá's southern coast and, mixed with oceanic waters, laves its Atlantic coast. Amapá has two large rivers, the Araguari and the Oiapoque, the latter shared by Brazil and French Guiana. Both rivers are less than 250 miles (400 km) long and have headwaters on the Guiana Shield. Although most of Amapá is still forested, there are large savanna areas on its eastern half. Coastal Amapá is one of the rainiest areas in the Amazon region. Annual totals are usually more than 120 in. (3,000 mm).

The Araguari was the first relatively large river in the Amazon to be dammed. The Coaracy Nunes Dam was constructed to supply energy for a local multinational manganese industry and for Macapá, the capital. The Araguari was impounded in 1972. Any associated environmental impacts have yet to be studied scientifically. Local fishermen have not reported any major effects on fisheries, and migratory species are still found below and above the dam.

The Serra do Navio manganese

▲ **THE SOUTHEASTERN COAST**
Relatively little sediment from the Amazon River makes it as far south as the eastern side of the outlet of Marajó Bay. Nearshore waters in this region are clearer and mostly brackish. During the high-water period of the Amazon River, a freshwater layer extends just outside Marajó Bay and along the eastern coast. Local rivers also contribute to this freshwater layer. Freshwater catfish species captured in this zone between February and May attest to the influence of fresh water on the Atlantic.

▲ **ROCKY HABITATS**
In the coastal region, rocky habitats of any extent are only found on the eastern side of Marajó Bay near its meeting with the Atlantic. Depending on the time of year, these habitats range from fresh water to brackish water, but the fauna is mostly of marine origin.

▼ **MARAJÓ BAY WATERS NEAR BELÉM**

Marajó Bay receives it waters from the Tocantins River, the Amazon River via the Breves Channel, the Pará River, and the Guamá River. Marajó Bay turbidity is largely due to sediments from the Amazon River. Water depths in Marajó Bay average 16.5–66 ft (5–20 m).

▶ **MARAJÓ BAY REGION**

Marajó Bay extends for nearly 125 miles (200 km) from the mouth of the Guamá River near Belém to the Atlantic. The giant river bay receives water and sediments from the Amazon River, although most of its freshwater discharge comes from the Tocantins River.

deposits in the headwater region of the Araguari River were largely depleted by the 1980s, and mining operations folded in the late 1990s. Gold mining in the upper Araguari Basin was intense between the early 1980s and mid-1990s. As in most of the Brazilian Amazon, gold mining has declined in Amapá since the mid-1990s. Cattle ranchers are now colonizing Araguari riparian forests below the dam, and deforestation is increasing.

Bordered on the south by the lower Araguari, and on the east by Cabo Norte (Cape North), the Piratuba Lakes region is an immense low-lying swamp inundated mostly by local rain water but also by tides at its eastern and southern borders. About one-half of this wetland region is a federal conservation unit. With its large open-water bodies and vegetation-covered islands, the Piratuba Lakes region is reminiscent of central Brazil's Pantanal. The Piratuba Reserve is rich in aquatic life and is an important rookery for egrets, ibises, and other wading birds.

The lakes are fished commercially for peacock bass (*Cichla*) to supply the Macapá market. The Piratuba Lakes region has not been developed for tourism despite having some open landscapes with large bird populations, as on the Pantanal. Cattle ranchers graze livestock on the periphery of the Piratuba Lakes region, but few people live inside the reserve. At present cattle ranching appears to pose the main threat to the Piratuba Lakes region.

Amapá is a staging ground for large-scale tree plantations in the Amazon Basin. The savanna-scrub regions between about Macapá to beyond the Araguari River have been cleared and planted with eucalyptus and pine. Headwaters of short coastal rivers originate in these scrublands. Swamp forests dominated by the buriti (*Mauritia flexuosa*) often form long palm corridors, but these are being rapidly destroyed by plantation development.

MARAJÓ BAY NEAR
CITY OF VIGIA

▲ MIXED TIDAL FOREST

Mangroves begin to give way to tidal forest near Vigia, approximately 35 miles (60 km) from the Atlantic. Tidal forests near Vigia are important to local fisheries for crab and freshwater fish species. The tidal forest shown here has a mix of mangrove and floodplain species.

▲ ISLANDS IN MARAJÓ BAY

Marajó Bay has hundreds of small forest-covered islands, most of which are near the eastern coast. These islands are subject to daily flooding by the tides. Few have been deforested.

▲ BELÉM

With a population of 1.3 million, Belém is the largest city in the eastern Amazon Basin. It is located at the confluence of the Guamá River and Marajó Bay. The muddy waters that bath Belém's port are a mixture of water from the Tocantins, Guamá, and Amazon Rivers. Much of Belém lies on swampy ground, and the city is still poorly drained.

▲ URBAN POLLUTION

Stream pollution in and near cities in the Amazon is a serious health problem. Belém is especially afflicted because of its low-lying terrain that is inundated by daily ocean tides. Trash and garbage are disposed of in urban streams, which exacerbates health threats and increases pollution.

▲ URBANIZED STREAM IN BELÉM

Sewage and other pollutants within Belém's tidal streams have led to astronomical densities of dangerous bacteria.

MARAJÓ BAY NEAR
BARCARENA

▼ INDUSTRY WITHOUT POLLUTION

The Barcarena bauxite processing plant near Belém, which has operated since the late 1980s, is the largest industrial complex in the Marajó Bay region. There have been no reports of serious pollution, and tailings are filtered in holding ponds and not discharged into Marajó Bay. Most bauxite processed by the Barcarena plant is shipped from the Trombetas Valley. Electricity for the plant is supplied by the large Tucuruí Dam on the Tocantins River.

▲ CLAY MINING

High-quality clay is mined along southeastern Marajó Bay for the ceramic industry near Belém.

FOREST USE WITHOUT DESTRUCTION
Tidal forests are exploited for palm hearts and fruits used locally for juices and ice cream. Local inhabitants manage the palm forests near Belém, and in general there has not been any large scale deforestation.

THE ASSAÍ PALM
The assaí is one of the most graceful palms in the Amazon. It is exploited for palm hearts and fruit and provides an excellent example of forest enhancement for economic return. The house of this particular tidal forest inhabitant is nearly surrounded by assaí palms.

MARAJÓ BAY AT THE TOCANTINS MOUTH
Little is known about this region despite construction of Tucuruí Dam on the Tocantins River. It has always been assumed that Tucuruí Dam has had no major impacts as far downstream as Marajó Bay, although this assumption was made without any field studies.

VENEZUELA

COLOMBIA

ECUADOR

PERU

BOLIVIA

BRAZIL

WESTERN MARAJÓ BAY

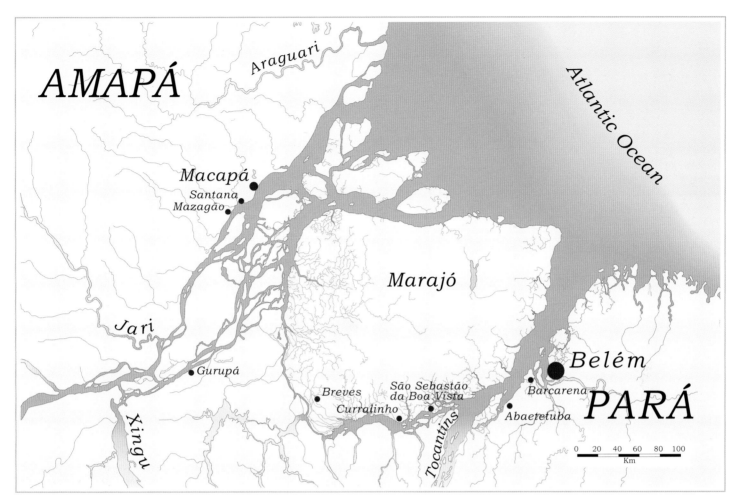

▲ Marajó Island

Encompassing nearly 18,900 square miles (49,000 km²) Marajó is one of the largest river islands in the world. Marajó is surrounded by muddy water. Most of the large Island is subject to tidal or seasonal flooding. The interior is inundated mostly by rain water. Although designated as a state conservation unit, little has been done to advance environmental protection on Marajó. Most of the eastern part of the Island is used for cattle and water buffalo ranching, and the western forests are being heavily logged.

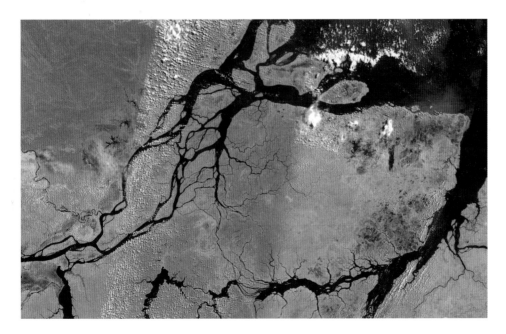

◀ Marajó from space

The eastern Amazon Basin is unusually cloudy, and there are few days when the entire region has been photographed clearly from satellites. The savannas (pink areas) of eastern Marajó Island stand out on satellite images: these are the main areas of livestock ranching. Most of the green area is forest-covered with intermittent savannas.

▲ RIPARIAN TIDAL FOREST

Marajó has about 20 rivers, most of which are less than 60 miles (100 km) long. Under natural conditions the tidal floodplains of Marajó's rivers are covered by forest. Mangrove forest dominates the lower Paracuari River shown here but is replaced by freshwater species approximately 6 miles (10 km) upriver.

MARAJÓ ISLAND, SOUTHERN COAST

▲ MARAJÓ UPLANDS

Most of Marajó is low-lying and subject to inundation from rain water or tidal flooding. Marajó, however, is not an alluvial island but was once part of the mainland before the formation of Marajó Bay. The tides appear to be denuding terra firma exposed on coasts.

⚠ TIDAL STREAMS THREATENED

Tidal streams on Marajó Island are important nursery habitats for fish. Stream headwaters of Marajó arise in the center of the Island. Savanna burning has destroyed the headwater forests of many of Marajó's rivers.

⚠ WESTERN MARAJÓ ISLAND

Western Marajó Island is dominated by floodplain forest subject to inundation by the daily tides. The area is rich in several valuable commercial timber species, and logging has dominated the local economy the past two decades.

⚠ LOGGING THE TIDAL FORESTS

Long-term logging without planting is not sustainable in tidal forests. Some of the most valuable species, such as virola (*Virola surinamensis*), have already been depleted. This giant log-raft is being hauled downstream to a sawmill near Belém.

▲ LAGO ARARI

Lago Arari is the largest lake of Marajó and has supported important fisheries for at least a century. Arari is fed by local rain water and connected to Marajó Bay by the Arari River, which is not navigable during the dry season. The shores of Lago Arari have been completely deforested.

MARAJÓ ISLAND INTERIOR

▲ THE TARTARUGA CANAL

The Tartaruga Canal is approximately 25 miles (40 km) long. It was constructed in the 1950s and runs from Lago Arari to the northern coast of Marajó Island west of Cape Maguari. Although the canal decreased the shipping distance between Belém and Macapá, it started draining Lago Arari and it became necessary to construct a dam.

▶ TOWNS ON STILTS

Cattle and water buffalo ranching dominate the economy of Marajó's savanna interior. The town of Jenipapo is built on stilts to stay above flood water during the rainy season.

▲ RETAINING WATER ON MARAJÓ

The local government of Santa Cruz de Arari constructed an earthen dam on the Rio Arari to maintain the water level in Lago Arari to increase fish production.

⚠ FIRES AND THE FUTURE

The aquatic habitats of the interior of Marajó Island have never been studied in any detail. One can only speculate on what the ecology of these immense wetlands might have been like without the burning.

⚠ LIVESTOCK ON MARAJÓ ISLAND'S WET SAVANNAS

Marajó's savannas have been used to graze livestock for several centuries. During the rainy season grasses and other herbaceous plants grow rapidly. The cattle egret first appeared on Marajó in the 1940s and has subsequently dispersed throughout the Amazon Basin, especially where there are livestock. Cattle egrets feed on insects and other prey that are attracted by livestock grazing.

⚠ HEADWATER DEFORESTATION

The riparian forests of eastern Marajó Island have been largely destroyed by fire. Shown here is the Arari River, which connects Marajó Bay with Lago Arari.

◀ MARAJÓ ISLAND IN FLOOD

The savannas of eastern Marajó are flooded mostly with local rain water. Depths rarely exceed 3 ft (1 m). Water buffalo are used to navigate the savannas during the floods.

▲ GALLERY FORESTS

Small streams in Marajó's savanna region are subject to desiccation during the dry season and become vulnerable to fires that sweep across the savannas.

▲ FIRE AND LIVESTOCK

Along with fire, livestock have led to the destruction of eastern Marajó Island's riparian forests. Water buffalo and cattle eat and trample seeds and seedlings in areas that have not been burned. Once savanna grasses are depleted, livestock will forage in forests for whatever is edible.

▲ Assaí palm forests

In addition to buriti, the assaí (*Euterpe oleracea*) forms the largest palm swamp communities on northern Marajó Island. Helicopters have been used to transport assaí palm hearts from the interior of Marajó. Virtually nothing is known about the ecology of these swamps.

◀ Palm swamps

North of the great savannas of Marajó are huge palm swamps dominated by buriti (*Mauritia flexuosa*). During the rainy season the palm swamps become inundated with approximately 3 ft (1 m) of water.

SOUTH-CENTRAL MARAJÓ ISLAND

VENEZUELA

COLOMBIA

ECUADOR

PERU

BOLIVIA   BRAZIL

▶ COASTAL STATE OF AMAPÁ

Although most of the state of Amapá is not technically in the Amazon Basin, its wetlands are ecologically linked to the Amazon River. The Araguari and Oiapoque are the two largest coastal rivers of Amapá. The Oiapoque River forms the border between Brazil and French Guiana. Most deforestation has been north of Macapá, although this area has largely been replanted with plantation pine and eucalyptus.

▼ FIRST LARGE DAM IN THE AMAZON

Although small compared with Tucuruí Dam on the Tocantins River, the Coaracy Nunes Dam on the Araguari, constructed in 1972, was the first large dam built in the Amazon region. The ecological impacts of the dam have never been studied.

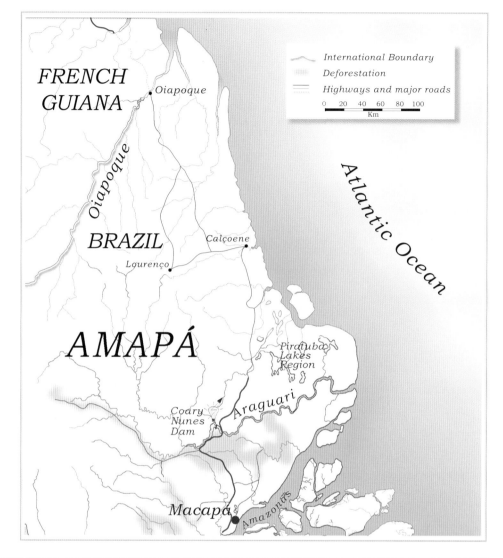

ARAGUARI,
AMAPÁ STATE

▲ RANCHES ON THE RIVER

Cattle ranchers have begun to deforest riparian forests downriver of Coaracy Nunes Dam. Average tides in this region are less than approximately 12 in. (30 cm).

▲ LOWER ARAGUARI

The lower Araguari embraces one the largest mangroves of the coastal region. There has been little deforestation in this region.

▲ Coastal lakes

The region north of the Araguari is an impressive landscape of shallow lakes and swamp vegetation. Generally known as the Piratuba Lakes region, a large portion of the swamp has been designated as a federal conservation unit. Sea breezes stir bottom sediments and render the lakes turbid, at least during the dry season.

PIRATUBA LAKES REGION, AMAPÁ STATE

▲ Flooded forests of Piratuba

Immense areas of swamp forest are inundated during the rainy season. Cattle ranchers, however, have begun to destroy Piratuba's forests through uncontrolled burning.

▲ Islands in the swamp

The Piratuba Lakes region is reminiscent of central Brazil's great Pantanal. Communities of plants and animals become isolated on islands by floodwaters during much of the year.

STATE INTERIOR

▲ HEADWATER DESTRUCTION

Amapá tree plantations are expanding from the savannas into forested regions. Dry forest, palm forest, and rainforest are replaced by one or two plantation species. A unique assortment of fish species, especially small species that evolved in isolation, lives in the coastal region's waters. With deforestation streams dry up and aquatic animals are decimated.

▲ AUSTRALIA IN THE AMAZON RAINFOREST

The multinational corporation Champion has invested extensively in tree plantations in Amapá. Eucalyptus and pine are the principal species planted for the export wood-chip market.

◀ EUCALYPTUS

Eucalyptus has proven to be more promising economically than pine in Amapá plantations. Eucyalyptus, however, also transpires more water, and large plantations will lead to water deficits in small streams that have survived deforestation.

CHAPTER SIX

THE AMAZON RIVER
The Giant

The Amazon River courses through three countries but does not maintain a single name for its entire length. It is identified on most maps as, beginning upstream, the Amazonas (Peru), the Solimões (Brazil), and the Amazonas (Brazil). Geographers sometimes consider the Ucayali River in Peru also to be part of the Amazon River because the Amazon's farthest headwaters are found there. South Americans often use the terms *"rio Amazonas"* (Portuguese) or *"río Amazonas"* (Spanish) to mean the Amazonas-Solimões-Amazonas.

In this book we use the common map interpretation to define the Amazon River. In this sense, starting upriver, the river is mostly oriented west to east-northeast and courses through five degrees of latitude before emptying into the Atlantic just north of the equator. The Amazon River—from the confluence of the Ucayali and Marañón Rivers in Peru to the Atlantic—is approximately 2,320 miles (3,750 km) long. The channel and floodplain of the river occupy more than 38,600 square miles (100,000 km²). More than 80 percent of the river is in Brazil, 18 percent is exclusively in Peru, and approximately 2 percent is shared between Peru and Colombia.

The Amazon River's flooding regime is complex because of large southern and northern drainages that receive peak rainfall at different times of the year. Between Santarém and Iquitos, average annual river-level fluctuation ranges from approximately 14.8 to 33.0 ft (4.5–10.0 m). The greater ranges are in the central Amazon near Manaus. Values decrease gradually upriver and more markedly downriver of the mouth of the Negro. Below the Xingu River, river level is largely controlled by the tides and ranges from approximately 6.5 to 13 ft (2–4 m). Tidal ranges are greater near the Atlantic. Between April and July the entire Amazon River upriver of the Xingu is in flood. Only in October and November can the entire Amazon River be said to be in its low-water period. River floods arrive earliest (October and November) in Peru and west of about the Juruá River in Brazil. Between Manaus and Santarém, rapidly rising river levels, and thus floods, start about two months later than in Peru.

The ecology of the Amazon River is obviously closely linked to that of its tributaries. The extent of the main stem across most of north-central South America, its central geographical position in the

Vortex formed where Xingu and the Amazon mainstream join.

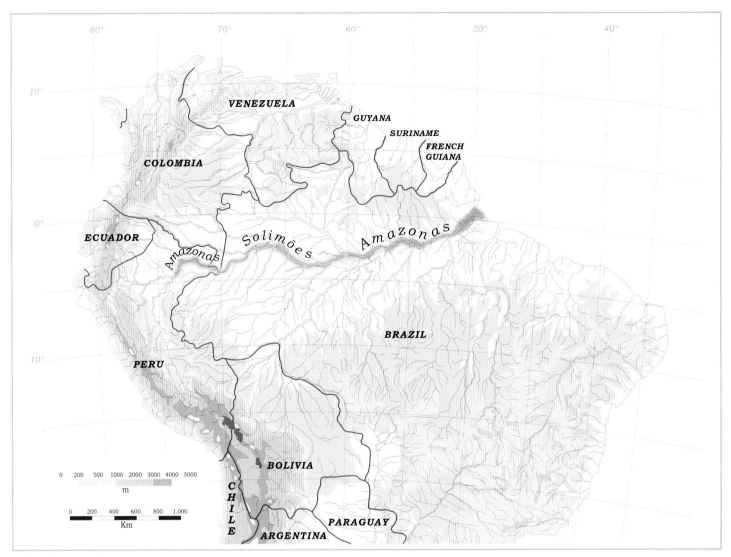

▲ THE AMAZON RIVER

Unfortunately the Amazon River as a whole does not have a universally accepted name in either Spanish or Portuguese. To Amazonians "the Amazonas" does not usually refer to the entire main stem in Brazil, Peru, and Colombia. Between the Brazilian-Peruvian-Colombian border and the mouth of the Negro the Amazon River is called "the Solimões." Technically the Amazon River is the "Amazonas-Solimões-Amazonas."

▶ AMAZON RIVER ALONG AMAPÁ COAST

Heavy tides and muddy soils have discouraged large-scale colonization of the Amazon River mouth region. Deforestation and fire from inland savannas, shown in the background here, however, are encroaching on these forests.

◀ AMAZON RIVER MOUTH

The Amazon River mouth on the Amapá shore has floodplain forest on the tidal levee and buriti (*Mauritia flexuosa*) palm forest inland. Almost the entire forest area shown here is subject to tidal flooding.

AMAZON RIVER MOUTH

▲ MACAPÁ

Macapá is the capital of the state of Amapá and located approximately 90 miles (150 km) up the Amazon River.

Amazon Basin, and the unmatched size of its floodplains contribute to its ecological complexity. Because the Amazon River is the main artery for urbanization, commerce, transportation, fisheries, and floodplain agriculture, its floodplains have also been modified more than those of any of its large tributaries, with the possible exception of those of the Tocantins River. Most proposed large-scale floodplain agricultural projects are aimed at the Amazon River floodplain because of its size, fertile soils, and proximity to major urban centers.

The Amazon River floodplain is molded by annual deposition and erosion cycles. Although not as unstable as Peruvian river floodplains such as those of the Ucayali, the Amazon's floodplain is nevertheless constantly undergoing morphological changes. For example, the erosion of floodplain banks reintroduces a quantity of sediments greater than the quantity of net sediment flux

that flows past Óbidos, approximately 550 miles (900 km) upstream of the Atlantic. Some floodplain areas, however, are very broad, often exceeding 12 miles (20 km), and may undergo only slight morphological changes, even over a century. Deforestation and floating meadow destruction appear to be leading to greater floodplain instability along the Amazon River, as discussed later.

Humans have used the Amazon River floodplain for at least 11,730 years—the age of the oldest known archaeological sites associated with the main river. Some anthropologists and geographers have argued that relatively dense populations lived along the Amazon River in pre-Columbian times. It has even been suggested that indigenous populations were, at times, larger than the rural populations now living on the floodplains. The extent to which Indians modified the Amazon floodplain is not clear, but deforestation at

any given time probably never reached present-day proportions. Large parts of the Amazon River floodplain might have been gradually modified during the past 10,000 or more years, but at any given time in history most of the floodplain forest was relatively natural although by no means pristine.

After the European Conquest ended, the first significant impact on the Amazon River floodplain from human activity appears to have taken place when steamships were introduced in the 1860s. Large quantities of firewood were needed. The main species cut was mulatto wood (*Calycophyllum spruceanum*), which was apparently largely depleted by the time steamships were abandoned in the 1930s. Cacao was a relatively important crop on the Amazon River floodplain in the Santarém region at the end of last century. Although considerable deforestation of levees took place, larger trees were left because cacao is best grown in shade.

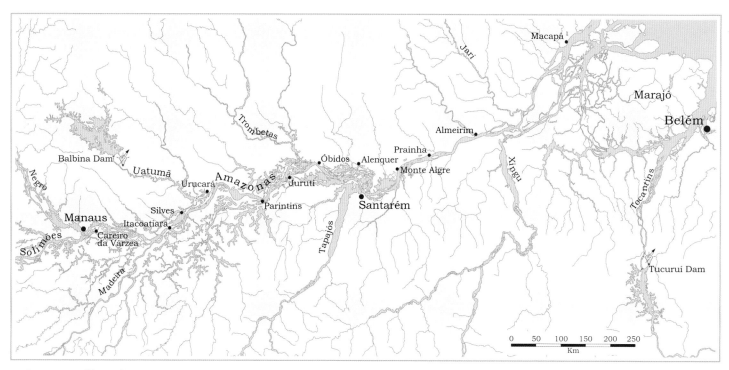

▲ AMAZONAS (BRAZIL)

Between the Negro in the west and the Atlantic, the Amazon River is called the Amazonas in Brazil. The Brazilian Amazonas is approximately 900 miles (1,450 km) long with 19,300 square miles (50,000 km²) of floodplain.

AMAZONAS REGION, BRAZIL

The introduction of floodplain jute farming in the 1930s greatly accelerated floodplain deforestation, especially on the high levees near channels. Jute farming was concentrated along the Amazon River from just upriver of the Negro to below Santarém. By the 1970s, when the jute boom was over, nearly all of the tall forest on high levees between the Negro and just downriver of Santarém had been highly modified.

When Manaus and other cities began to grow rapidly in the 1960s, central and western floodplain forests were the main sources of timber. By 1980 most of the Amazon River floodplain had been logged. Even the magnificent kapok tree (*Ceiba pentrandra*) was largely destroyed along most of the main stem. Illegal floodplain logging is a problem even in the Mamirauá Sustainable Development Reserve (at the confluence of the Solimões and Caquetá-Japurá Rivers) and in the mouth region of the Amazon River.

Other than for logging, which is not sustainable, Amazon River forests appear to have few commercially valuable direct uses. Ecotourism is limited because tourists prefer blackwater or clearwater tributaries, where there are fewer biting insects and the general environment seems cleaner than the muddy Amazon River. The economic philosophy of Amazon River floodplain development has almost dictated the removal of forest. What has been forgotten, however, is that the Amazon River's most valuable sustainable resource—fish—depends on flooded forests and floating meadows. The value of fish is seldom factored into floodplain-development plans.

Agronomists and private-sector entrepreneurs believe large-scale livestock ranching and rice farming are the most profitable ways to utilize Amazon River floodplains. Government agricultural institutes publish exaggerated estimates of potential livestock productivity and almost never consider serious

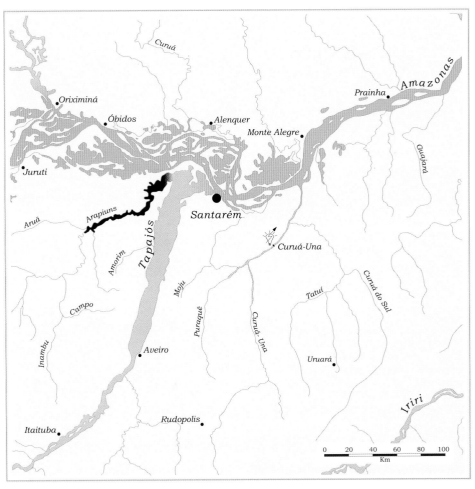

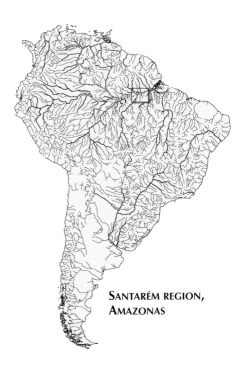

SANTARÉM REGION,
AMAZONAS

▷ **SANTARÉM REGION**

Santarém is approximately 500 miles (800 km) inland at the confluence of the Amazon and Tapajós Rivers. Three major water types are found in close proximity in the Santarém region.

environmental impacts. Floodplain rice farming is still largely experimental. Large-scale soybean farming has also been suggested as a profitable use of the Amazon River floodplain.

The benefits of any floodplain-development scenario should be weighed against its impact on the floodplain's three main habitats: forests, floating meadows, and lakes. Cattle ranchers destroy floodplain forest to increase the production of grass and other herbaceous plant species on which livestock feed. Livestock, in turn, destroy floating meadows and other herbaceous plant communities. Large-scale cattle ranching thus sets up a destructive cycle for floodplain ecology.

Floodplain forests, often called "flooded forests," are important habitats

for fish in the Amazon Basin. Many fruit- and seed-eating fishes have evolved in the Amazon. During the annual floods, fish spend about six months in flooded forests, feeding on fruits, seeds, insects, and spiders that fall out of the trees. Other species feed on flooded-forest detritus, and a myriad of predatory fish species hunt their prey among inundated saplings, stems, and branches. In addition, many fish species breed in flooded forests. Flooded forests also offer seasonal protection from commercial and subsistence fishermen. During the floods fish become widely dispersed in a complex environment where they are difficult to catch.

The floating meadows of the Amazon River floodplain are some of the most productive plant communities in

▲ **SANTARÉM**

Santarém is the largest city along the Amazon River between Macapá near the mouth and Manaus 1,100 miles (1,800 km) upstream at the confluence of the Solimões and Negro. Santarém was the urban hub for the gold rush in the Tapajós Valley, but more recently logging and cattle ranching are generating revenue for the city.

AMAZON RIVER IN FLOOD

Near Santarém the Amazon River is carrying more than 80 percent of its discharge at any given time into the Atlantic. Millions of tons of organic debris flow past Santarém to the ocean. The seasonal flotsam is especially extensive when floodwaters are rising.

THE AMAZON RIVER CHANNEL

Near Santarém the Amazon River channel averages approximately 0.6–1.9 miles (1–3 km) in width. Floodplains, however, are much wider and between upland shores on either side of the river can be 12–24 miles (20–40 km) wide.

MEETING OF AMAZON AND TAPAJÓS RIVERS

The Amazon River's two largest clearwater rivers—the Tapajós and the Xingu—are right-bank tributaries of the Amazonas. The city of Santarém is located at the confluence of the Tapajós and Amazonas.

the world. Although floodplain forests store more carbon, floating meadows have higher net primary production. Standing biomass of Amazonian aquatic grasses can reach 69 short tons per acre (150 mt/ha) per year fresh weight, or 13 short tons per acre (30 mt/ha) per year dry weight. Livestock, however, cannot digest most of this plant mass. Nearly 400 species of herbaceous plants grow in floodplain areas in the central Amazon. Approximately 10 percent of them are aquatic, whereas most of the other species are terrestrial in the sense that their roots penetrate the soil. More than 350 fish species are usually found in the floating meadows of a large floodplain area of the Amazon River—more than are found in the entire Mississippi River system.

Cattle have been tended on the Amazon River floodplain for at least 150 years. Before the 1970s herds were small, and relatively little forest was cut for pasture development. The existing floating meadows were sufficient to feed small herds. The large island of Careiro near the mouth of the Negro may have been an exception. A relatively large dairy herd was established there by the 1940s, and considerable deforestation took place.

After the mid-1960s, vegetable, manioc, and watermelon farming near Manaus and Santarém also increased floodplain deforestation near these urban centers. Floodplain manioc is used mostly to make gritty flour, a process that requires large quantities of firewood. Floodplains were also sources for urban firewood until upland highways and roads were built in the 1980s. There are no longer enough firewood trees on much of the floodplain near

Santarém to sustain manioc flour processing, and roots are taken to uplands.

By the mid-1980s relatively large herds of cattle and water buffalo began to be introduced onto the Amazon River floodplain between about the Xingu and Madeira Rivers. Pasture development has greatly accelerated either floodplain deforestation or floodplain modification. Even where forest is left intact, seedlings are destroyed by trampling livestock. Today at least 90 percent of the floodplain forests of the Amazon River between the mouth of the Negro and that of the Xingu have been heavily modified. Tidal forests of the Amazon River mouth archipelago and Amapá shore have not been used extensively for cattle ranching and have largely been spared.

The number of cattle and water buffalo on the Amazon River floodplain is not accurately known but probably exceeds 300,000. Average floodplain production of cattle and water buffalo ranges from approximately 11 to 18 lb per acre (30–50 kg/ha) per year. In comparison, the fish harvest is more productive, and beef and water buffalo meat is often two to three times more expensive than fish. Cattle ranchers on the Amazon River floodplain pay few taxes, and ranch workers often earn less than minimum wage. Ironically then, although livestock ranching on the Amazon River floodplain is not significantly fulfilling the rising need for animal protein, it nevertheless is destroying an already existing source that is cheaper.

Much of the floodplain forest that remains along the Brazilian Amazonas may appear to be natural, but in fact it is in some stage of secondary succession subsequent to the decline of jute farming in the early 1970s. An interpretation of aerial imagery without ground reconnaissance, for example, gives the impression that significant amounts of natural forest remain. Most of the closed-canopy forest seen on aerial imagery of the Amazonas is relatively low in species diversity compared with that found in natural communities. Often one or a few species dominate closed-canopy secondary forests. Tachi (*Tachigalia paniculata*) is one such species. Tachi trees are easily recognized by their huge flower crops and the species is well known locally because of the enormous populations of stinging ants that live on the trees.

Even where forest remains along the Brazilian Amazonas, it may be functionally dead when large numbers of cattle or water buffalo are present. This is because the animals destroy seeds and seedlings by eating or trampling on them. Water buffalo have been especially devastating to ground vegetation. Cattle and water buffalo also open floodplain forests for further invasion by pigs, sheep, and goats that are commonly raised with the bovines. Together these livestock can destroy the reproductive ability of a standing forest.

In addition to the effects mentioned previously, floodplain livestock ranching is devastating herbaceous plant communities—the livestock's main food source. The favorite grasses of cattle and water buffalo are pirimembeca (*Paspalum repens*) and canarana (*Echinochloa polystachya*). Unfortunately these two grasses also form the main floating meadows used by fish communities. If ranchers graze two or more head of cattle or water buffalo per

▲ **LOW WATER PERIOD**
Water marks on trees show flood levels along the Amazon River. Tides are evident as far as Santarém during the low-water period, but they are less than 6 in. (15 cm).

THE FORESTED LEVEE

Under natural conditions floodplain forest was the dominant plant community on the levees bordering the Amazon River. Tall emergent trees graced the skyline, and roots stabilized river banks.

THE DEFORESTED LEVEE

The levees bordering the main channel are the highest parts of the floodplain and thus the favored sites for agriculture and settlement. Floodplain dwellers seldom leave forest uncut at the river's edge because it would decrease sunlight to crop plants.

hectare, the animals will destroy an entire floating-meadow community within two to three months. The bovines are introduced even before dry land is available. Cattle can feed in water up to approximately 3 ft (1 m) deep, whereas water buffalo can stay afloat or at least partly buoyed by the floating-meadow communities they eat in deeper waters. Livestock that feed in the water can destroy large areas of floating meadows four to six weeks before the meadows would decrease in size under natural conditions. The otherwise permanent floating-meadow communities along channels are also destroyed when cattle and water buffalo swim in to feed on them after they have devoured the grasses on the upper levees.

Scientists have not studied the effects on the fish population of the destruction of floating meadows by livestock. In addition to the destruction of the structural integrity of floating meadows, another potentially serious

problem is deoxygenation of waters due to the large biomass of rotting stems. Under natural circumstances most of the grass biomass rots on dry land rather than in the water.

Perhaps the most serious threat posed by livestock is the destruction of floating meadow fish nurseries. The area and biomass of floodplain meadows is reduced naturally by as much as 80 percent during the low-water period, when little if any forest is inundated. Under natural circumstances young fish seek refuge in the remaining floating meadows. Without these floating meadows, young fish are more susceptible to predators and unsuitable aquatic conditions and perish in greater numbers.

In addition to the destruction of biodiversity and fisheries, livestock ranching on floodplains may be leading to the loss of land. Cattle and water buffalo are heavy animals. Floodplain soils are soft when not matted together by roots. Livestock tend to travel the

AMAZONAS UPRIVER
OF SANTARÉM

▲ LEVELING THE LEVEES

Between about the mouths of the Xingu and
the Negro, levee vegetation was largely
destroyed between the 1930s and 1960s to
plant jute. More recently levees are being
used for annual crops and livestock ranching.

▼ SEEING THE PASTURE BUT NOT THE FOREST

Livestock ranches on the Amazon River
floodplain are usually one-dimensional
enterprises that show little respect for the
forest. A major problem is that most ranch
owners live in cities and have never considered that parts of their lands should be left
forested to protect lake fisheries and wildlife
in general.

▲ AQUATIC LAWNMOWERS

During the annual floods floodplain cattle spend about five to six months on upland pasture.
Cattle often undergo severe malnutrition on nutrient-poor upland pastures, and they are literally starving when returned to the floodplains. The zebu and other local breeds can spend
long periods in the water. Floating meadows are devastated at the same time as they are also
being used by fish as important nurseries.

▲ Harvesting floodplain grass

Although there has been talk of using machines to harvest floodplain grass during the floods, only manual labor has been used.

▼ Fish below the belly

Water buffalo destroy the structural integrity of floating meadows and pollute floodplain waters at the same time. The large quantities of feces introduced into the water, along with decomposing grass, leads to rapid deoxygenation. Release of hydrogen sulfide gas from bottom sediments by walking and scuffling livestock further deoxygenates the water column. Along with flooded forests, floating meadows are the most important floodplain habitat of fish. If herd size is not controlled, an enormous amount of fish habitat could be destroyed.

▼ No escape from water buffalo

Once edible grass is gone near corrals where water buffalo sleep at night, the bovines range farther each day to find new pastures. Herds easily traverse lakes and channels to reach floating meadows. Water buffalo can remain propped in floating meadows for long hours, even when they cannot touch ground. Piranha attacks on floodplain livestock are highly exaggerated in natural history films, but few if any livestock are lost to these fish.

same paths, and daily trampling leads to sunken trails that become artificial ditches. These "trail-ditches" are further excavated by rainwater run-off when floodplains are drained. Trail-ditches are having two important effects: affected floodplains drain faster, and they break up and erode faster. Erosion is also accelerated by destruction of forests whose roots would otherwise hold soil in place. Large-scale livestock ranching along the Amazon River may cause its floodplain to become highly unstable.

At least three million people live in cities along the Amazon River. Manaus and Iquitos each has more than one million inhabitants and, along with Macapá and Santarém, will undoubtedly continue to be the urban centers driving the economy on the Amazon River floodplain. Manaus, Iquitos, and Macapá have free trade-zone status to subsidize weak local economies. Only Manaus has major industries and factories. Urban markets will continue to drive floodplain fisheries, cattle ranching, and crop farming.

Considering its size the Amazon River is very poorly protected. The mouth region and western floodplain areas are in general less deforested than the heavily modified Brazilian Amazonas and the lower Solimões within 125 miles (200 km) of Manaus. There are no functional protected areas alongside the lower 1,250 miles (2,000 km) of the Amazon River. Neither Peru nor Colombia has any significant protected areas alongside the Amazon River. The Tikuna Indians of Brazil near the Brazilian-Colombian-Peruvian border are the only indigenous peoples with any significant claim to Amazon River floodplains.

Located at the confluence of the Amazonas and Caquetá-Japurá Rivers, the Mamirauá Sustainable Development Reserve is the only functional conservation unit alongside the Amazon River. The Brazilian government established the Mamirauá Reserve in 1992, but ownership and control were ceded to the state of Amazonas. The reserve includes more than 4,250 square miles (11,000 km^2), nearly all of which is considered floodplain. More than 10,000 people live on or near the reserve. It has been zoned for multiple uses, and about one-third of its area has been designated as a protected zone. Fish and timber are the two most important resources extracted from the reserve. Uncontrolled logging is illegal but has proven difficult to prevent.

The Mamirauá Reserve represents a large-scale experiment based on community management of protected areas. In fact the experiment should be seen as a combination of academic and community efforts, because academics have been at least as involved as the local residents in establishing zoning regulations for the reserve. It will probably take two or three decades to see whether the Mamirauá Reserve experiment is successful. Challenges will certainly emerge when the highly dedicated academics that founded Mamirauá Reserve move on and its management is handed over to a new generation of community residents. Considering the general fate of the Amazon River floodplain, however, the Mamirauá Reserve provides a hopeful note for conservation in the region.

SMALLER LIVESTOCK

In addition to cattle and water buffalo, pigs, goats, and sheep are also raised on the Amazon River floodplain. The five species together have a negative synergistic impact on floodplains because they wreck havoc on a larger spectrum of vegetation.

🔺 Giant lilies are no match for water buffalo

The green disks are giant Amazon water lilies. This floodplain area has been deforested and livestock have grazed through most of the herbaceous vegetation. Giant water lilies have defensive spines that deter cattle but do not seem to deter tough-legged water buffalo. Water buffalo eventually destroy the giant water lily colonies, probably more by trampling than by consumption.

🔺 Lily of the lowlands

The giant Amazon water lily (*Victoria amazonica*) is found throughout most of the lowlands of the Amazon Basin. It grows in colonies in floodplain waters less than approximately 10 ft (3 m) deep and where there is protection from the wind. At the site shown here the giant lily has colonized the edge of the small floodplain lake and the edge of the floodplain channel.

🔺 A livestock path becomes a dissecting stream

Although scientific data are not available to confirm their observation, floodplain dwellers commonly state that livestock trails are leading to loss of land. The more the floodplain becomes dissected by livestock trails, which turn into drainage ditches, the faster it erodes. It is possible that cattle and water buffalo could lead to a massive loss of relatively stable floodplain in the central and lower Amazon River region.

🔺 The floodplain is drying faster

Livestock-excavated ditches cause the floodplain to drain faster and many ditches have also caused an increased amount of water to drain from lakes.

▶ BOVINE CANALS

This floodplain cattle trail was once approximately 6.5 ft (2 m) higher but became excavated by retreating waters at the end of various annual floods. In effect the trail has become a floodplain canal.

▲ THE PATHS TO FLOODPLAIN LOSS

Once forest is removed and livestock are introduced, floodplain drainage is altered. Cattle and water buffalo trails become ditches that cause the floodplain not only to drain faster but also to become more susceptible to erosion.

AMAZONAS NEAR
SANTARÉM

▲ BEACH BEANS

When the floodplain emerges after the annual floods, crops are planted immediately to ensure sufficient growing time before water rises. Beach beans have become a favorite crop because of a ready market and their drought-resistant properties.

▲ RICE

Wild rice is a native species of the Amazon River floodplain and, unsurprisingly, developers are planning to farm the domestic species on the rich alluvial soils. This floodplain area near Santarém is being prepared for mechanized rice farming.

▼ HEAVY MACHINERY ON THE FLOODPLAIN

Both rice and soybeans have been considered for large-scale agriculture on the Amazon River floodplain. To date heavy machinery has only been used in the Brazilian Amazon for experimental rice farming. At this site near Santarém the floodplain has been leveled by bulldozers and tractors and is being prepared for irrigation.

▶ DROUGHT-RESISTANT CROPS

Although the Amazon River floodplain borders the largest river in the world, its soils are subject to intense desiccation during the dry season. Most farmers cannot afford irrigation. Watermelons are drought-resistant and have proven to be a highly productive crop during the dry season.

▲ RICH SOILS BUT LONG FLOODS

The Amazon River floodplain has long been considered to have great agricultural potential because of its rich alluvial soils. Long flooding seasons, however, greatly decrease productivity. Most vegetable farming takes place within a day's boat journey to urban centers. Floodplain crops must also compete with upland agriculture and imports from more productive regions outside of the Amazon. Vegetable and fruit farming have been responsible for only a small fraction of floodplain deforestation.

▼ MAIZE

Maize was an important crop along the Amazon River floodplain when the Portuguese and Spanish arrived in the sixteenth century, but it was generally replaced by manioc. Developers are now experimenting with maize varieties that could be used in large-scale farming. Ironically, such varieties might have existed before indigenous farming was destroyed. An eye should be kept on floodplain maize because of its large potential market for local chicken farms.

▲ THE QUESTION OF PESTICIDES

Most crop farms are small and cannot afford large-scale use of pesticides. The availability of pesticides has increased in the past decade and more farmers are selectively spraying crops. Pesticides are of special concern on Amazon River floodplains because they accumulate in isolated water bodies and easily enter the food chain.

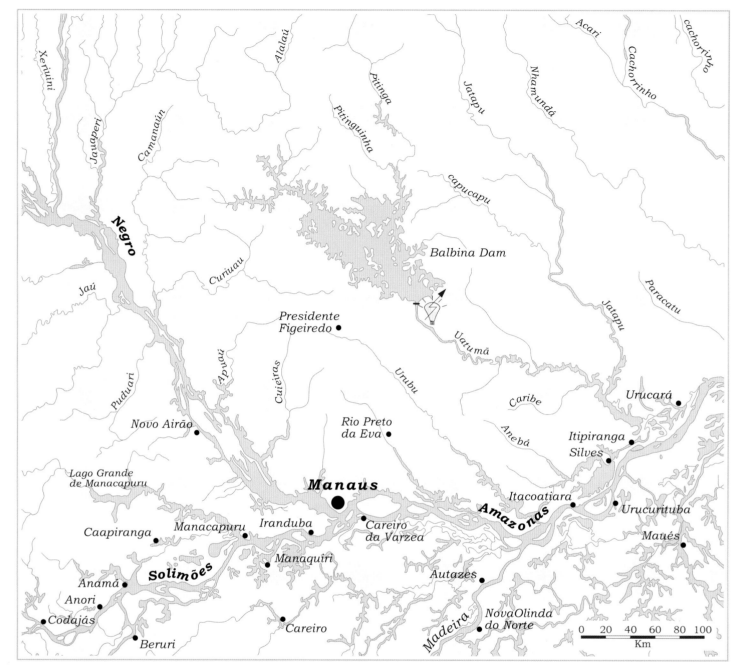

▲ MANAUS REGION

Manaus is the largest city in the lowland Amazon Basin. Located at the confluence of the Negro and Solimões-Amazonas (Amazon River), the free trade zone in the city drives the economy of the central Amazon. Within 125 miles (200 km) of Manaus aquatic resources are heavily exploited for the large urban market, and the Amazon River floodplain has been heavily modified for farming and cattle ranching, although less than near Santarém. The Balbina Reservoir is the largest lake or reservoir in the central Amazon.

◀ SOLIMÕES CHANNEL NEAR MANAUS

The channel of the Solimões near Manaus averages 1.2–1.9 miles (2–3 km) in width. Floodplains on either side average approximately 3–6 miles (5–10 km) in width. Shown here is a large floating meadow being transported downstream in the middle of the channel.

Meeting of
Amazon River
and Rio Ngro

▲ THE MANAUS PORT

The center of Manaus is approximately
7 miles (12 km) up the Negro. The city has
grown so rapidly in the past two decades,
however, that it has reached the Amazon
River. Its geographical site is now at the
confluence of the Negro and Amazon River.
This means that Manaus borders two of the
Amazon Basin's largest rivers and urban
pollutants are entering both of them.

▼ THE AMAZON RIVER NEAR MANAUS

Near Manaus the Amazon River flows between its largest tributary, the blackwater Negro,
and one of the main river's largest islands, Careiro, which is shown in the upper part of
the photo.

▲ MIGRATION FROM THE FLOODPLAIN

Manaus has experienced rapid growth since
the creation of a free trade zone in 1967.
The population along the floodplain
decreased as riparian dwellers flocked to
the capital city in search of jobs and better
education opportunities for children.

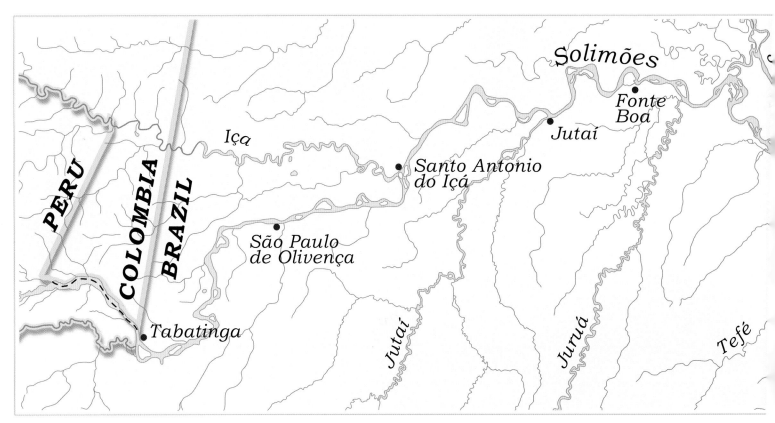

▲ SOLIMÕES (BRAZIL)

The Amazon River between the Negro and the Brazilian-Colombian-Peruvian border is called the Solimões in Brazil. The Solimões is approximately 1,000 miles (1,600 km) long and has 15,400 square miles (40,000 km²) of floodplain. Approximately 46 percent of the Amazon River's discharge is delivered before the confluence of the Solimões and Negro. The Solimões has a large number of small blackwater tributaries and floodplain lakes. Floodplain deforestation is less along the Solimões than along the Brazilian Amazonas farther downstream.

SOLIMÕES REGION

▲ THE SOLIMÕES DURING THE LOW-WATER PERIOD

During the low-water period the depth of the Solimões is reduced to approximately 23–33 ft (7–10 m), floodplains are largely drained, and beaches emerge along the channel banks and islands.

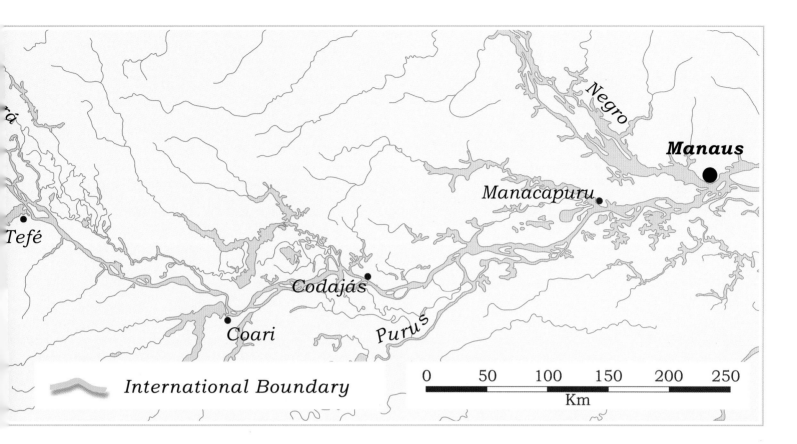

Negro

Manaus

Manacapuru

Tefé

Codajás

Coari

Purus

~~~~~~~~~~ **International Boundary**

| 0 | 50 | 100 | 150 | 200 | 250 |

Km

VENEZUELA

COLOMBIA

ECUADOR

PERU

BOLIVIA

BRAZIL

SOLIMÕES, MAMIRAUÁ SUSTAINABLE DEVELOPMENT RESERVE

▲ THE SOLIMÕES CHANNEL

Near Tefé 1,750 miles (2,800 km) upstream from the mouth of the Solimões (Amazon River), the channel averages approximately 1.2–1.9 miles (2–3 km) in width and 66–132 ft (20–40 m) in depth. At this point the Amazon River is already transporting approximately 30 percent of its total discharge to the ocean.

▶ THE SOLIMÕES IN FLOOD

The Solimões overflows it banks at the height of the annual floods and the levees become inundated along with the houses on them. The floodplain forests are invaded with a massive sheet of water that can reach depths of approximately 16–19.5 ft (5–6 m). The annual floods enrich the floodplains with nutrients derived from the Andes.

▲ LOCAL COMMUNITIES

The Mamirauá Sustainable Development Reserve cannot function without local community participation. Academics have organized communities to develop zoning and other management strategies. The degree to which management strategies can be maintained in the long run will be one of the principal lessons of Mamirauá.

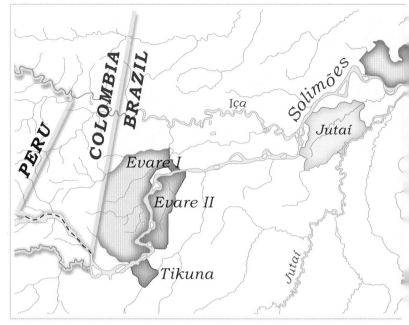

▲ DIVERSE FLOODPLAINS

The Mamirauá Sustainable Development Reserve has diverse aquatic habitats, ranging from tall floodplain rainforest inundated with muddy water to blackwater areas with shorter and more open forests. There are also large areas of floating meadows. Most economic activity in the reserve is extractive and timber and fish are the two most important resources exploited.

▼ RELATIVELY NATURAL FLOODED FOREST

The flooded forests of the Mamirauá Sustainable Development Reserve are among the green mansions of the Amazon River floodplain. There are few places along the Amazon River where deforestation has not altered tall floodplain rainforest. The greatest impact on Mamirauá's floodplain forests has been logging.

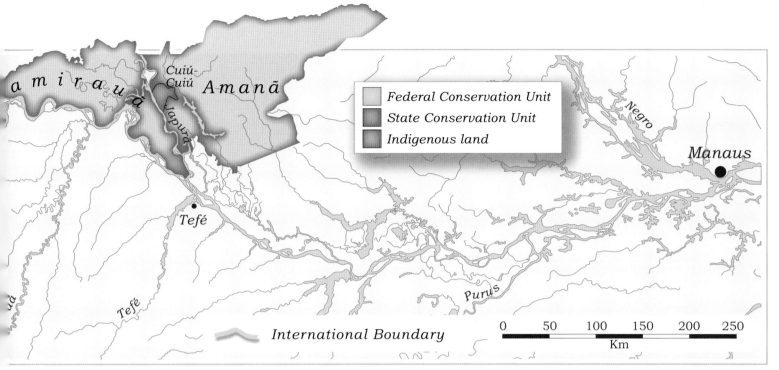

Federal Conservation Unit
State Conservation Unit
Indigenous land

International Boundary

0   50   100   150   200   250
Km

▲ SOLIMÕES (BRAZIL) CONSERVATION UNITS

The Mamirauá Sustainable Development Reserve at the confluence of the Solimões and Japurá River is the largest protected Amazonian floodplain region in Brazil. Approximately 10,000 people live near or within the reserve's 46,300 square miles (12,000 km²). Mamirauá is managed by local communities in conjunction with academics but under jurisdiction of the state of Amazonas.

SOLIMÕES, MAMIRAUÁ SUSTAINABLE DEVELOPMENT RESERVE

◄ PEOPLE AND PROTECTED AREAS

The degree to which people and protected areas are compatible is still intensively debated. Mamirauá offers a test case of utmost importance because of the large number of people that live near or in the reserve and depend on extractive resources, such as fish and timber. If rice farming, cattle ranching, and other activities that lead to large-scale deforestation can be prevented from entering the Mamirauá Sustainable Development Reserve, then the structure of the forest, the most important conservation component, can probably be maintained.

▲ BLACKWATER RIVER MOUTHS

The southern bank of the middle Solimões has several large blackwater river mouth-lakes. The mouth-lake of the Tefé River is shown here during the low-water period when its sandy beaches are exposed. Blackwater rivers, which are highly acidic and poor in nutrients, usually have many fish species not found in muddy rivers.

▲ BLACKWATER LAKES

The Amazon River has numerous blackwater lakes that are connected to its floodplain by small channels. Blackwater lakes are generally poor in nutrients although some, depending on their exact location on the floodplain, can be invaded at the peak of the annual floods by nutrient-rich muddy water. Shown here is Lago Amanã east of the Mamirauá Sustainable Development Reserve at the confluence of the Solimões and Japurá. Lago Amanã has been designated as a state protected area contiguous with Mamirauá.

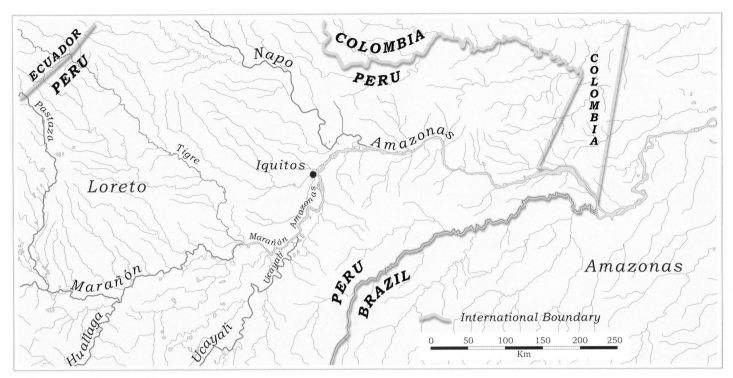

⛰ AMAZONAS (PERU AND COLOMBIA)

The Amazon River is called the Amazonas in Peru and Colombia. Cartographically the Amazon River (Amazonas) is the reach between the confluence of the Marañón and Ucayali Rivers and the Brazilian-Colombian-Peruvian border. The Peruvian-Colombian Amazonas is approximately 400 miles (650 km) long and has perhaps 7,700 square miles (20,000 km²) of floodplain. Colombia and Peru share approximately 60 miles (100 km) of the lower Amazonas. More than 80 percent of the upper Amazonas, however, is in Peru. Floodplain deforestation has been much less in this region than farther downstream in Brazil.

⛰ IQUITOS ON THE FLOODPLAIN

Iquitos is located partially on the Amazonas floodplain between the small Nanay River and the main stem. Shown here is the stilted neighborhood of Belén, just upriver of the center of Iquitos.

⛰ HIGH-WATER PERIOD OF AMAZONAS IN PERU

At this site on the Amazonas west of Iquitos, floodplain dwellers have left most of the levee forest uncut and enriched it with tree species with edible fruits. The floodplain forest is heavily inundated between about March and June.

▲ AMAZONAS NEAR CONFLUENCE OF UCAYALI

Amazonas floodplains in Peru are relatively small compared with those found in Brazil. They are also better preserved, and intact floodplain forest is still found along much of the Amazonas in Peru.

◀ AMAZONAS FLOODPLAIN UPRIVER OF IQUITOS, PERU

At this floodplain site riparian dwellers use beachfront and the first high levees for agriculture. Most of the floodplain forest has been little altered. The small channel that connects to the Amazonas is used to access the floodplain.

⚠ COW PEAS ON THE PLAYAS

A favorite crop on Amazonas beaches in Peru is the cow pea. Mature pods can be harvested in two to three months after seeds have been planted in the rich beach soils. During the dry season water deficit can become a problem.

⚠ HARVESTING RICE WITH THE COMING OF THE FLOODS

When river level begins to rise rapidly rice fields become flooded. This farmer along the Amazonas in Peru is taking the last of his rice crop before the floods destroy it.

⚠ FLOODPLAIN RICE IN PERU

Floodplain rice farming in Peru is more extensive than in Brazil. This level floodplain area has been deforested for rice. The levee forest in the background has been enriched with tree species that have edible fruits and seeds.

⚠ RICE AND RICH SOILS

The rich soils of the Amazonas floodplain are capable of sustaining relatively high levels of rice production with minimal inputs, such as fertilizers. Pesticides are still used sparingly but could become a problem to floodplain waters if used widely.

CHAPTER SEVEN

THE TOCANTINS
The Dammed River

The Tocantins is the easternmost large river in the Amazon Basin. With more than 289,600 square miles (750,000 km^2), the Tocantins Valley is more than twice the size of Ecuador and larger than France. It is the largest river valley restricted to one country in the Amazon Basin.

Some scientists do not consider the Tocantins River to be part of the Amazon Basin, because it does not discharge directly into the Amazonas, but rather into the Pará River south of Marajó Island. Amazonas waters, however, also discharge into the Pará via channels around western Marajó Island. The Tocantins debouches into a mixture of Amazonas and Pará waters and thus technically could be considered part of the Amazon Basin. More importantly, the ecosystem of the lower Tocantins River is directly linked to that of the Amazon River mouth region. The fauna and flora of the lower Tocantins are closely related to Amazonian species. The Tocantins flows so far south, however, that its headwaters are more than 1,850 miles (3,000 km) from Marajó Bay. The river's headwaters are south of Brasília in the *cerrado,* or scrub-savanna, region of central Brazil.

The Tocantins Valley is the only river valley in the Brazilian Amazon whose drainage encompasses more than three states. The largest of those states is Tocantins, a relatively new state founded in 1989, whose capital is Palmas. The Tocantins River has only one large tributary, the Araguaia. In the middle stretch of the Araguaia River is Bananal, one of the largest scrub-savanna wetlands in the Amazon Basin.

Most of the Tocantins Valley is outside of the Amazon rainforest because annual precipitation is less than 60 in. (1,500 mm). Many Amazonian species, however, live in and along rivers and streams deep in the central Brazilian scrubland.

The Tocantins River is the most heavily modified large tributary of the Amazon Basin. By the early 1970s the Belém-Brasília and Transamazon highways opened the Tocantins Valley to large-scale development. Cattle ranching expanded along the major highways and led to extensive deforestation in the states of Goiás, Tocantins, and Pará. In the 1990s the soybean-farming frontier pushed north

◀ **TUCURÍ DAM**
Tucuruí Dam on the Tocantins is the largest dam in the Amazon Basin and has supplied the energy that has enabled large-scale industrialization in the eastern Amazon.

BRAZIL

State Boundary
States: Brazil

Deforestation

Highways and
major roads

Cametá

Tucuruí

Tucuruí Dam

Tocantins

Maranhão

Marabá

Imperatriz

Araguaia

Pará

Estreito

Tocantins

Couto de Magalhães

Piauí

Caseara

Palmas

Bahia

Tocantins

Mato Grosso

Goiás

Brasília

Alto Araguaia

0   50   100   150   200   250
Km

THE TOCANTINS VALLEY

Some scientists do not consider the Tocantins River to be part of the Amazon Basin because it discharges into the Pará River south of the Amazonas. The Tocantins, however, is linked ecologically to the Amazon River mouth and its flora and fauna are related to Amazon Basin species. The Tocantins Valley lies within five Brazilian states and is the only tributary in the Brazilian Amazon region whose drainage includes more than three Brazilian states. Most of the Tocantins Valley is in the state of Tocantins, a relatively new Brazilian state that was created in 1989.

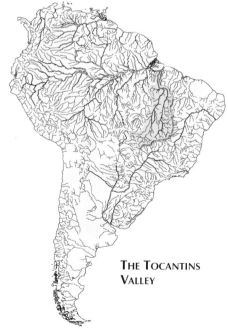

THE TOCANTINS
VALLEY

into the scrub-savanna and rainforest areas of Goiás and Tocantins.

The largest high-grade iron ore deposits in the world are in the Carajás region in the lower Tocantins Valley. Manganese, copper, gold, and other minerals also exist in the Carajás region. Manganese and copper mined in the region are transported by rail to the port of Itaqui near São Luís in the state of Maranhão. The Itacaiunas River is the main tributary that drains the Carajás region. Gold mining significantly impacted the river in the 1980s. The highly organized iron-ore operations, however, appear to have had little impact on the ecology of the Itacaiunas.

The three significant wetland features of the Tocantins Valley are the huge river-mouth, Tucuruí Reservoir, and Bananal Island. The lower 90 miles (150 km) of the Tocantins River is a giant mouth-bay, which formed when the river channel was excavated during the most recent Ice Age. Tides exert a noticeable influence on the lower Tocantins, but there is never an invasion of saltwater. The mouth-bay supports many pelagic fish species, including commercially important plankton-feeding mapará catfish (*Hypophthalmus* spp.). These species have been heavily targeted for the Belém market since the 1950s. The mapará fishery in the mouth-bay declined drastically after Tucuruí Dam was completed in 1988. The factors that caused the fishery to crash are not clearly known. Two possibilities are the disturbance of spawning areas near the dam and a lack of nutrients or plankton.

The Tocantins Valley appears to

▲ **CONSERVATION UNITS AND INDIGENOUS AREAS OF THE TOCANTINS VALLEY**

The Tocantins is probably the most extensively modified large river valley in the Brazilian Amazon. The only major protected wetland area in the Tocantins Basin is Araguaia National Park in the northern Bananal Island region. Most of the headwater region of the Tocantins Valley has already been heavily modified, and large-scale agriculture will undoubtedly continue to degrade watersheds in this region.

▲ THE TOCANTINS RIVER ON THE BRAZILIAN SHIELD

The Tocantins drains a large part of the eastern Brazilian Shield. Valley-edge tablelands and cataracts are the most obvious geological telltales of the ancient Brazilian Shield. At several places, such as these cataracts downriver of Palmas in the state of Tocantins, the River is very narrow.

▲ LOWER TOCANTINS RIVER

The Tocantins is a clearwater river. Water levels within its lower 60 miles (100 km) are controlled by oceanic tides. Farther upstream in the lower section, water levels are controlled mostly by water release from Tucuruí Dam Reservoir. The Tocantins River is shown here downriver of Tucuruí Dam.

▲ BANANAL WATER BODIES DURING THE DRY SEASON

During the dry season fish and other aquatic life are confined to small streams and lakes that represent only a small percentage of the habitat available to them during the rainy season. The dunelike sand bodies in the stream channel, here visible during low water, probably move downstream during episodes of high water

▲ ARAGUAIA RIVER

The Araguaia River is the largest tributary of the Tocantins. During the low-water period the Araguaia is often reduced to depths less than 3 ft (1 m) and parts of the river can become choked with sandbars.

BANANAL ISLAND,
TOCANTINS STATE

▲ FOREST AND SAVANNA OF THE BANANAL
The Bananal, also called Bananal Island, is
a large seasonal savanna- and forest-swamp
located along the middle Araguaia. The
Bananal is flooded for about six months
each year, at which time there is an explo-
sion of aquatic life.

have the greatest hydroelectric potential
of any area in the Amazon region. More
than 20 dams have been planned for the
Tocantins and Araguaia Rivers, along
with an enormous electrical distribution
network that would serve not only the
eastern Amazon Basin but also northeastern and central Brazil. Three dams
have been built or are nearly completed.
Tucuruí Dam was the first major dam
constructed on a large river in the Amazon. The energy produced by the dam
spurred economic development in the
state of Pará, although it was insufficient
to satisfy rapidly growing urban and
industrial demands in the 1990s. More
turbines are being added to the dam to
boost energy capacity.

The new Lajeado Dam on the
Tocantins River will produce energy for
the Palmas region in the state of Tocantins. Farther upstream the Serra da Mesa
Dam in the state of Goiás will supply
the immediate region and Brasília in the
Federal District. The ultimate impact

that dams will have on the Tocantins
and Araguaia will largely depend on
how many are constructed and how
close they are to each other. The Tucuruí, Lajeado, and Serra da Mesa Dams
are at least 250 miles (400 km) apart
from one another.

Encompassing more than 920
square miles (2,400 km^2), Tucuruí
Reservoir is the second largest lake or
reservoir in the eastern Amazon. Tucurí
Dam should have served as an example
of the need for adequate environmental
impact studies prior to dam construction
in the Amazon Basin. In retrospect it
appears to have done no such thing: federal and state governments still do not
require adequate environmental impact
studies before dams are constructed.

Tucuruí Dam was constructed
without any major study of the potential
effects on migratory fish species or of its
impact beyond the immediate region of
the impoundment. It appears that the
dam has prevented some migratory

species from moving upstream and has
destroyed the spawning habitats of other
fish species. The dam has affected the
commercially important mapará catfish,
especially those living downstream of it.
Many noncommercial species have
probably declined in number as well.

Upriver of Tucuruí Dam, population sizes of commercially valuable fish
increased tenfold in the decade after the
dam was constructed. Commercially,
the most valuable fish living in Tucurí
Reservoir are plankton-feeding mapará
catfish. The large numbers of pelagic
prey available in the reservoir allowed
predatory fish populations, such as peacock bass (*Cichla* spp.) and croakers
(*Plagioscion* spp.), to increase significantly. Some long-distance migratory
species, such as curimatá (*Prochilodus*
sp.), adapted to the new reservoir and
use it as a nursery, migrating upstream at
the beginning of the floods to spawn
where the river channel is still more or
less natural.

▲ **DEFORESTATION NEAR TUCURUÍ DAM**
Little is being done to protect the watershed near Tucuruí Reservoir and the hilly region has been heavily deforested for cattle ranching. Increased erosion could accelerate sedimentation in the reservoir, thus decreasing water storage capacity.

TUCURUÍ DAM REGION

Bananal Island is a low-lying island 250 miles (400 km) long and up to 75 miles (120 km) wide between two channels of the Araguaia River. The Island covers approximately 7,700 square miles (20,000 km²) of a much larger low-lying floodable region of perhaps 15,400 square miles (40,000 km²). The Island's terrain is very flat and subject to flooding every year for about six months during the rainy season.

This large river island has been used for cattle ranching for at least a century. During recent decades indigenous peoples have also begun to raise cattle on the Island. Cattle and water buffalo are now found on most of the Island, although the northern part of Bananal is a national park. With approximately 100 lakes, Bananal Island supports commercial and sport fishing. Ecotourism on the Island has blossomed in the past decade. Despite the size of Bananal's wetlands, there have been few studies of the ecology of the giant river island.

The cerrado region of central Brazil covers much of the headwater regions of the Tocantins, Xingu, and Tapajós Rivers. In the past four to five decades thousands of streams have been destroyed in the region as the cattle ranching and agricultural frontiers advanced northward. Once riparian forest is destroyed, streams are subject to complete desiccation during the dry season. One of the characteristic aquatic habitats of the cerrado region is buriti (*Mauritia flexuosa*) palm swamp, which occupies low-lying areas along streams. Hundreds of shade-loving animal species depend on these aquatic forests in an otherwise precarious desertlike environment during the dry season. Palm swamps are rapidly disappearing due to stream impoundment, brush fires in exceptionally dry years, and aggressive deforestation of riparian vegetation.

Dams, cattle ranching, road construction, and large-scale crop farming will continue to transform the Tocantins Valley. Industries will be attracted as hydroelectric projects make more energy available. A functional interstate river basin commission has yet to be established to assess the long-term and far-reaching consequences of headwater deforestation, dam construction, pesticide pollution, and other activities that can cause significant downstream impacts. As development continues, most of the middle and upper Tocantins Valley will gradually be transformed into a dry, nonforested landscape reminiscent of northeastern Brazil.

Araguaia National Park, which now covers the northern third of Bananal Island, was the first national park decreed in the Brazilian Amazon. It is the only major conservation unit protecting wetlands in the Tocantins Valley and is probably Brazil's best hope for protecting wildlife associated with savanna wetlands. Most other savannas in Brazil are being rapidly converted to cropland.

▲ FISHERMEN OF THE TUCURUÍ RESERVOIR

Tucuruí Reservoir did not become a giant fish pond for the Amazon region as government personnel claimed in the 1980s. Tucuruí fisheries are small-scale and could eventually collapse, as often happens in reservoirs created by dam after nutrients from decaying vegetation are exhausted.

▲ TUCURUÍ RESERVOIR BAYS

Tucuruí has hundreds of bays but the reservoir appears to have little appeal to sport-fishing enthusiasts and other tourists.

▲ TUCURUÍ DAM

Tucuruí Dam is located approximately 150 miles (250 km) up the Tocantins River and is the largest dam in the Amazon Basin (Belo Monte Dam on the Rio Xingu will soon surpass Tucuruí in hydroelectric capacity). Tucuruí Reservoir floods approximately 925 square miles (2,400 km²). The large dam was closed in 1984, but satisfactory studies were never carried out to determine its impacts on fish migrations.

▼ SITE OF LAJEADO DAM

The Lajeado Dam is located approximately 625 miles (1,000 km) upstream and in a narrow part of the middle Tocantins River. Lajeado is 25 miles (40 km) downriver of Palmas, capital of the state of Tocantins. Of special environmental concern in this region will be minimal water release from the dam during the dry season, especially in low rainfall years when the reservoir does not fill to desired levels.

UPPER TOCANTINS VALLEY

◄ PALM SWAMP AT EDGE OF TABLELAND
This habitat may not look like wetland, but it is a palm oasis in the central Brazilian cerrado.

▲ CERRADO HEADWATERS
Most of the upper Tocantins Valley is in the savanna-scrub region of central Brazil called cerrado. Although the cerrado has an intense dry season, unique aquatic habitats are found along its streams. Palm swamp exists at the bottom of the cerrado canyon shown here.

CHAPTER EIGHT

THE XINGU AND TAPAJÓS RIVERS
Clearwater Reflections

The Xingu Valley is the fourth largest tributary basin in the Amazon. Covering approximately 194,500 square miles (504,000 km²), the Valley is nearly the size of France. Two-thirds of the Valley is in the state of Pará; the remaining one-third is in the state of Mato Grosso. The Xingu River is almost 1,550 miles (2,500 km) long and contributes approximately 4 percent of the Amazon River's total annual discharge. The confluence of the Xingu and Amazon Rivers is approximately 260 miles (420 km) from the Atlantic via the main river. Oceanic tides are evident at least 60 miles (100 km) up the Xingu.

Most of the Xingu Valley lies within the Amazonian rainforest zone. Scrub-savanna dominates the headwaters area of the Xingu. The rainy season in most of the Xingu Valley is from December to May, and this is also the period of highest river levels. Where tides are felt in the lower Xingu, average annual river-level fluctuation is only 6 ft (2 m). Elsewhere along the main stem, the average ranges from 13 to 14.8 ft (4–4.5 m). The range between the lowest and highest known water levels is approximately 26 ft (8 m).

The outstanding aquatic features of the Xingu Valley are the large mouth-bay of the Xingu River, numerous cataracts, beautiful waterfalls in the hilly Serra do Cachimbo region drained by the Iriri River, and a low-lying headwater basin subject to seasonal inundation. The mouth-bay has a large archipelago and is bordered by sandy beaches for six to eight months each year. Some of the beaches are important nesting sites for the giant Amazon River turtle (*Podocnemis expansa*). Fishermen target mapará catfish (*Hypophthalmus* spp.) in the mouth-bay for the Belém and Macapá markets.

The Xingu River and most of its tributaries are studded with cataracts. The most impressive cataract stretch on the main river is between the mouth-bay and Altamira on the Transamazon highway. A large part of the 3- to 12-mile-wide (5–20 km) riverbed in this region is rocky, and numerous islands split the main channel into a complex maze. During the low-water period, river depths in this stretch fall to less than 20 in. (50 cm). The Volta Grande Rapids downriver of Altamira are a major geographic divide between aquatic life in the central Amazon Basin and that in most of the Xingu Valley.

◄ **INSIDE CLEARWATER FLOODED FOREST OF THE TAPAJÓS**
Clearwater forests growing on sandy soils are usually more open and trees are smaller than counterparts on alluvial soils of muddy river floodplains.

▶ THE XINGU VALLEY

The Xingu Valley is nearly the size of France
and is the third largest tributary basin in the
Amazon. Most the Xingu Valley is within the
Amazonian rainforest zone. Headwaters of
the Xingu River are approximately 1,550
miles (2,500 km) from the Amazon River
and flow through the Brazilian states of
Mato Grosso and Pará. Outstanding aquatic
features include the giant mouth-bay, the
Volta Grande rapids near Altamira, Serra do
Cachimbo waterfalls, and a large headwater
basin subject to long seasonal flooding.
Deforestation has been the most extensive
in the headwaters, near Altamira on the
Transamazon highway, and near São Felix
do Xingu in the middle Xingu region.

THE XINGU VALLEY

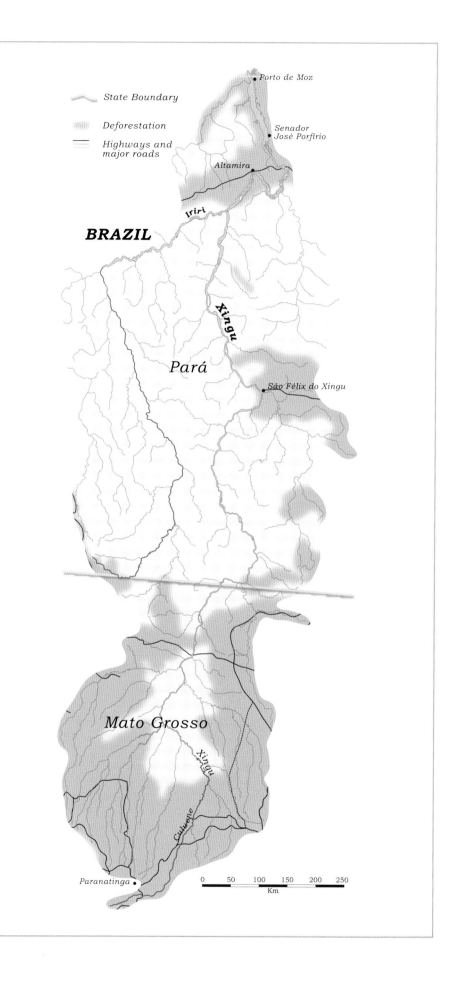

Large river turtles, dolphins, and the Amazonian manatee are not found above the rapids. The fish species below and above the rapids are also strikingly different. No migratory fish species swimming from the Amazon River pass the cataracts.

The Volta Grande Rapids have not escaped the attention of dam builders. Plans for the Belo Monte Dam were drawn up in the 1980s, but have faced heavy criticism from environmental and indigenous-rights groups. Journalists and artists gathered several times in Altamira to protest any major development project on the Xingu River that would infringe on areas inhabited by indigenous peoples. The Belo Monte Dam is now scheduled for completion by 2005.

The Serra do Cachimbo is an ancient upland that forms the major divide between the middle stretches of the Xingu and the Tapajós. Weathered tablelands covered mostly by savannas are common at higher elevations. As tributaries descend from the tablelands, they flow over granite and resistant sandstones that form perhaps the most spectacular waterfalls in the Amazon Basin.

Little is known about the aquatic life of the Serra do Cachimbo. In comparison, botanists have studied the terrestrial plant life in the area and found many endemic species. Presumably, the tributaries above the waterfalls each have distinct populations of fish species and other aquatic life.

The headwaters of the Xingu River drain into a large, internal low-lying sedimentary basin that is reminiscent of Bananal Island in the Tocantins River. Perhaps 30 percent of the Xingu

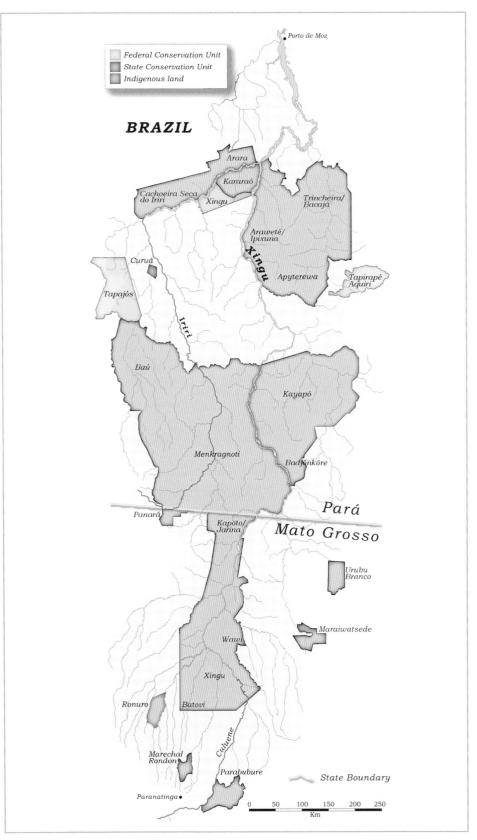

▲ **CONSERVATION UNITS AND INDIGENOUS AREAS OF THE XINGU VALLEY**

Indigenous areas encompass about one-half of the Xingu Valley. Miners, loggers, and others, however, have invaded many of these lands. The largest wetlands of the Xingu Valley are in the southern headwaters and generally within indigenous areas.

▲ RAINFOREST RIVER

The Xingu Valley is one of the most extensively forested tributary basins in the Amazon Basin. Rainforest is still found along most of the Xingu River and its large tributaries. Large indigenous areas have also provided a buffer against the massive deforestation characteristic of the neighboring Tocantins Valley.

MIDDLE XINGU REGION

headwater basin is subject to seasonal flooding for four to seven months each year. Major aquatic habitats include very large lakelike lagoons, flooded forests, and grass savannas that are inundated during the rainy season. Open rainforest and savanna vegetation dominate the uplands. Water in the headwater basin is more nutrient-rich than water downriver in the Xingu and supports an abundance of aquatic herbaceous plants and mollusks, two groups that are relatively scarce elsewhere in the basin.

The three most extensively deforested regions in the Xingu Valley are (1) the region peripheral to the headwaters, (2) the region around São Felix do Xingu in the middle stretch, and (3) the region along the Transamazon highway near Altamira in the lower reaches. Most of the Xingu Basin is still inaccessible by road, and the Santarém-Cuiabá highway, the main north-south link, skirts only the western edge of the valley.

More than one-half of the Xingu Valley is classified as indigenous area. Gold miners, loggers, and others have invaded much of the area. There are no large national parks that protect wetlands of any size in the Xingu Valley. The headwater wetlands are largely under the control of indigenous groups.

The Tapajós Valley is the fifth largest tributary basin in the Amazon. Covering approximately 188,800 square miles (489,000 km²) the Tapajós Valley encompasses approximately 7 percent of the Amazon Basin. Its headwaters are almost 1,650 miles (2,700 km) from the Amazon River mouth and nearly reach Cuiabá, the capital of Mato Grosso, in central Brazil. The mouth of the Tapajós River is approximately 500 miles (800 km) from the Amazon River mouth. More than 95 percent of the Tapajós Valley is divided between the states of Mato Grosso and Pará, with the states of Amazonas and Rondônia

skirting the western drainage. For at least two decades, political movements have been underway to create the state of Tapajós in a large part of the Tapajós Basin.

The Tapajós Valley lies mostly on the Brazilian Shield and within the Amazon rainforest zone. Headwaters arise in the central Brazilian scrub savanna less than 125 miles (200 km) from the giant Pantanal swamp. Average annual precipitation is approximately 90 in. (2,300 mm). There is a pronounced three- to four-month dry season. The rainy season in the upper Tapajós Valley begins in late September, whereas in the lower Valley it begins in late December or January. The peak of the annual floods in the middle and upper Tapajós Valley is usually in March. Near the Tapajos River mouth, the highest water levels are normally in May or June. This is because water levels in the lower river are controlled by the Amazon River. Annual river-level

▶ WATERFALLS OF THE SERRA DO CACHIMBO

Magnificent waterfalls drop off the Serra do Cachimbo tablelands. A few small blackwater rivers are found in the sandy parts of the Serra do Cachimbo, but most rivers are crystalline. Fish populations have probably been isolated in the areas above the waterfalls and there are probably many endemic species.

▼ BEACHES AND ROCKS

The Xingu is a relatively shallow river during the low-water period, and depths average less than 3 ft (1 m). The main stem is studded with rocky outcrops, cataracts, and huge beaches.

▶ CLEAR WATERS OF THE XINGU RIVER

Xingu drainage is mostly on the highly eroded Brazilian Shield that is covered with rainforest. Nutrient levels are too low in most of the river to support floating meadows. During the low-water period when river depths are minimal and current is slowed, phytoplankton blooms give water in the Xingu River a green cast.

fluctuation of the Tapajós and its two main tributaries, the Juruena and the Teles Pires, averages 13–16.5 ft (4–5 m). The ranges between the highest known floods and lowest river levels are 26–29.5 ft (8–9 m).

The Tapajós Valley has fewer wetlands than any of the Amazon's other large tributaries. Most tributaries of the Tapajós flow through the relatively high terrain of the Brazilian Shield. Hilly regions, such as the Serra do Cachimbo, Serra dos Caiabis, and Serra do Tombador, are drained by the Juruena and the Teles Pires.

The first major cataracts on the Tapajós River are near Itaituba, approximately 125 miles (200 km) from its mouth. Migratory fish, however, are able to pass these rapids. Numerous rapids stud the middle and upper Juruena and Teles Pires Rivers. The lower Juruena has floodable forests, and there are small low-lying areas subject to seasonal inundation scattered throughout the Tapajós Basin.

As with the Tocantins and Xingu Rivers, the Tapajós has a giant mouth-lake bordered by high cliffs and low beaches. The beaches are inundated for

six months each year and support sandy-flooded-forest species such as wild cashew (*Anacardium* spp.). The southern half of the mouth-lake has a large archipelago that is covered with floodable forest. In the mouth region of the Tapajós, muddy water, clear water, and black water exist in close proximity. The blackwater Arapiuns, a left-bank tributary, drains sandy soils and flows into the clearwater Tapajós near its confluence with the muddy Amazonas. The Arapiuns has large palm swamps in its headwaters region.

The Santarém-Cuiabá and

VENEZUELA

COLOMBIA

ECUADOR

PERU

BOLIVIA

BRAZIL

TRANSAMAZON HIGHWAY REGION NEAR LOWER RIO XINGU

◀ CATTLE RANCHING

Altamira on the Transamazon highway is one of the fastest-growing cattle ranching areas in the Amazon Basin. The Transamazon highway traverses the narrow lower part of the Xingu Valley and therefore has had a relatively minor impact on deforestation in this tributary basin.

◀ LOGGING THE XINGU BASIN

After cattle ranching, logging is the most important economic activity of the lower Xingu region. Timber is cut mostly to make boards and flooring, which are transported to southern Brazilian states.

◀ PASTURES OF ALTAMIRA

A deforested swath following the Transamazon highway now nearly divides the lower and middle Xingu Valleys.

Transamazon highways opened the Tapajós Valley to large-scale development in the 1970s. Although neither has been paved and transit is difficult during the rainy season, the highways have been used as arteries for cattle ranching, gold mining, logging, and soybean farming. Current transportation project proposals include an industrial waterway and a railway between Cuiabá and Santarém to export agricultural products from central Brazil. Constructing the industrial waterway, called Hidrovia, would require channel deepening and excavation of cataracts.

Gold mining has probably impacted the Tapajós Valley more than any other tributary valley in the Amazon Basin. Gold mining in the valley was concentrated in the auriferous area between the Tapajós, Jamaxim, and Teles Pires Rivers. Most gold was extracted from alluvial deposits. The number of streams excavated for gold is unknown, but it undoubtedly is in the thousands.

Prior to gold mining in the region, crystalline waters flowed in nearly all of its streams. Excavation, sluicing, and placer mining transformed clearwater streams into turbid slurries. Heavy loads of stream sediments, in addition to dredge mining in the larger channels, turned the clearwater Tapajós into a slightly turbid river until the gold rush largely ended in the mid-1990s, when new deposits were difficult to find and gold prices fell.

Tapajós gold mining created two principal environmental problems—destruction of clearwater streams and mercury pollution. The fish fauna of the gold mining region of the Tapajós is very poorly known. Fish species living in the Brazilian Shield tributaries of the Tapajós appear to have evolved in clear water. High turbidity would probably kill them.

The Tapajós gold rush ended nearly a decade ago. It would be valuable to know if the diversity of fish species in the gold mining region is as high as that found in similar Brazilian Shield areas that were not mined. A scientific study would help ecologists understand the resiliency of fish faunas in heavily mined areas of the Amazon Basin.

The fate of the mercury used for gold mining in the Tapajós Valley is not clearly known. Scientists generally assume that enough time has passed that large-scale mercury contamination, especially through food chains, will not be a problem in the Tapajós Basin. Numerous deaths or poisonings linked to contaminated food chains have not been reported. This in part may be because fish are not a major food source for people in the middle Tapajós region.

The huge mouth-bay is the main deposition zone for the Tapajós River, and some mercury may be buried there. Sediment loads were greater during the 1980s, when the gold rush was in full swing. The length of time that Tapajós sediments might remain in the mouth-bay is not known. The formation of islands, however, suggests that it could be decades if not centuries in some stretches. Buried mercury will perhaps be carried slowly downstream in sediments and discharged into the Amazon River. Another possibility is that dangerous levels of mercury could eventually build up near Santarém at the confluence of the Tapajós and the Amazonas, an area of important commercial fisheries.

With the decline of the gold rush,

LOWER XINGU NEAR ALTAMIRA

▲ THE BIOLOGICAL IMPORTANCE OF THE VOLTA GRANDE RAPIDS

It might be assumed that a dam would have few important consequences on fish faunas that were already separated naturally by rapids acting as a barrier. The opposite is probably truer because distinct upstream and downstream faunas double the chances that unique species or ecologies will be destroyed. If the fish fauna were the same below and above the dam, then there would probably be a greater chance of adaptability in at least one part of the modified river. The construction of a fish ladder would not solve the problem because it would lead to a mixing of faunas that evolved separately.

▶ **THE TAPAJÓS VALLEY**

The Tapajós River has the fifth largest tributary basin in the Amazon and is the most terrestrial. Unlike the Tocantins and Xingu, the other two large Brazilian Shield rivers, the Tapajós River does not have a large swampy area. Gold mining has ravaged streams in the middle drainage since the early 1980s, and headwater forests are rapidly disappearing as the central Brazilian agricultural frontier moves north into the Amazon Basin.

THE TAPAJÓS VALLEY

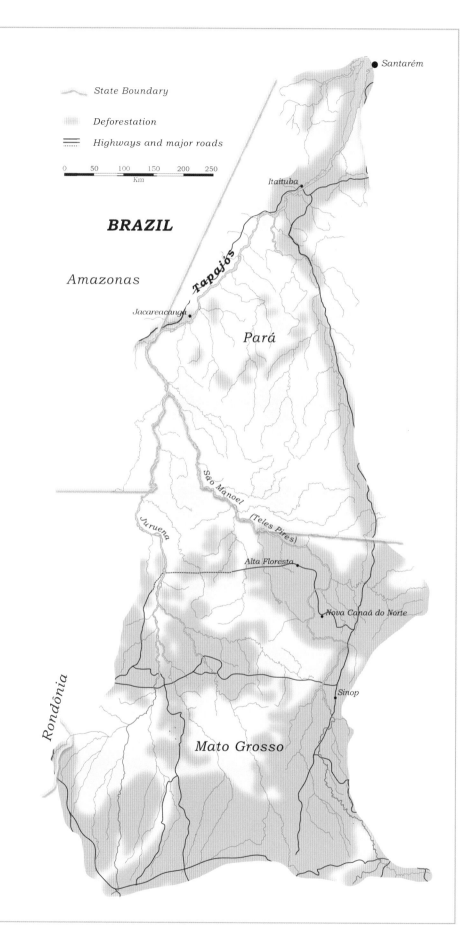

entrepreneurs in the middle and lower Tapajós Valley began to invest heavily in cattle ranching and logging. Itaituba, on the Transamazon highway, was transformed from a gold-driven economy to a cattle and logging center. Itaituba is located in a narrow part of the Tapajós Valley, and deforestation appears to be advancing westward along the Transamazon highway into the Madeira Basin. Landscape alteration in the Tapajós Valley is most noticeable in the Mato Grosso headwater region along the Santarém-Cuiabá highway and near the city of Peixoto de Azevedo on the Teles Pires. The latter area is in the heart of the central Brazilian agricultural frontier, from which soybean farming is rapidly expanding northward.

Relatively few areas are designated for protection in the Tapajós Valley. Most are in the lower drainage, and gold miners, squatters, or loggers have invaded them. No significant areas around headwaters are protected. In the next two to three decades, the headwater region of the Tapajós River will be converted largely into pastureland and cropland as the agricultural frontier advances north. The right bank of the Arapiuns is designated as protected but is an area of heavy logging. The Arapiuns River near the mouth of the Tapajós deserves special attention because it is the easternmost relatively large blackwater river in the Amazon Basin. As with the blackwater Negro River, many endemic species probably live in the Arapiuns.

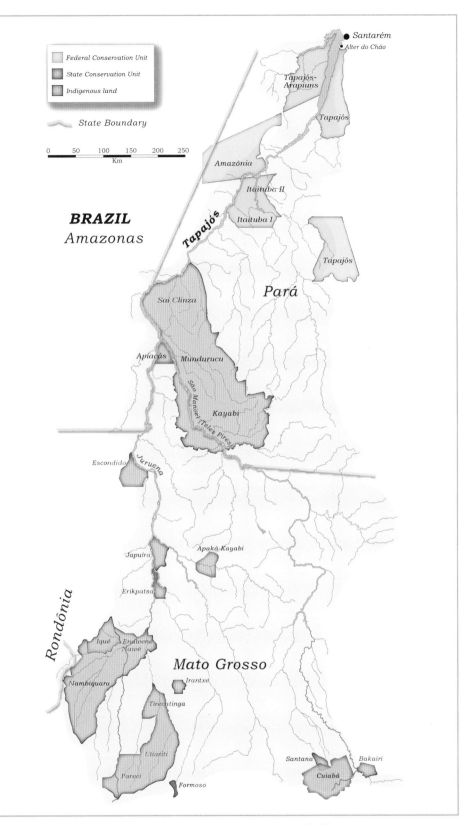

▲ **CONSERVATION UNITS AND INDIGENOUS AREAS OF THE TAPAJÓS VALLEY**

The Tapajós Basin has relatively few designated protected areas. All of the large protected areas that have received any significant attention from authorities or scientists are in the lower drainage. Indigenous lands have been invaded by gold miners and loggers and are no longer isolated enough to ensure long-term protection.

▲ THE GIANT MOUTH-LAKE

The Tapajós mouth-lake is more than 12 miles (20 km) wide and is nearly 90 miles (150 km) long. Mouth-lakes are called *rias* by geologists and some scientists believe they were formed when sea levels were lower and rivers were steeper and ran faster than they do today, thus widening and deepening their channels. Other geologists suggest that Amazon mouth-lakes fill structural depressions originating from tectonic activity.

◀ THE CLEARWATER TAPAJÓS

The Tapajós is a clearwater river that contrasts sharply with the muddy Amazonas. Santarém at the confluence of the Tapajós and Amazonas enjoys one of the most spectacular waterfronts in the Amazon.

LOWER TAPAJÓS

▲ **TAPAJÓS FLOODED FOREST**

Flooded forests of the lower Tapajós are often found on sandy soils. Tapajós flooded forests have species often associated with both muddy rivers and blackwater rivers. The tall palms are assaí (*Euterpe*).

▲ **STRANGLERS IN THE WATER**

This flooded forest strangler of the genus Clusia (*Guttiferae*) stands alone in an area near the Tapajós mouth that has been extensively deforested.

CHAPTER NINE

THE MADEIRA
South America's Core

Encompassing 540,000 square miles (1.4 million km²), the Madeira Valley covers approximately 20 percent of the Amazon Basin. The Valley is larger in size than any Amazonian country except Brazil.

The mouth of the Madeira River is approximately 800 miles (1,300 km) from the mouth of the Amazon River. The farthest headwaters of the Madeira rise near Cochabamba, Bolivia. They are approximately 2,050 miles (3,300 km) from the mouth of the Madeira and approximately 2,850 miles (4,600 km) from that of the Amazon River. The Madeira is the longest tributary in the Amazon Basin and accounts for 15 percent of the Amazon River's total discharge to the Atlantic.

About 50 percent of the Madeira Valley is in Bolivia, 40 percent in Brazil, and 10 percent in Peru. Brazil and Bolivia share a 600-mile-long (1,000 km) border along the Mamoré and Guaporé-Iténez Rivers. Within the three countries there are 14 administrative regions (called "states" in Brazil; "departments" in Bolivia and Peru) in the Madeira Valley.

The largest cities in the Madeira Basin are La Paz, Santa Cruz de la Sierra, and Cochabamba, all of which are in Bolivia. All three cities are located along small tributaries. La Paz and Cochabamba are located in the highlands at elevations above 9,850 ft (3,000 m). Porto Velho, in the state of Rondônia, Brazil, with a population of approximately 300,000, is the fourth most populous city in the Madeira Basin.

The Madeira Valley is probably the most geographically complex tributary basin in the Amazon. The headwaters of the Madeira River arise in the southernmost Andes within the Amazon Basin, in the eastern Bolivian lowlands, and on the Brazilian Shield. Except in the south, most of the Madeira Basin is within the lowland rainforest zone. Savanna predominates throughout the southern part of the Basin.

Most of the Madeira Basin's lowland region in eastern Bolivia is below approximately 1,000 ft (300 m). Annual precipitation in this region is 40–60 in. (1,000–1,500 mm). Annual rainfall totals 80–100 in. (2,000–2,500 mm) in most of the rest of the basin. Along the Andean foothill region of the basin exposed to eastern or southern moisture-laden

◀ **MADRE DE DIOS HEADWATERS AT 9,850 FT (3,000 M)**
The last wisps of Amazonian moisture make it to approximately 9,850 ft (3,000 m). Rivers above this elevation run shallow for most of the year.

▶ THE MADEIRA VALLEY

Occupying approximately 540,000 square miles (1.4 million km²) the Madeira Valley encompasses more than 20 percent of the Amazon Basin. The Madeira River is the largest tributary in terms of both drainage area and water discharge. About one-half the Madeira Valley is in Bolivia, 40 percent is in Brazil, and 10 percent is in Peru. Within the three countries there are 14 states or departments. At least 2,250 miles (3,600 km) long the Madeira is the longest tributary in the Amazon Basin and delivers 15 percent of the Amazon River's total annual discharge. The headwaters of the Madeira are near Cochabamba, Bolivia, which is approximately 2,850 miles (4,600 km) from the Amazon River mouth.

THE MADEIRA VALLEY

winds, the amount of annual precipitation ranges from 195 to 390 in. (5,000–10,000 mm). These high-rainfall areas, however, are relatively small.

The rainy season in the Madeira Valley begins in the lowland headwaters area of Bolivia and Peru in November and lasts through April. Farther downstream the rainy season is between December and April. Flood peaks in eastern Bolivia are in February, whereas in Brazil, downstream of Porto Velho, peak floods are usually in March or April. Between December and May, nearly all rivers below 1,000 ft (300 m) in the Madeira Valley are in flood. Water levels in rivers are lowest each

year between August and October.

River-level fluctuations vary greatly in the Madeira Basin. Within the upper drainage in Bolivia and Peru, average annual river-level fluctuation is approximately 16.5–23 ft (5–7 m). Ranges between extremes in river level can reach 29.5 ft (9 m). The relatively narrow channel of the Madeira between the mouth of the Beni River in Bolivia and Porto Velho in Brazil cause a backwater effect, which prolongs the duration of flood peaks in the lower Beni and Mamoré Rivers.

Some of the most dramatic river-level fluctuations in the Amazon Basin take place downriver of the Madeira

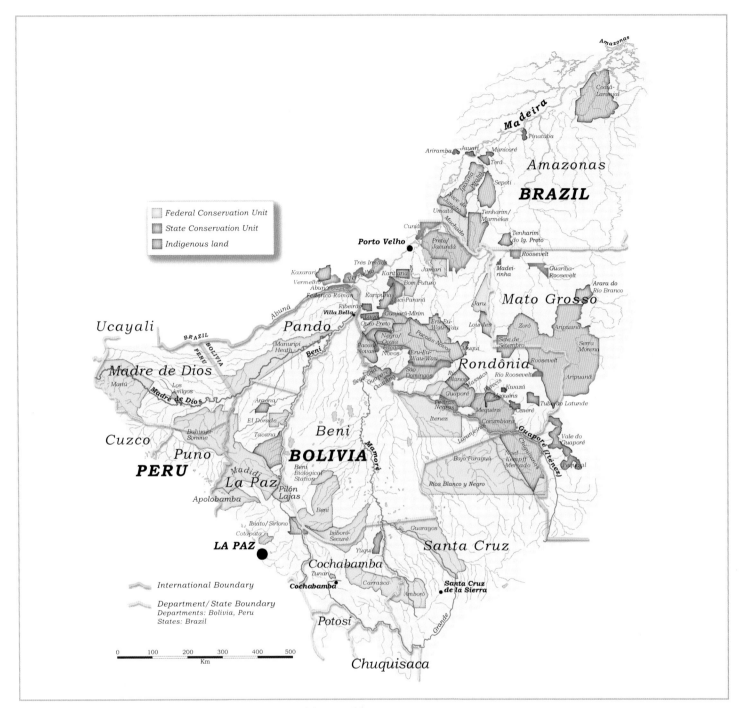

▲ Conservation units and indigenous areas of the Madeira Valley

The Madeira Valley is being heavily developed in its middle sections, and gold mining, deforestation, and logging have heavily impacted rivers and wetlands. The Llanos de Mojos of eastern Bolivia is the largest wetlands in the Madeira Valley, and the area was transformed in pre-Columbian times by large-scale raised-field agriculture. Few aquatic areas are protected in Brazil, and the Madeira floodplain has only one significant designated protected area, which is the Cuniã Reserve near Porto Velho in the state of Rondônia. The right-bank tributaries of the Madeira drain the Brazilian Shield and have relatively large clearwater flooded forests. Only flooded forests of the lower Machado (Ji-Paraná) are theoretically protected. The best-protected areas are Manu National Park, Tambopata-Candamo Reserved Zone, and Bahuaja-Sonene National Park in the upper Madre de Dios drainage in Peru. Both Brazil and Bolivia have designated protected areas in the upper Guaporé-Iténez, but deforestation by squatters and cattle ranchers has been widespread in Brazil. Bolivia has two large designated protected areas within the Beni watershed. The area of Madidi National Park ranges from lowland rainforest to the high arid Andes in the headwater region. Manuripi Heath National Park in Bolivia includes most of the left bank of the Madre de Dios, the Beni's largest tributary.

▲ CONFLUENCE OF THE CLEARWATER
MACHADO (JI-PARANÁ) AND THE MUDDY
MADEIRA

The large right-bank tributaries of the
Madeira are clearwater rivers that contrast
sharply with the muddy Madeira. All forest
shown in this photo is flooded for about six
months each year. The clearwater right-
bank tributaries of the Madeira have some
of the most deeply flooded forests in the
Amazon. The clearwater flooded forests
often have plant and animal species that are
also found in muddy river and blackwater
river floodplains.

UPPER MADERIA, BRAZIL

▲ THE MUDDY MADEIRA

The Madeira is one of the two muddiest
large tributaries of the Amazon River and
contributes nearly one-half of all sediments
delivered to the Atlantic by the main stem.

rapids, between Porto Velho and the
mouth of the Manicoré River. Annual
river-level fluctuation averages in this
region range from approximately 35.4
to 40.7 ft (10.8–12.4 m). The range
between the highest known flood mark
and the lowest water point for rivers in
this region is approximately 50.5–71.5
ft (15.4–21.8 m). Downriver of the
mouth of the Manicoré, water levels in
the Madeira are largely controlled by
the backwater effect of the Amazon
River. At the mouth of the Madeira,
river-level fluctuation averages approximately 19.5 ft (6 m).

The Madeira is an extremely
muddy river during most of the year.
The Beni and its principal tributary, the
Madre de Dios, deliver the heaviest
sediment loads, followed by the
Mamoré. Some of the tributaries that
arise in the eastern Bolivian lowlands,
such as the Yata near the confluence of
the Beni and Mamoré, are also turbid.

Most of the tributaries that arise on
the Brazilian Shield have clear water.

The largest of these clearwater rivers—
such as the Aripuanã and Machado (Ji-
Paraná)—are right-bank tributaries of
the Madeira. The Guaporé-Iténez,
another clearwater tributary, drains the
southern Brazilian Shield and eastern
Bolivian lowlands. Clearwater tributaries are also found in the Andean headwater region above approximately 1,300
ft (400 m). They are clear, however, for
only about only the six to eight months
each year, when rainfall is minimal.

Most blackwater rivers of the
Madeira Valley—such as the Camunã
and Igapó-açu—are near the mouth
region. Blackwater streams and small
rivers less than approximately 330 ft
(100 m) wide, however, are scattered
throughout the Madeira Valley. There
are also blackwater floodplain lakes,
such as in the Cuniã Reserve near
Porto Velho.

Wetlands cover an extensive area—
at least 23,200 square miles (60,000
km²)—within the Madeira Valley.
Downriver of the Bolivian-Brazilian

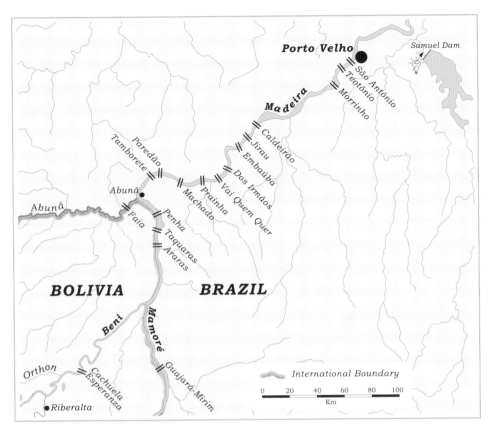

▲ THE TEOTÔNIO RAPIDS OF THE MADEIRA

The Teotônio rapids are approximately 12 miles (20 km) upstream of Porto Velho and are the principal barrier to navigation of the Madeira. The rapids also represent a major geographical divide in the Madeira Valley and many fish species do not pass them. The Teotônio rapids are shown here during low water when there is a 6.5–10 ft (2–3 m) difference between smooth water above (right) and below (left) the cataracts.

▲ THE MADEIRA RAPIDS

The Madeira rapids are telltales of the ancient underlying Brazilian Shield. There are 16 major cataracts in the 225-mile-long (360 km) stretch between Porto Velho and Guajará-Mirim at the Brazilian-Bolivian border. The lower Beni in Bolivia also has the Esperanza rapids. Historically the Madeira rapids presented a major barrier to transportation, and the Madeira-Mamoré railway was constructed in the early twentieth century to bypass the cataracts. A highway, now paved between Porto Velho and Guajará-Mirim, replaced the railway. There have been proposals to blow up the cataracts to deepen the river channel or to build locks to allow barge and boat transportation.

▲ THE ESPERANZA RAPIDS OF THE LOWER BENI

The Brazilian Shield is exposed in Bolivia at the Esperanza rapids, approximately 35 miles (60 km) upriver of the mouth of the Beni. The Esperanza rapids are a geographical barrier to dolphins, the Amazonian manatee, and the giant Amazon River turtle. Large catfish, however, easily swim through the Esperanza rapids during their upstream migrations to the Andean foothills.

▲ THE TEOTÔNIO RAPIDS DURING THE LOW-WATER PERIOD

During the low-water period, the Madeira channel at the Teotônio rapids is reduced to less than approximately 165 ft (50 m) in width.

UPPER MADEIRA
REGION, BRAZIL

▲ **GOLD-DREDGING THE MADEIRA**

Rondônia had relatively large quantities of alluvial gold that originated either in the Andes or on the Brazilian Shield. Alluvial gold concentrations were especially high in the region of the Madeira rapids. During the 1980s and 1990s the riverbed of the Madeira in the state of Rondônia was heavily dredged for gold. Dredge densities became so great that normal boat transportation was impeded. Fishermen reported that migratory fish were frightened by the dredges and schools returned downstream. Dredges still operate in the Madeira Channel, but their numbers are only a small percentage of what they were during the 1980s and early 90s. Dredge operations discarded large quantities of mercury into the Madeira, but ecological impacts have never been satisfactorily determined. It is possible that most of the mercury became bound to sediments and was buried or carried away downstream.

border, the Madeira River floodplain is relatively narrow, covering approximately 770 square miles (2,000 km²). A large part of the floodplain is blanketed with floodable forest that is inundated for four to six months each year. The floodplain forest has been selectively logged but not extensively deforested.

The middle and upper reaches of the Guaporé-Iténez River are bordered by gallery forest and extensive tracts of low-lying floodable savanna. This stretch of the river is reminiscent of the headwaters area of the Xingu and of Bananal Island in the Araguaia River. There has been extensive deforestation on the Brazilian side of the Guaporé-Iténez, and ranchers are grazing cattle on the savanna grasslands.

The most extensive wetlands within the Madeira Valley are the floodable savannas of the Llanos de Mojos region in the center of the department of Beni in Bolivia. Occupying approximately 69,500 square miles (180,000 km²), the Llanos de Mojos wetlands are also the most extensive savanna wetlands in the Amazon Basin. Rainfall and overflow from the Mamoré River and its tributaries keep most of the savanna area underwater for four to eight months each year. Water depth on the savannas during the floods is generally less than 3 ft (1 m); the average appears to be less than approximately 20 in. (50 cm). The Llanos de Mojos savannas are interspersed with levees and their remnants, dunes, shallow lakes, palm swamps, riparian forests, and upland forests.

The duration of seasonal floods is shorter on floodplains within 185 miles (300 km) of the Andes compared with those farther away due to their

increased elevation. In Manu National Park, for example, which is close to the Andes, floodplains are inundated for only one to four weeks each year.

Heavy deposition and fast currents make riverbanks highly unstable near the Andes. Floodplain forests are often less than 100 years old before the river channel begins to change course and undercut them. The changing channels and undercutting currents cause many trees to fall into the water. Giant kapok (*Ceiba pentandra*) trees are common in the woody flotsam that studs rivers close to the Andes. Mahogany trees, prized for their wood in the western Amazon, were common amongst the tree-fall that forms large tangled rafts in rivers such as the Beni and the Madre de Dios. Mahogany has been extensively logged, and there are few if any harvestable trees left near the riverbank. Rio Madeira means "Wood River" in Portuguese—a fitting name, given the thousands of floating and sunken trees that enter the river each year from Bolivia and Peru during the floods.

Most of the rivers in the pre-Andean region meander, and there are many oxbow lakes. The oxbow lakes become shallow during the low-water season—often less than 3 ft (1 m) deep—and usually do not support the vast floating meadows found in floodplain lakes within the central Amazon. *Mauritia flexuosa* palm swamps are another type of important wetland near the Andes. They are found in low-lying and semipermanently flooded areas up to at least an altitude of 1,300 ft (400 m).

Terrestrial and aquatic habitats in the Andes above 1,300 ft (400 m) change radically with elevation and their geographical position relative to moisture-laden winds. In general, there are three humid zones: a foothill region between approximately 1,650 and 3,950 ft (500–1,200 m); a montane rainforest region between 3,950 and 8,200 ft (1,200–2,500 m); and cloud-forest between 8,200 and 11,500 ft (2,500–3,500 m). Some plant species can grow in more than one zone; for example,

cloud-forest vegetation is commonly found as low as 4,900 ft (1,500 m).

Above the cloud forest are high Andean valleys that receive less than 40 in. (1,000 mm) of annual precipitation. Windward slopes of these valleys are often covered with forest, whereas leeward or rain-shadow slopes can be barren. A tundralike zone with grassy tussocks, called the "puna," is found between approximately 11,500 ft (3,500 m) and the snowline at 14,750 ft (4,500 m).

The steep slopes of the montane zone ensure that its aquatic habitats are characterized by fast-moving water. Pools in many of the streams can reach depths of 13–26 ft (4–8 m). Montane streambeds and riverbeds are generally rocky. Water transparency ranges from nearly crystalline when rainfall is minimal to highly turbid when there is heavy precipitation.

Floodplains are narrow—often only a few meters wide—but overhanging trees are usually the rule along montane streams and rivers. Waterfalls

▲ **CATTLE RANCHING IN RONDÔNIA**
Rondônia is the most deforested state in the Brazilian Madeira Valley. Livestock ranching has been the principal agricultural focus in the state since the early 1980s. Major headwater areas, such as those of the Machado (Ji-Paraná) and the Guaporé-Iténez in Brazil, are rapidly being converted to pastures.

RONDÔNIA STATE, UPPER MADEIRA, BRAZIL

commonly emerge from the tops of steep but forest-clad slopes. The humid eastern slopes of the Andes, called the Yungas in Bolivia, are drained by headwaters of the Mamoré and Beni Rivers.

Since at least the mid-nineteenth century, developers have dreamed of linking the Amazon with central and southern Brazil via the Madeira. The 225-mile-long (360 km) stretch of rapids between Porto Velho and Guajará-Mirim, in addition to the shallow Guaporé-Iténez, however, are formidable obstacles to an interbasin transportation network.

The Cuiabá-Porto Velho highway, constructed in the early 1970s, connected central and southern Brazilian states with the western Amazon and allowed large-scale migration into the Madeira Valley. During the 1970s most development in the Valley took place in the territory of Rondônia, which later became a state. Colonists originally settled mostly along the Cuiabá-Porto Velho highway, which cut across

the divide between the Machado (Ji-Paraná) and Guaporé-Iténez Rivers. The highway was paved in the mid-1980s and numerous feeder roads branched into the Guaporé-Iténez Valley and north into Machado (Ji-Paraná) Basin.

The Porto Velho-Manaus highway opened in the mid-1970s and sliced through the low-lying left-bank drainage of the middle and lower Madeira. The Transamazon highway traversed all the large tributary headwaters of the middle and lower Madeira. Finally, the Porto Velho–Guajará-Mirim highway replaced the Madeira-Mamoré railway, which had been used since the early 1900s to bypass the Madeira rapids.

More than two-thirds of Rondônia has been moderately to heavily deforested in the past three decades. The agricultural frontier is still expanding in Rondônia and colonization is heavy in the Guaporé-Iténez Valley. The Porto Velho-Manaus highway, which was

originally paved, has proven prohibitively expensive to maintain because of the swampy terrain it traverses. Less than 10 percent of the Madeira Basin's watershed is in the left-bank area, where the highway was constructed.

The only large dam in the Madeira Valley is Samuel Dam on the Jamari River, which is a right-bank tributary downriver of Porto Velho. There are also proposals to dam the Machado (Ji-Paraná), an even larger clearwater tributary near the Rondônia-Amazonas border. Neither a fish ladder nor a diversion canal was built to allow migratory fish to continue upriver past Samuel Dam.

Rondônia was one of the principal gold-mining regions in the Amazon Basin in the 1980s and early 1990s. Gold miners concentrated their efforts in two areas: in the cataract stretch of the Madeira River between Porto Velho and the Bolivian border and in small right-bank tributaries of the same region. Hundreds of large dredges

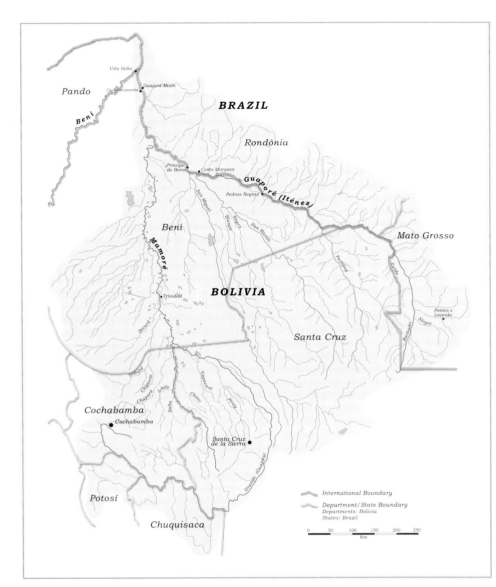

▲ DRAINING THE WET SAVANNAS OF RONDÔNIA

All of the Brazilian state of Rondônia is in the Madeira Basin. Colonists from central and southern Brazil have transformed Rondônia into one of the most active agricultural regions in the Amazon Basin. Farmers are now draining the wet savannas northeast of Porto Velho to plant soybeans and other crops. The plowed land shown here was originally savanna up to the forest shown in the background.

▲ THE MAMORÉ BASIN

Covering approximately 20,300 square miles (525,000 km²) the Mamoré Basin is the largest tributary area in the Madeira Valley. Brazil and Bolivia share a 450-mile-long (700 km) border along the Madeira, Mamoré, and Guaporé-Iténez. The tributary basin of the Mamoré is the fourth largest in the Amazon Basin. Only the Madeira, Tocantins, and Negro have basins larger than that of the Mamoré, and the Mamoré is part of the Madeira basin. The Mamoré is nearly 1,350 miles (2,200 km) long and the headwaters farthest from its mouth are near the city of Cochabamba in Bolivia. The Mamoré has two major tributaries: the 1,100-mile-long (1,800 km) clearwater Guaporé-Iténez, which has headwaters on the Brazilian Shield in the hilly Chapada dos Parecis and the 700-mile-long (1,100 km) muddy Grande (Guapay) that drains the eastern Bolivian lowlands. The Mamoré is a muddy river that joins the Beni to form the Madeira. The Mamoré Basin lies within five Bolivian departments and two Brazilian states. Santa Cruz de la Sierra—Bolivia's second largest city—is the largest city in the Mamoré Basin.

MAMORÉ BASIN

▲ THE MAMORÉ AT GUAJARÁ-MIRIM

Brazil and Bolivia share approximately 90 miles (150 km) of the 1,350-mile-long (2,200 km) Mamoré. Guajará-Mirim in Brazil and Gua-yaramerín in Bolivia are sister cities that are growing rapidly and dominate the economy of the lower Mamoré Valley. Fishing boats are shown here at port in Guajará-Mirim, Brazil.

▲ RAISED FIELDS OF THE EASTERN BOLIVIAN SAVANNAS

Indigenous peoples in pre-European Conquest times transformed large parts of the eastern Bolivian savannas for agriculture. Raised fields were constructed to prevent crops from being flooded. Traces of the fields are still easily seen from the air.

▲ THE MAMORÉ NEAR TRINIDAD (BOLIVIA)

The Mamoré meanders through the savannas of eastern Bolivia before entering rainforest close to the Brazilian border. The Mamoré has thousands of oxbow lakes and other flood-plain water bodies. During the floods the Mamoré inundates large areas of savanna, which are also flooded by local rainwater.

sucked bottom sediments and churned the streambed for gold.

In the 1980s scientists presented evidence that predatory fish living in the Madeira River had relatively high levels of mercury possibly coming from gold mining sites. They were uncertain, however, of the extent to which humans might have been contaminated. One problem was that no control studies were done to detect what the natural levels of mercury might be in fish populations of the Madeira. Gold mining has declined drastically in Rondônia, although a few large dredges continue to operate in the main channel.

The most extensively modified wetlands in the Amazon at the time of the European Conquest in the sixteenth century were probably those that existed on the eastern Bolivian plains. Arawak Indians transformed the swampy savannas by constructing earthworks to provide dry ground for crops, dwellings, and roads. Large earthen weirs were also constructed to trap and retain fish. The Llanos de Mojos landscape was so extensively modified that the raised fields, large settlement mounds, and earthen causeways can be easily spotted from a plane.

Scholars believe that the pre-Columbian population of the eastern Bolivian plains may have reached 350,000: a figure much higher than presently found in the region. Ironically, forest appears to have encroached after the European Conquest and decimation of the Indians, which suggests that much of the savanna may originally have been forested. Today cattle ranchers use the savannas for extensive grazing. Urban services can be found in the city of Trinidad, but the Llanos de

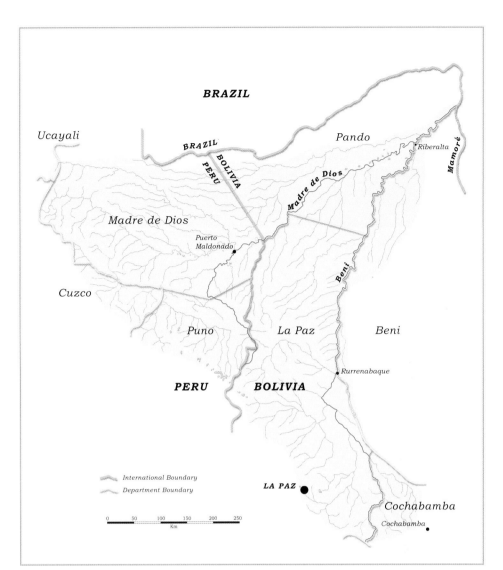

International Boundary
Department Boundary

0   50   100   150   200   250
Km

BENI BASIN

▲ THE BENI BASIN

The Beni Basin encompasses approximately 66,400 square miles (172,000 km^2) and lies within Bolivia and Peru. The 1,000-mile-long (1,600 km) Beni is a muddy river, as is its large tributary, the Madre de Dios. Most of the Beni's headwaters are in the Andes. The Beni Basin includes three Bolivian and three Peruvian departments. Peru's territory within the Beni Basin is almost entirely in the upper Madre de Dios drainage. La Paz is the largest city along a headwater stream in the Amazon Basin, but Puerto Maldonado on the Madre de Dios is the largest city along a major river in the Beni Basin.

▲ CONFLUENCE OF MADRE DE DIOS
AND TAMBOPATA

It rained heavily in the Tambopata Basin
(right) a day before this photograph was
taken, resulting in the cocoalike slurry of
sediments that color the water. At the same
time there were no large rainstorms in the
Madre de Dios Basin whose waters
remained the color typical of the low-
water period.

▼ UPPER BENI FLOODPLAIN

Near the Andes the Beni floodplain is relatively unstable and alluvial soils are a mix
of alluvium and gravel. The high floodplains
are dominated by forests rich in palms.

MADRE DE DIOS,
PERU

Mojos region remains isolated due to
the poor condition of the roads to La
Paz and to Guayará-Mirin at the Brazilian border.

Santa Cruz de la Sierra—the second largest city in Bolivia—is the only
large urban center within the eastern
Bolivian savanna region. Bolivia's agricultural frontier is expanding rapidly
around the city and along the lowland
stretch of the Cochabamba-Santa Cruz
highway. A road from Bolivia to Brazil
has yet to be built, but the two countries are connected by the Santa Cruz-
Corumbá railway. A pipeline to export
natural gas from the Santa Cruz de
la Sierra area to Brazil was completed
in 2001.

The Chapare region, in the upper
Mamoré Basin, is the second most
extensive agricultural frontier in the
Amazon headwaters region of Bolivia.
The Chapare was one of the world's
main coca-growing areas for the production of cocaine until the late 1990s,
when Bolivian authorities began to

eradicate the country's cocaine trade.
International organizations, such as
US-AID, and European countries,
helped by financing banana, orange,
and other crop farming for the region.
Although the amount of coca grown in
the Chapare is far less than before,
alternative-crop farming and migration
of people to the area from the highlands has accelerated deforestation of
the foothills.

A road between La Paz and Rurrenabaque—a Bolivian city in the
upper Beni Valley—has begun to spur
agricultural colonization in the upper
Beni Valley. Rurrenabaque has developed inexpensive ecotourism to attract
people interested in river trips. The
Beni River flows through a narrow and
scenic gorge in the Cerros de Bala near
Rurrenabaque. People in favor of
attracting industry to the region consider the gorge a prime site for a dam.
The Bala site alone is reported to represent approximately one-fifth of the
hydroelectric potential of Bolivia. Two

▲ **FLOODPLAIN OF THE BENI**

The Beni transports enormous quantities of sediments, and its floodplain is relatively unstable, especially within 185 miles (300 km) of the Andes. When river level drops, banks can cave in and trees, shrubs, and other debris are carried downstream. The unstable bank shown here has been colonized by cane grass (*Gynerium sagittatum*) and umbrella trees (*Cecropia*).

▲ **FLOODPLAIN LAKES OF MADRE DE DIOS**

Oxbow lakes are formed when the river channel changes course. The unstable upper Madre de Dios has numerous floodplain lakes, most of which are shallow and surrounded by floodable forest. Fish become densely packed into the cochas, as the floodplain lakes are called locally, during the low-water period.

obstacles to erecting a dam in the gorge exist: the heavy sediment load of the Beni and major opposition from environmental groups that oppose flooding part of Madidi National Park.

The Madre de Dios is the largest tributary of the Beni River. Its headwaters are almost entirely in Peru. A tortuous highway over the Andes connects Cuzco at 10,800 ft (3,300 m) with Puerto Maldonado at 1,150 ft (350 m) at the confluence of the Madre de Dios and Tambopata Rivers. The highway continues to the Brazilian border and on to Rio Branco, the capital of the state of Acre. Puerto Maldonado is a rapidly growing city on Peru's agricultural frontier in the upper Madre de Dios region and driven economically by gold mining, logging, and ecotourism centered mostly on rivers

The second highway from the highlands into the Madre de Dios Basin is from Cuzco to Boca Manu at the confluence of the Manu and Alto Madre de Dios (after which the Madre de Dios is formed). Most of the lowland stretch, however, is usually not passable. Highland peoples are colonizing the foothills and lowlands along the Cuzco-Shintuya highway that skirts Manu National Park. Ecotourism has blossomed, especially with tourists taking boat trips to Manu.

The upper Madre de Dios region is presently the most heavily mined area in the Amazon Basin for alluvial gold. Coarse gravel and sand that trap alluvial gold are found throughout the region in riverbeds, levees, and many floodplains. According to miners, gold is constantly being deposited in the region, but it takes four to five years after an area has been mined before quantities are sufficient for their extraction to be economically viable again. In this short of period, however, gold quantities are minimal compared to

those found in virgin sediments.

Miners excavate for alluvial gold in the levees, floodplains, and river channels. They have blasted hundreds of kilometers of levees with high-pressure spray and completely turned them over. Large-scale operations use heavy machinery to excavate floodplains. Even floodplain lakes are dredged. Aerial flights over tributaries of the Madre de Dios—such as the Inambari and the Colorado—reveal a landscape that has been transformed into a giant gravel pit. Gold mining here has been so extensive that its signature is now a major feature on satellite images of the region.

Wood, primarily from mahogany trees, is the main product transported from the upper Madre de Dios to Cuzco. Fuel trucks transport diesel and gasoline to Puerto Maldonado and return with thick boards stacked on top of empty tanks. Passengers ride on top of the boards. Harvestable mahogany

△ WOODY SHORES OF THE MADRE DE DIOS

The Madre de Dios contributes huge quantities of wood to the Madeira. Tree-fall is heaviest when river level is dropping rapidly. Large trees, however, are transported downstream mostly during the floods. It probably takes several decades in some cases for river-transported trees to reach the Amazon River more than 950 miles (1,500 km) downstream.

◁ WOOD JAMS

Small tributaries, such as the Los Amigos downriver of Manu National Park, can become choked with fallen trees, often making navigation very difficult. The role of such enormous quantities of wood in aquatic habitats near the Andes is unclear but probably creates enormous habitat areas for fish and other animals.

◁ MANU FLOODPLAIN FOREST

Manu National Park in the Madre de Dios headwaters has extensive floodplains. Manu's floodplains are high and only inundated for one to four weeks each year, compared with about six months for floodplains in the central Amazon. Manu's floodplain forest is rich in plant and animal species and characterized by giant kapok trees that tower above the canopy.

and other commercially valuable species are scarce on the floodplains near Puerto Maldonaldo. Loggers are moving up the tributaries in search of new sources.

The Madeira Valley is the most transnational of the Amazon's great tributary basins and Brazil, Bolivia, and Peru each have different types of conservation units. As in most of the Amazon, conservation areas in the Madeira Valley are still being designated and debate continues on how they should be managed.

In Brazil most of the designated protected areas are in the heavily deforested state of Rondônia. Squatters, loggers, and cattle ranchers have invaded nearly all of Rondônia's protected areas. Consequently, they do not attract tourists. The only protected floodplain along the Madeira River in Brazil is Cuniã, located approximately 25 miles (40 km) downriver of Porto Velho. Despite being relatively small (15 square miles [40 km²]), Cuniã is a geographically important reserve. Blackwater lakes and streams can be found within the reserve. Each year when the Madeira is in flood, muddy water from the river invades the reserve.

Cuniã is managed by the state of Rondônia as a sustainable development reserve. Commercial fishing is the principal economic activity taking place within Cuniã. The greatest dangers confronting the reserve are agricultural expansion in the savanna and forest region west of the reserve and new feeder roads into the reserve from the Porto Velho-Manaus highway.

Relatively large areas of seasonally flooded forest exist alongside the lower courses of the Machado (Ji-Paraná),

Manicoré, Aripuanã, and other large-right bank tributaries of the Madeira. These forests are uncommon because relatively little flooded forest grows alongside other large clearwater rivers, such as the Tapajós and Xingu. Only the lower Machado, however, has been granted protection status. Little consideration has been given to designating conservation areas in the clearwater tributary region of the Brazilian Shield, perhaps because it is so isolated and few scientists have worked there.

The Madeira rapids are among the most spectacular muddy-river cataracts in the Amazon Basin. There have been various plans to remove the rapids by deepening the river channel or by building a series of locks to flood the rapids. The Cachoeira do Teotônio, approximately 12 miles (20 km) above Porto Velho, is probably the best place in the Madeira Valley to observe and study the upstream migrations of large catfish and other fish species. The value of the Madeira rapids for studying fish migration suggests that they should be given protection status. The Cachoeira do Teotônio is also the major tourist attraction near Porto Velho.

Brazil and Bolivia have shown little cooperation in devising means to protect the enormous wetlands of the middle and upper Guaporé-Iténez Valley. Deforestation is heaviest on the Brazilian side and shows no signs of abating. There are large designated protected areas along the Guaporé-Iténez, but those in Brazil have been heavily invaded.

Bolivia's largest wetlands in the Madeira Valley are the Llanos de Mojos. The wet savannas and gallery forests of the Llanos de Mojos were extensively

VENEZUELA

COLOMBIA

ECUADOR

PERU

BOLIVIA

BRAZIL

MANU RIVER, PERU

▶ **MANU IN CONSTANT CHANGE**
Although there is little deforestation by humans in Manu National Park, shifting river channels take a continuous toll on floodplain trees. Currents cut away at soft floodplain banks and eventually bring down even the largest trees. In the same process, however, new floodplain and forest is created in areas, such as oxbows, where the old channel has been abandoned.

▶ **MANU FLOODPLAIN LAKES**
Forests and lakes are the two characteristic features of the Manu floodplain. The floodplain lakes of Manu National Park are probably among the most natural in the Amazon, as neither commercial nor subsistence fishing is allowed in them and there has been little deforestation.

UPPER MADRE DE DIOS REGION, PERU

▲ **SETTLEMENT ON THE MADRE DE DIOS**

Most permanent settlements along the upper Madre de Dios consist of recent generations of Andeans who migrated to the lowlands. These communities have yet to develop adequate economies, and most people depend on precarious gold mining or logging for employment.

modified in pre-Columbian times. It is probable than much, if not most, of the savanna region was originally forest. The decimation of the native population allowed forests to become reestablished in many areas. The large native population of the Llanos de Mojos supported itself mainly by transforming the savanna wetlands for raised agriculture and earthen fish weirs. We know too little about the biology of the Llanos de Mojos to understand to what extent native populations might have impacted wetland ecology. The destruction of riparian forests would undoubtedly have affected local fish populations, in addition to affecting the extensive arboreal biodiversity of the forests. Llanos de Mojos native populations possibly destroyed flooded forest habitats and the associated fish habitats. Consequently, they may have had no choice but to depend more on other species for food, many of which they could easily capture and retain in earthen weirs.

Amazonian Indians generally recognize the value of "fish forests." In savanna regions that have intense dry seasons, however, it may have been difficult for Indians to control the large numbers of fires that were set each year. Gradually floodable forests would have been destroyed as happened on Marajó Island at the mouth of the Amazon River and in much of the Bananal Island region of the Araguaia. Protecting areas of the Llanos de Mojos from large-scale human impacts will probably result in the continued reversion to gallery forests. However, maintaining the typical indigenous landscape of the Llanos de Mojos would probably result in decreased biodiversity.

Bolivia's most important designated protected area in the Beni Basin is Madidi National Park. The region around the park is relatively sparsely populated but has been invaded by loggers. The lower reaches of the park, including the Tuichi, are used extensively by ecotourists taking upriver boat trips from Rurrenabaque on the Beni. Erecting the proposed Bala Dam discussed previously would flood a part of the park. Another large designated protected area in the upper Beni is the Isiboro-Secure National Park. Both Madidi and Isiboro-Secure parks have relatively large indigenous populations as well. The Manuripi-Heath National Park along the Madre de Dios is probably the most important protected area for eastern Bolivian wetlands because of its relatively sparse human population and the long stretch of the main river included within the park.

Manu National Park in the upper Madre de Dios watershed in Peru is the most highly publicized protected area in the Madeira Valley. Manu has probably received more media attention than all other protected areas in the Madeira Basin combined. Due to a combination of natural beauty, scientific interest, relatively pristine natural conditions, and proximity to South America's most visited tourist attraction—Machu Picchu in the Andes near Cuzco—Manu National Park has become one of the ecotourism hotspots of the rainforest world. More scientific investigations have been carried out in the park than any in any other area of the Madeira Basin. Few of them, however, have focused on aquatic subjects. The park

▲ **AGRICULTURAL COLONIZATION OF THE AMAZON-ANDEAN INTERFACE ZONE**

The soils in the lowlands along the Andean foothills are richer than those of most of the Amazon. Farmers are beginning to experiment with rice and other crops in the valley bottoms. Within the next several decades there will probably be large-scale deforestation as farming techniques and technologies improve.

▲ **DEFORESTATION IN ANDEAN FOOTHILLS OF THE UPPER MADRE DE DIOS**

In great contrast to what happened at higher elevations in the Andes, native peoples apparently did not heavily deforest the eastern foothills. Andeans have a long history of cultivating steep slopes, and the foothills present few obstacles to them. Deforestation of high-elevation watersheds by native peoples probably had little impact on Amazonian rivers. Foothill deforestation by modern colonists, however, could have much greater consequences because of destruction of both terrestrial and aquatic habitats.

BENI LEAVING ANDES

△ BENI IN FOOTHILL REGION DURING THE LOW-WATER PERIOD

Water transparency increases in the upper Beni during the low-water period when there is little rainfall in the headwaters region. The muddy river takes on a greenish color because of increased phytoplankton production. The foothills of the Beni are still largely forested.

△ THE CERROS DE BALA GORGE OF THE UPPER BENI

The Beni leaves the Andean foothills through a very narrow gorge near the Bolivian city of Rurrenabaque in the department of La Paz. The Cerros de Bala Gorge has been surveyed as a potential site for a dam and is reported to have the single greatest hydroelectric potential of Bolivian rivers. The Beni, however, carries a heavy sediment load, which would shorten the life of the reservoir, and the impoundment would inundate a large part of the Madidi National Park.

△ ROLLING ROCKS FROM THE ANDES

Riverbeds in and near the Andes are layered with washed rocks that strong currents have carried out of the mountains. The rocky substrates do not become buried with sediments because swift currents carry the lighter materials downstream to become part of the vast quantities of alluvium found along rivers in the lowlands. The Beni site shown here is west of the Cerros de Bala Gorge in Bolivia.

▲ ANDEAN CLEARWATER RIVERS

Foothill streams are clear for at least six to seven months each year. Swift currents remove sediments, and the main rivers become turbid only below approximately 1,300 ft (400 m).

occupies approximately 695 square miles (1,800 km²) and covers a wide range of habitats, including lowland and montane rainforest, cloud forest, and high-elevation grasslands.

The Manu River meanders extensively and forms hundreds of oxbow lakes. The Manu's floodplain is large but is sufficiently above the River to remain inundated for only one to three weeks each year. Most of the floodplain is occupied by floodable forest. Biodiversity is very high on the floodplain and contiguous uplands. Most of Manu National Park is off-limits to everyone except the indigenous groups that live there. Approximately 20 percent of the park is open to scientists and tourists. People who live along the portion of the River in the park occupy approximately 10 percent of its area.

Compared with other designated protected areas in the Amazon Basin, Manu National Park is undoubtedly one of the most pristine in terms of abundance of wildlife. Armed park guards control entrance into the park, and squatter invasions have not been a major issue. The park demonstrates that wildlife abundance and thus ecotourism are highest in areas where there are few human settlements. The park is also an important protected area for fish species that migrate to the Andean foothills to spawn.

The second major designated protected area in the upper Madre de Dios region is in the Tambopata-Candamo and Heath Basins south of Puerto Maldonado. Protected areas include the Bahuaja-Sonene National Park and the Tambopata-Candamo Reserved Zone, where conservation strategies are being studied. The area is rich in aquatic and terrestrial habitats, including wet savannas, floodplain forests, palm swamps, and lowland and upland rainforest. Most of Tambopata-Candamo-Heath region is sparsely populated though gold mining has heavily impacted tributaries near the Andes. Exxon-Mobil has contracts to extract oil in the Tampopata-Candamo Basin but to date only one experimental well has been drilled.

Manu National Park and areas around Puerto Maldonado are likely to experience notable increases in ecotourism, which offers an optimistic note for conservation in the upper Madre de Dios region. The great hope of conservationists is that conservation areas in the region will eventually be linked with Madidi National Park in Bolivia to form an enormous and functional transnational conservation corridor.

FOOTHILL FORESTS AND RIVERS

Forest-covered slopes decrease erosion. Most of the sediments eroded from the Andes came originally from elevations above the foothills.

MADRE DE DIOS HEADWATERS

PERUVIAN FOOTHILLS OF UPPER MADRE DE DIOS

The foothill region is cloudy most of the year because moisture-laden winds from the Amazon clash with the Andes. As the humid air rises water vapor condenses, creating the characteristic cloud cover. The Araza Valley shown here at approximately 1,650 ft (500 m) is representative of a foothill landscape without significant human impacts.

ANDEAN FOOTHILLS OF THE INAMBARI OF THE UPPER MADRE DE DIOS

The meeting of the rainforest with the steep Andes is one of the most magnificent sights in the Amazon drainage. Although a significant amount of rain falls on the eastern Andean slopes, water clarity and other properties in the rivers vary from season to season. For about six months most of the riverbed is dry.

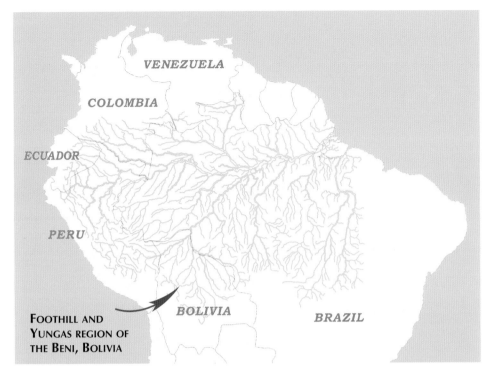

FOOTHILL AND YUNGAS REGION OF THE BENI, BOLIVIA

▲ FOOTHILL DEFORESTATION IN THE UPPER BENI BASIN

Foothills often have relatively rich volcanic soils that are attractive to Andean farmers. Montane forests are cleared to plant maize, potatoes, and other crops.

▲ CHAPARE OF UPPER MAMORÉ VALLEY

Until the mid-1990s the Chapare region of Bolivia was famous as the world's center for coca paste, from which cocaine was produced, either locally or in Colombia. The foothill region of the upper Mamoré Basin in Bolivia has been heavily impacted by coca growers and other agricultural colonists from the high Andes. At this foothill site on the Chapare, coca farmers have only deforested small patches of forest.

◀ MONTANE FOREST OF THE BOLIVIAN YUNGAS

Under natural conditions montane forests of the Yungas are dense and rich in plant and animal species. The Yungas, however, have been extensively deforested and agricultural colonization is expanding rapidly.

**CLOUDFOREST REGION
MADRE DE DIOS, PERU**

▲ CLOUD FOREST WATERFALLS AND POOLS
Millions of rivulets flow hidden beneath the
cloud forest. Some merge to form beautiful
waterfalls and pools. Although fish and
other aquatic diversity is low in montane
waters compared to lowland rainforest
streams, many unique species can be found.

▶ MONTANE FOREST AND CLOUD FOREST
Andean slopes between approximately
4,900 and 9,850 ft (1,500–3,000 m) that are
exposed to constant moisture-laden winds
have either dense montane forests or cloud
forests. Conditions radically change where
slopes are not exposed to high humidity, as
can be seen on the dry hill in midframe in
the background.

▲ FOREST IN THE CLOUDS
The moisture-saturated environment of the
cloud forest can almost be classified as a
wetland. Most of the aquatic habitats are
hidden beneath the dense vegetation.

BENI HEADWATERS,
BOLIVIA

▲ HEADWATER ARIDITY

Headwater areas above 9,850 ft (3,000 m) are generally dry, and the amount of annual precipitation is less than 20 in. (500 mm). There can be torrential storms between January and April that fill the river channels and their floodplains.

◀ DESCENT INTO THE AMAZON FROM HUALLA HUALLA

At 13,100 ft (4,000 m) average temperatures are always below 20°C, and only small streams are found. This small headwater stream drains the slopes of the Hualla Hualla Peak of the eastern Cordillera Vilcanota in Peru.

▲ THE PUNA

The puna, a type of tussock grassland, exists at elevations above 11,500 ft (3,500 m). The puna grassland shown here is in the headwaters area in Manu National Park.

MADRE DE DIOS
HEADWATERS, PERU

VENEZUELA

COLOMBIA

ECUADOR

PERU

BOLIVIA   BRAZIL

▲ ICY STREAMS NEAR THE SNOW LINE

Stream temperatures near approximately 13,100 ft (4,000 m) are only 12°C compared with an average of approximately 28°C at elevations below approximately 325 ft (100 m) in the central Amazon.

▲ THE SNOWS OF HUALLA HUALLA

The amount of snowfall in the Andes is not enough to have any significant impact on river levels in the lowlands. Arid conditions dominate until the snowline at approximately 2,700 ft (4,300 m).

Beni headwaters, Bolivia

▲ HIGHLY MODIFIED STREAMS OF THE UPPER ANDES

Trout are not native to the Andes, but widespread introductions now make them the most dominant fish species in many high-elevation streams. Andean streams are commonly dammed for trout farming, as shown here in headwaters of the Beni east of La Paz. Trout require cold water, and can live in Andean streams above approximately 8,200 ft (2,500 m).

▲ ARID HEADWATERS OF BENI

Beni headwaters arise in the high Andes near La Paz. Crop farming and grazing in nearly all the river valleys in the high and arid Andes, which has been going on since before the European Conquest, have extensively transformed the valleys. In this headwater valley at 11,500 ft (3,500 m) east of La Paz, humans have transformed the entire landscape, from the highest peaks to the stream bottom.

▶ HEADWATER DEFORESTATION

Upper Amazon watersheds above approximately 9,850 ft (3,000 m) in Bolivia have been heavily modified for thousands of years. Because rainfall is generally less than 25 in. (600 mm) in the high Andes, increased erosion at high elevations has probably had relatively little if any significant impact on sediment loads delivered to the lowlands. The local impacts on streams have not been studied in any detail.

CHAPTER TEN

THE PURUS AND JURUÁ VALLEYS

Lands of Meandering Rivers

The Purus and Juruá Valleys are ecologically similar and together occupy nearly 231,000 square miles (600,000 km²). The Purus Valley is larger and wider and covers approximately 144,800 square miles (375,000 km²), whereas the Juruá Valley (83,800 square miles [217,000 km²]) is relatively narrow in its middle and lower reaches.

The Purus and Juruá Rivers—both tributaries of the Amazon—have an extensive number of meanders and huge floodplains studded with thousands of lakes. Although their valleys lie within Brazil and Peru, more than 90 percent of each river is within the Brazilian states of Amazonas and Acre. The headwaters of the Purus arise in the Peruvian departments of Ucayali and Madre de Dios. Those of the Juruá are in the department of Ucayali in Peru.

The exact lengths of the Purus and Juruá Rivers are subject to debate because of the difficulty in measuring rivers that have huge numbers of meanders. Measurements depend on where they are taken within the channels. Reasonable estimates indicate that each river is about 2,000 miles (3,200 km) long, making them the second and third longest tributaries of the Amazon, after the Madeira. Measured against

river discharge, the Purus and Juruá have more floodplain than any of the other large tributaries of the Amazon River. Within the Purus Basin there are approximately 15,400 square miles (40,000 km²) of floodplain, and approximately 10,800 square miles (28,000 km²) of floodplain exist alongside the Juruá River.

The Purus and Juruá Valleys are entirely within the rainforest zone. Their large tributaries arise at elevations generally below 1,300 ft (400 m) in a hilly area east of the Ucayali Valley. Andean sediments were perhaps deposited in the Purus and Juruá Valleys when headwaters still tapped the high mountains millions of years ago. The Ucayali Valley now lies between the headwaters of both rivers and the Andes.

The headwaters of the Juruá River are located higher in elevation than those of the Purus. They are in the "Serra do Divisor," as it is called in Brazil, or the "Sierra Contamana," as it is called in Peru. The highest peak in the region is approximately 2,880 ft (878 m) tall.

Water from the Purus River accounts for approximately 5 percent of the Amazon River's total annual discharge, and the Juruá River contributes another

◀ **LAND OF MEANDERS**
The highly meandering Purus has huge floodplains studded with magnificent oxbow lakes.

▷ THE PURUS VALLEY

Headwaters of the Purus River arise in Peru at elevations less than 1,650 ft (500 m). The Purus Valley is mostly within the Brazilian states of Amazonas and Acre but its head-waters are largely in the Peruvian depart-ments of Ucayali and Madre de Dios. The Purus is approximately 2,000 miles (3,200 km) long and its basin occupies approximately 144,800 square miles (375,000 km²). Most deforestation has been in Acre near the capital city of Rio Branco and along the main highway that traverses the state.

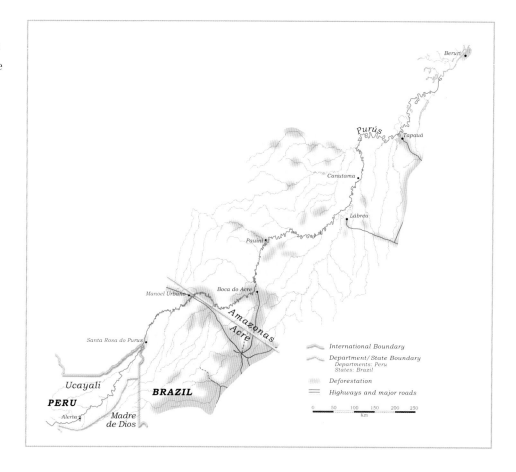

THE PURUS VALLEY

2 percent. Both rivers are generally considered to be muddy-water rivers with high nutrient levels compared with those of the large clearwater and blackwater tributaries of the Amazon River. The amount of sediment dis-charged by the Purus and the Juruá, however, is minimal compared to that of the Madeira River or Ucayali River. This is because, unlike the Madeira and the Ucayali, the Purus and the Juruá do not have headwaters in the Andes. The tributaries of the Purus and the Juruá that arise in the central lowlands are either clearwater or blackwater rivers; many are transitional between these two general types at different times of the year.

The amount of annual precipita-tion in the Purus and Juruá Valleys typ-ically ranges from approximately 70 to 85 in. (1,800–2,200 mm). Annual river-level fluctuations in the middle sec-tions of both tributaries range from 39 to 49 ft (12–15 m). This range is among the highest known in the Ama-zon Basin. The difference between the highest and lowest water levels ever recorded in the middle courses of the two rivers ranges from 53 to 80.4 ft (16–24.5 m). The Purus and Juruá are usually in flood from December through mid-May. In their lower courses, floods last until August because of the backwater effect of the Solimões (Amazon River).

The Purus and Juruá Rivers are constantly shifting courses across their broad floodplains, resulting in thou-sands of meanders and oxbow lakes. The combination of numerous flood-plain lakes, extensive flooded forests, and huge floating-meadow communi-ties within the two rivers makes them

▲ CONSERVATION UNITS AND INDIGENOUS AREAS OF THE PURUS VALLEY

The Purus Valley has few functional conservation units and little scientific research has been carried out in the protected areas. Peru has given Purus headwaters areas temporary protection status, and the human population is still sparse in that region. The Purus is the most important tributary fished to supply the large Manaus market.

UPPER PURUS

⚠ **UPPER PURUS**

The Purus is a muddy river with a large floodplain. During the low-water period, as shown here, the Purus is confined to its relatively narrow channel.

among the most productive of the Amazon River's tributaries. The Purus is the most important tributary fished to supply Manaus, the Amazon's largest fish market.

From the perspective of river-basin management, the political boundaries of the fast-growing state of Acre present daunting challenges. The Porto Velho-Rio Branco and Rio Branco-Cruzeiro do Sul highways cut across all of the large headwater tributaries of the Purus and Juruá. The economy in Acre is largely centered on cattle ranching, and the rate of deforestation in Acre is among the highest in the Amazon Basin.

Much of the highway between Rio Branco and Cruzeiro do Sul is in poor condition. During the rainy season, most of the highway is impassable. Peru and Brazil have plans to build a road between the cities of Pucallpa (located on the Ucayali River) and Cruzeiro do Sul (located in Brazil along on the Juruá River). If this transportation artery is completed, colonization, deforestation, and cattle ranching can be expected to increase in Acre. The areas that have been the most extensively deforested are near Rio Branco along the Acre River, near Sena Madureira along the Iaco River, and near Cruzeiro do Sul along the Juruá River. The only major road outside of Acre in the Purus Valley is the Rio Branco-Boca do Acre highway. Boca do Acre is in the state of Amazonas at the confluence of the Purus and Acre Rivers.

The most extensive impacts of floodplain logging and commercial fishing on the Purus and Juruá Rivers have been downriver of the Acre-

▲ **ACRE RIVER OF UPPER PURUS REGION**

Purus headwaters, such as the Acre River that passes through the city of Rio Branco (Acre's capital), arise at low elevations in the Alluvial Extension Zone of soft sediments. Headwaters of the Purus are muddy throughout the year.

Amazonas border. Urban centers are few and small and getting to these remote areas requires a long boat trip. As a result, relatively little biological and conservation research has been carried out in the middle and lower Purus and Juruá Valleys. Likewise, little scientific research has been done in the headwaters regions of the rivers, although they lie within federally protected areas. The headwaters of the Purus arise in Peru in the Alto Purus protected area. Those of the Juruá arise in Brazil in Serra do Divisor National Park.

Environmental groups and the media brought Acre into the international spotlight in the 1980s because of the murder of Chico Mendes—a rubber collector who organized his fellow workers to confront large-scale cattle ranchers. Acre has continued to attract attention because its government is favorably disposed toward politicians, academics, and journalists interested in conservation issues. The plans of environmental groups in Acre, however, are highly localized and do not take into account the state's critical role in managing the upper watersheds of the Purus and Juruá Valleys. One major exception to this lack of strategic planning is the establishment of the Serra do Divisor National Park, occupying approximately 32,800 square miles (85,000 km²) in the upper Juruá watershed in Brazil.

At present Serra do Divisor

National Park is relatively isolated. Dirt roads, however, from the main Acre highway and from Cruzeiro do Sul are expanding westward and southward toward the park's boundary. This expansion will open up areas close to the park to logging and cattle ranching. Conservation groups have proposed expanding the size of Serra do Divisor by protecting the Sierra Contamana (the Peruvian side of the Serra do Divisor). The waters of this area drain into the Ucayali River. The proposed Pucallpa-Cruzeiro do Sul highway would cut through the park and might increase problems related to protecting the park's ecosystems.

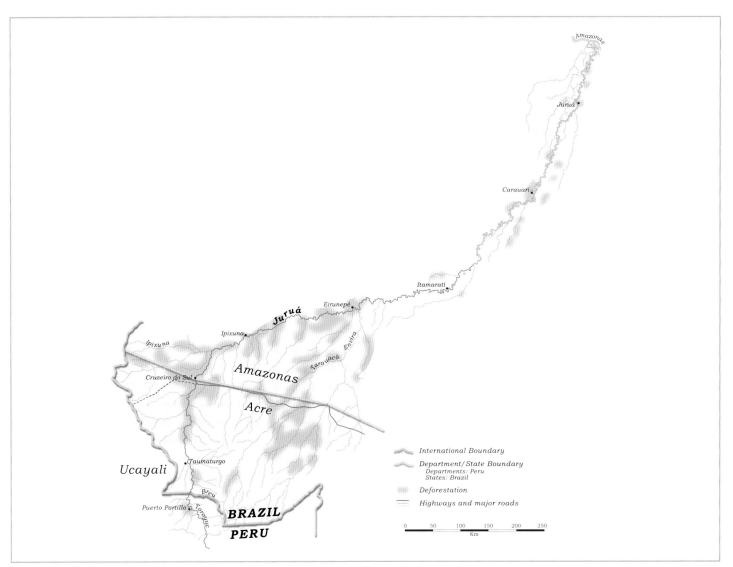

▲ THE JURUÁ VALLEY

Juruá headwaters are born in the Serra do Divisor, low hills generally less than 1,650 ft (500 m) whose summits delineate the Brazilian-Peruvian boundary. The Juruá Valley lies in the Brazilian states of Amazonas and Acre; a small headwater region is in the Peruvian department of Ucayali. Three-fourths of the Juruá Valley is less than 60 miles (100 km) in width. Most tributaries are found in the headwater region. The Juruá is approximately 2,000 miles (3,200 km) long and its basin occupies approximately 83,800 square miles (217,000 km²). Cruzeiro do Sul is the largest city it the Juruá Basin. Cattle ranching and logging are expanding rapidly in the region around the city.

THE JURUÁ VALLEY

▲ **CONSERVATION UNITS AND INDIGENOUS AREAS OF THE JURUÁ VALLEY**

As within the Purus Valley, there are few designated protected areas within the Juruá Valley. The most important is Serra do Divisor National Park, which includes about three-fourths of the Juruá's upper headwaters. The planned highway from Cruzeiro do Sul in Brazil to Pucallpa on the Ucayali in Peru would cut through the park.

UPPER JURUÁ SEDIMENTS

Streams in the Serra do Divisor have supplied sediments to most of the Juruá Valley.
The clays and sands shown here on an
exposed riverbank near Cruzeiro do Sul are
part of the Alluvial Extension Zone of sediments that were deposited in the Juruá and
Purus Valleys from non-Andean sources.

UPPER JURUÁ AND FLOODPLAIN IN
ITS NATURAL STATE

The Juruá has relatively large floodplains
from its mouth to just below Cruzeiro do
Sul in the Brazilian state of Acre. Floodplains are mostly covered with forest that is
inundated for five to six months annually.

UPPER JURUÁ DURING THE
LOW-WATER PERIOD

The upper Juruá becomes very narrow and
shallow during the low-water period and is
choked with sediments.

▲ HEADWATER DEFORESTATION IN THE JURUÁ VALLEY

The rolling hills characteristic of the upper Juruá Valley are being deforested as the cattle ranching frontier expands across Acre. There has been little effort to convince ranchers to leave riparian forest.

◀ UPPER JURUÁ DURING THE LOW-WATER PERIOD

During the low-water months the upper Juruá is often less than 3 ft (1 m) deep. Boats in this region have flat keels and are powered by maneuverable engines with long drive shafts so that propellers can be raised.

◀ CRUZEIRO DO SUL

Cruzeiro do Sul on the upper Juruá in Acre is one of the most isolated yet fastest growing cities in the Amazon Basin. Cattle ranching and logging support the economy of this outpost city. There is plane service between Cruzeiro do Sul and Rio Branco and Manaus.

CHAPTER ELEVEN

THE UCAYALI AND MARAÑÓN VALLEYS
In the Shadow of the Andes

The Ucayali River is generally considered to be the main headwater tributary of the Amazon River. Its length is usually included as part of the total length the Amazon River. The Ucayali is approximately 1,675 miles (2,700 km) long. It is the fifth longest tributary of the Amazon River. The River's headwaters arise at nearly the same latitude as northern Lake Titicaca. They are approximately 3,950–4,200 miles (6,400–6,800 km) from the mouth of the Amazon River. Occupying approximately 130,300 square miles (337,500 km²), the Ucayali Basin is relatively smaller in area than basins of other long tributaries of the Amazon River. All of the Ucayali is in Peru and its drainage basin is divided among 11 departments. More than 90 percent of the basin's area is in the large departments of Loreto, Ucayali, and Cuzco.

The Ucayali generally flows southward between the high Andes to the west and the low hills to the east. The hilly region east of the river is too low to interrupt the western flow of moisture-laden Amazon air. The amount of annual precipitation ranges from 80 to 120 in. (2,000–3,000 mm) at elevations less than approximately 1,650 ft (500 m).

Rainforest occupies most of the Ucayali Valley up to approximately 3,300 ft (1,000 m), where montane forest starts to grow. Montane forest and cloud forest are common on the eastern slopes of the Valley to as far south as the confluence of the Urubamba and Vilcanota Rivers, approximately 185 miles (300 km) south of Cuzco.

The Ucayali meanders over a broad valley bottom that generally lies below 1,000 ft (300 m). The river's two main headwater tributaries are the Urubamba and the Tambo-Ene-Apurimac, whose headwaters arise above 16,400 ft (5,000 m). Three spectacular mountain ranges—the Cordillera Azul, the Cordillera Vilcabamba, and the Cordillera Vilcanota—lie within the Ucayali Valley. The Cordillera Azul is in the lower Valley, west of Pucallpa. The Cordillera Vilcabamba and the Cordillera Vilcanota lie within the headwaters region of the Ucayali near Cuzco.

Climatic conditions in the Ucayali Valley vary from arid highlands to wet lowlands. An average of approximately 20 in. (550 mm) of rain falls annually in the Vilcanota Valley near Cuzco, which is at 9,850 ft (3,000 m). In the lowlands, the average

◀ **THE VILCANOTA FLOODPLAIN AT URUBAMBA**
Urubamba is located along the Vilcanota in the Sacred Valley of the Incas approximately 12.5 miles (20 km) north of Cuzco. To control flooding of the relatively broad floodplain, the Incas built canals running from the Vilcanota River. Floodplains in the Sacred Valley have been farmed for at least 2,000 years.

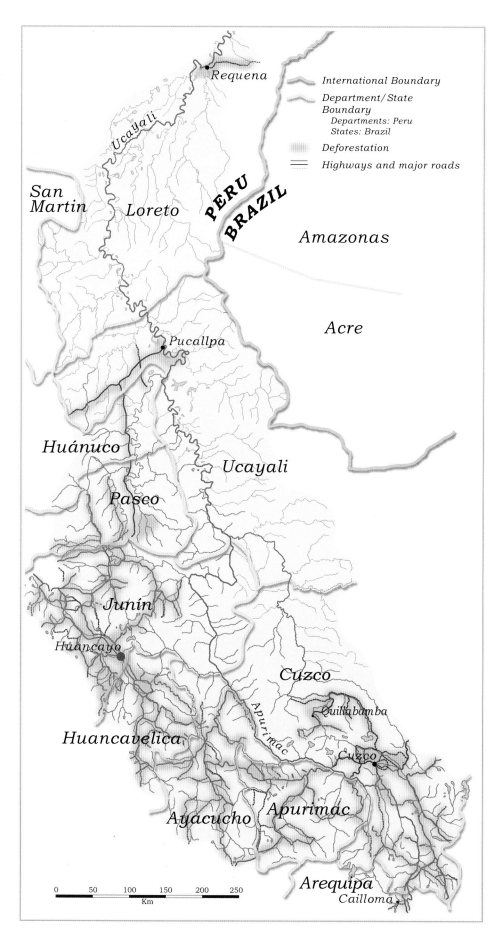

San
Martin

Loreto

Ucayali

Requena

PERU

BRAZIL

Amazonas

Acre

Pucallpa

Ucayali

Huánuco

Pasco

Junin

Huancayo

Cuzco

Quillabamba

Apurímac

Cuzco

Huancavelica

Ayacucho

Apurimac

Arequipa

Cailloma

International Boundary

Department/State
Boundary
   Departments: Peru
   States: Brazil

Deforestation

Highways and major roads

| 0 | 50 | 100 | 150 | 200 | 250 |

Km

◀ THE UCAYALI VALLEY

The Ucayali River is considered the main headwater tributary of the Amazon River, and its entire basin is in Peru. The 1,700-mile-long (2,750 km) Ucayali is the fifth longest tributary of the Amazon River. Occupying approximately 130,500 square miles (338,000 km²) the Ucayali has the eighth largest tributary basin in the Amazon and lies within 11 Peruvian departments. Its geography ranges from wet rainforest-covered lowlands to high snow-clad mountain peaks. The center of the Inca Empire was located along Ucayali headwaters in what is now the Peruvian department of Cuzco.

THE UCAYALI VALLEY

annual amount of rainfall is approximately 85 in. (2,200 mm) at Pucallpa, which is at 1,000 ft (300 m). Some montane areas exposed to moisture-laden eastern or southern winds can receive more than 200 in. (5,000 mm) of precipitation annually.

There are few data available for average annual river-level fluctuation in the Ucayali Basin, but it appears to be approximately 26 ft (8 m) in the lowlands. The Ucayali River is in flood from December to May. The highest water levels near Pucallpa usually occur in March. Upland tributaries rise and fall rapidly, and annual river-level fluctuations vary greatly due to narrow valleys.

The Ucayali has a broad floodplain dotted with thousands of small bodies of water. The river and its floodplain form a highly unstable network of levees, side channels, sandbars, mud bars, back swamps, lakes, and islands. The oxbow lakes are usually less than 0.3 mile (0.5 km) wide, but some are more than 12 miles (20 km) long. Large beaches appear during the low-water period and often become wider than the main river channel.

Although the Ucayali River is unstable, its floodplains in general last long enough for forest to become the dominant vegetation in areas not subject to deep permanent flooding. In areas of relatively permanent but shallow flooding, palm swamps dominated by aguaje (*Mauritia flexuosa*) are common. Extensive mats of floating herbaceous vegetation are found in floodplain water bodies reached by nutrient-rich Ucayali floodwaters.

Crops have been grown extensively on the floodplains of the Ucayali

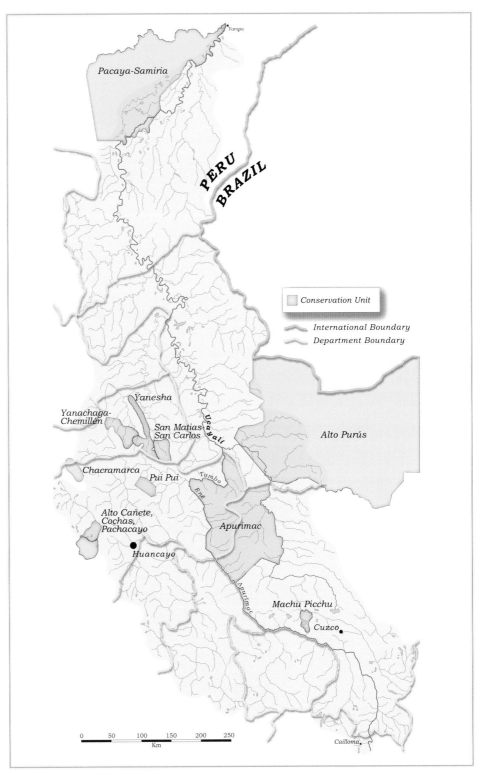

▲ **CONSERVATION UNITS AND INDIGENOUS AREAS OF THE UCAYALI VALLEY**
The Ucayali has few large protected areas. Reserved zones—areas whose definitive use has yet to be determined—account for most of the potentially protected areas. A part of the large Pacaya-Samiria National Reserve is in the Ucayali Valley, although most of this important protected floodplain area drains into the Marañón.

▲ **UCAYALI**

The Ucayali near Pucallpa, nearly 3,100 miles (5,000 km) from the mouth of the Amazon River, is still very large. The width of its channel can reach from 1.2 to 1.9 miles (2–3 km) during the floods. The flood-plain often is nearly 12.5 miles (20 km) in width.

River since pre-Columbian times. Manioc, maize, bananas, watermelon, beans, peanuts, sugarcane, and various fruit trees such as citrus are currently planted. Near Pucallpa rice farming is expanding on the Ucayali floodplains. Most of the Ucayali floodplains, however, are still forested, although there has been considerable disturbance from human activities.

Upstream of the confluence of the Urubamba and the Tambo-Ene-Apurimac Rivers, at 4,900 ft (1,500 m), the climate becomes drier because the Cordillera Vilcabamba and the Cordillera Vilcanota divert moisture-laden air coming from the south and east. During the nonrainy months, headwaters of the Ucayali above approximately 2,650 ft (800 m) have relatively clear water that is greenish in color. The Pongo de Mainique, a gorge recently strewn with huge boulders from a landslide, is a major obstacle to boat travel on the Urubamba.

Humans have significantly altered the highland areas above approximately 6,550 ft (2,000 m) in the Urubamba, Vilcanota, and Apurimac Valleys. Ecosystem modification in these areas started at least 2,500–4,000 years ago, when people began to graze llamas, alpacas, and vicunas—species belonging to the camel family—on the slopes. The animals graze on even the steeper slopes. Llamas roam and forage from 7,550 to 13,100 ft (2,300–4,000 m), alpacas from 13,100 to 15,750 ft (4,000–4,800 m), and vicunas from 12,150 to 15,750 ft (3,700–4,800 m). Farmers also graze sheep, goats, and cattle at higher elevations. Livestock paths, which look almost like terraces, are ubiquitous in the high Andes.

A distinctive feature of high Andean landscapes is terracing. Among other things, terracing was used to control erosion, facilitate irrigation, increase soil moisture, and increase sunlight exposure for crops. The Incas

relied extensively on terracing, and the practice remains widespread today.

The ecological impacts of llama, alpaca, vicuna, and livestock grazing and of terracing on the upper watershed of the Ucayali are difficult to assess. Most of the sediment load in the Ucayali River comes from elevations below 1,650 ft (500 m). Although grazing likely increases erosion and sediment runoff in the upper Andes, it is responsible for little if any of the sediment load in the main stem of the Ucayali. Terracing does decrease erosion and sediment runoff; however, terraces cover only a relatively small area of the total landscape.

The most famous headwater region of the Ucayali is the Sacred Valley of the Incas, centering on the Vilcanota River near Cuzco. Most of the Vilcanota Valley lies at approximately 9,850 ft (3,000 m). The Inca ruins of Ollantaytambo overlook the Vilcanota River. The better-known ruins of Machu

The Ucayali River meanders extensively and is noted for its broad floodplain, many side channels, and numerous sandbars during the low-water period. Floodable forest covers most of the floodplain.

▲ THE LOW-WATER PERIOD OF THE UCAYALI IN PERU
The thick alluvial sediments of the lower Ucayali floodplain can be seen at this village waterfront during the low-water period. River level rises sufficiently in most years to inundate level ground where the houses stand. The Ucayali discharges more sediment into the Amazon River than any other tributary except the Madeira.

Picchu are located a few kilometers away from the main stream.

The Incas farmed the Sacred Valley intensively and grazed animals on the floodplains and slopes of the Vilcanota Valley. They also built canals that diverted water from the Vilcanota River and its tributaries. Archaeologists have found at least 14 miles (23 km) of canals within a 125-mile-long (23 km) stretch of the Valley. The canals were built to increase the amount of available land on floodplains and to control flooding and erosion.

Human activities, more than anything else in the past 1,000 years, have shaped the landscape of the Ucayali Valley's upper watershed. The upper watershed lies within the Peruvian departments of Cuzco and Apurimac. The great Inca ruins are the most visited sites in South America. Little attention is given to conservation of natural landscapes in the Vilcanota and Apurimac valleys because of the overwhelming historical shadow of the Incas and the great works they constructed.

Deforestation of hillsides without terracing is recognized as a problem and there are many government reforestation projects. Pine or eucalyptus are typically planted and are also cut for timber and firewood. Local pollution of streams near urban centers has also been acknowledged as a serious problem. The Huatanay River, along which the city of Cuzco is located, discharges a large quantity of pollutants into the Vilcanota. The Huatanay empties into the Vilcanota at the beginning of the Sacred Valley.

There are few roads into the Ucayali Valley. Most of the vehicle transportation network is around Cuzco. The Cuzco-Quillabamba railway, which trains began to use in the 1950s, has been replaced by a dirt road that crosses over the high cordillera. The road now extends into the Urubamba Valley and is within 12.5 miles (20 km)

URUBAMBA AND
LOWER VILCANOTA

▲ URUBAMBA WATERS

At approximately 3,300 ft (1,000 m), the Urubamba is a relatively clearwater river during its six to seven month low-water period. The Urubamba has little floodplain, but riparian forest dominates the banks.

▲ CRYSTALLINE STREAMS OF THE CORDILLERA VILCABAMBA

Headwater streams of the Urubamba are crystalline and cool. Livestock have grazed most of the Cordillera Vilcabamba, but there are patches of low forest along the streams.

of the Pongo de Mainique Gorge. Settlers from the high Andes have used the road to extensively colonize the upper Urubamba Valley and the lower Vilcanota Valley. These valleys have become important tea-producing regions; citrus, coca, coffee, and bananas are also grown. Within the next few decades, a large part of these areas between approximately 2,650 and 4,900 ft (800–1,500 m) will likely be extensively deforested.

The Lima-Pucallpa highway— Peru's main artery into the Amazon—is the primary road to the middle Ucayali Valley. Although the highway has existed since the 1940s, Pucallpa did not start to grow rapidly until the mid-1980s. Both upland and floodplain deforestation is extensive near Pucallpa. Uplands have been deforested mostly for cattle ranching, whereas floodplain forests have been cleared to grow a wide variety of locally sold crops. The recent expansion of rice farms has also increased flood-

plain deforestation. Upland and floodplain forests are also being extensively logged for commercial timber.

There are few functionally protected areas in the Ucayali Basin. With the exception of Pacaya-Samiria National Reserve at the mouth of the Ucayali, most protected areas are relatively small and confined largely to the cordilleras. The Pacaya-Samiria National Reserve, most of which is in the Marañón drainage, is discussed later.

Efforts are underway to establish an important park in the Cordillera Azul— a mountainous area with sheer rock escarpments, lowland valleys, highaltitude lakes, and marshlands. The Cordillera Azul lies west of Pucallpa. There are two large, sparsely populated reserved zones in the Ucayali Basin, the Alto Purus and the Apurimac. The Alto Purus Reserved Zone abuts Serra do Divisor National Park in Acre, Brazil; the Apurimac Reserved Zone is in the region of the middle section of the

Apurimac River. Peruvian reserved zones legally belong to the government or to indigenous groups. For each reserved zone, a definitive list of sanctioned uses will eventually be established.

The Marañón is the westernmost large tributary of the Amazon River. The Amazon River (or "Amazonas," as it is called in Peru) is usually considered to begin after the confluence of the Marañón and Ucayali Rivers. Flowing for approximately 850 miles (1,400 km), the Marañón is the 11th longest tributary of the Amazon River. Its basin covers 138,200 square miles (358,000 km²) and is the seventh largest in the Amazon. The headwaters of the Marañón are approximately 90 miles (150 km) north of Lima and approximately 60 miles (100 km) from the Pacific.

Approximately 80 percent of the Marañón Valley is in Peru; the other 20 percent is in Ecuador. There are nine Peruvian departments and nine Ecuadorian provinces in the Marañón Basin (Ecuadorian provinces are the equivalent of Peruvian and Bolivian departments and Brazilian states). Most of the Basin's northern drainage, which is larger in area than all of the Marañón Basin within Ecuador, lies within the large Peruvian department of Loreto.

Most of the Marañón River flows through a narrow and high intermountain valley. Only the lower 350 miles (600 km) are in the Amazon lowlands below 1,000 ft (300 m). Before emerging from the Andes, the Marañón is marked by a series of rapids. The most spectacular rapids are those in the Pongo de Manseriche Gorge, which lies at 1,885 ft (575 m). River craft of any

▲ **VALLEY BOTTOM MONTANE FOREST**
Humid air penetrates far up the Urubamba Valley, and luscious forest can be found on valley bottoms as high as 10,500 ft (3,200 m). Cold steams issuing from snowfields flow through some of these thick forests.

▲ **HEADWATERS OF THE URUBAMBA**
At approximately 9,850 ft (3,000 m) in the Cordillera Vilcabamba, scrub vegetation dominates and streams nearly disappear during the dry season.

▲ **FARMING THE LOWER VILCANOTA**
Highland colonists have settled the slopes of the Vilcanota Valley during the past two decades. Deforestation has been extensive. Tea and maize are common crops at approximately 6,550 ft (2,000 m).

AREA NEAR CONFLUENCE OF URUBAMBA AND VILCANOTA

significant size are not able to navigate most of the Marañón.

The longest tributary of the Marañón River is the Huallaga. It is at least 625 miles (1,000 km) long and flows between the Cordillera Central and Cordillera Azul in Peru. Only the lower part of the river is navigable. The other large tributaries of the Marañón—the Pastaza, the Tigre, the Morona, and the Santiago—start in Ecuador. They are all less than 425 miles (700 km) long. The Pastaza, the largest, has headwaters near the Cotopaxi Volcano.

The lower Marañón River is muddy, whereas in most of the inter-Andean region, the river is clear. All of the Marañón's large tributaries are muddy from the Andean foothills downriver; within the Andes they are clear except during heavy rainstorms. The northern drainage of the Marañón has numerous small blackwater tributaries between the Santiago and Tigre

Rivers. The lower sections of the Marañón tributaries meander extensively and have large floodplains. Few measurements have been made to assess accurately annual river-level fluctuation in most of the Marañón Basin. River-level fluctuation of the lower Marañón is similar to that of the Amazonas near Iquitos—approximately 27.9 ft (8.5 m).

Most of the Marañón Basin in Peru is relatively isolated. The main road through the headwater region of the River is the Lima-Pucallpa highway. It crosses the Huallaga River at Tingo Maria. Another road follows the Huallaga as far as Yurimaguas, which is 125 miles (200 km) upriver from its confluence with the Marañón. A variety of treacherous roads from coastal cities such as Chimbote, Trujillo, Chiclayo, and Piura cross over the Andes and go into the Marañón Basin. Oil-exploration roads cross the northern tributaries of the

Marañón in both Peru and Ecuador.

Huánuco on the upper Huallaga River is the largest city in the Marañón Basin. There are no large-scale agricultural-colonization projects in the Marañón Basin; however, indigenous groups have farmed and grazed most of the highland area. The most heavily colonized areas in the lowlands are near Yurimaguas on the Huallaga and along the Marañón, upriver of Nauta. Numerous copper, zinc, silver, iron, mercury, antimony, and gold mines exist near Andean tributaries of the Marañón and of the Huallaga. The impacts of mining on the aquatic ecology of these headwaters and rivers have not been investigated in any detail. Most environmental attention in the Marañón Basin has focused on the effects of oil exploration, especially in Peru, where large deposits have been found.

There are oil wells both north and south of the Marañón River. Pipelines

⛰ ENTERING THE SACRED VALLEY OF THE INCAS

In the high Andes floodplains are generally narrow, but their relatively rich soils are intensively farmed. Pine and eucalyptus have been planted along the Vilcanota and floodplain edge in modern times.

transport crude oil from the rainforest regions across the Andes to refineries in the Peruvian coastal department of Piura. One of these, the North Peruvian pipeline from the Pacaya-Samiria National Reserve, follows the Marañón and is met by the main northern conduit just downriver of the Pongo de Manseriche. Here, the pipeline crosses the Marañón River and continues to follow it for a short distance, after which it crosses the Andes. The North Peruvian pipeline has a capacity of 200,000 barrels per day. Currently, however, less than one-half that amount is being pumped through it.

The settlement of the Ecuador-Peru border dispute in 1998 opened the possibility for Ecuador to transport crude oil to Peru from its border region with the northern tributaries area of the Marañón. The North Peruvian pipeline passes through regions in the Andes that are subject to earthquakes and mudslides. In 1999 the pipeline rup-

tured but was quickly repaired. In 2000 a barge transporting crude from the Pacaya-Samiria National Reserve went aground and released approximately 5,500 barrels of oil into the Marañón River, although the spill was apparently contained and no large-scale downstream impacts were reported.

Only two large areas have been designated for protection in the Marañón Valley. The Pacaya-Samiria National Reserve is the largest protected area in Peru and is also the largest protected floodplain in the Amazon Basin. It is located between the juncture of the Marañón and Ucayali Rivers. The reserve is named after two smaller rivers whose headwaters are within it. Most of the reserve is within the Marañón Basin. It encompasses approximately 8,300 square miles (21,500 km²), nearly all of which is floodplain. Within Pacaya-Samiria, there are at least 85 lakes. Palm swamps (especially *Mauritia flexuosa*) and

⛰ URUBAMBA

Montane forest is found far up the Urubamba, one the Ucayali's main southern tributaries. Colonists have begun deforesting hills and the valley bottoms in the march of agriculture down the Urubamba Valley. This site is at approximately 3,300 ft (1,000 m) and tea, coca, and citrus have been planted.

▲ FLOODPLAIN MEADOWS OF THE VILCANOTA

Cattle, sheep, and goats graze floodplain meadows of the Vilcanota, whereas llamas, alpacas, and vicunas range mostly at higher elevations.

▲ THE UPPER VILCANOTA

The entire landscape of the upper Vilcanota has been transformed by humans. Even the steepest hills are used for agriculture and grazing. Pine and eucalyptus have been planted for timber and firewood.

◀ HUATANAY

Cuzco, the largest city in the upper Ucayali watershed, is located on the Huatanay River, which in turn discharges into the Vilcanota near the entrance to the Sacred Valley of the Incas. The Huatanay is extremely polluted and discharges contaminants into the Vilcanota.

floodable mixed forest cover most of the reserve. The reserve has been selectively logged, but there has been relatively little large-scale deforestation.

Pacaya-Samiria was established mainly to protect and manage aquatic wildlife. Its lakes are fished to supply the large Nauta and Iquitos markets; however, inadequate refrigeration facilities limit the amount of fish caught. Somewhere between 75,000 and 100,000 people live in villages and towns around the reserve. Most of them, however, live in three large towns: Nauta along the Marañón River, Lagunas on the Huallaga River near its confluence with the Marañón, and Requena on the Ucayali River. The population inside the reserve is sparse—most communities have less than 100 people—and includes a minority of indigenous groups. Most residents of Pacaya-Samiria practice subsistence agriculture, fishing, and hunting, and collect palm fruits for consumption and sale to urban centers.

The Peruvian government and conservation groups have developed a two-pronged strategy to manage the reserve. The first part of this strategy uses trained guards at established posts to control entry to the reserve, and will be supplemented by a zoning system now being developed. The second part is an ongoing effort to develop sustainable economic activities around communities, such as controlled catches of aquarium fish and artificial incubation of turtles. Other economic activities include improving planting and cultivation practices. These activities alone, however, do not appear to be raising local incomes and other efforts, such as promoting ecotourism, are being explored.

UPPER VILCANOTA

▲ REFORESTATION

Most of the natural vegetation in the Vilcanota Valley was probably cut before the arrival of Europeans. Recent reforestation is done using either eucalyptus or pine. The trees are usually planted in areas that have ground moisture, such as near streams or in the outwash fans of hillsides. At this site only eucalyptus has been planted.

▶ CANAL BUILDING IN THE SPIRIT OF THE INCAS

Under natural conditions, rivers and streams of the high Andes are very poor in fish production. None of the native fish species living above approximately 6,550 ft (2,000 m) are considered commercially valuable. The introduction of trout from Europe and North America provided the high Andes with first-class food fish. Trout farming is widespread, and many headwater streams have been modified for aquaculture.

▶ AUSTRALIA IN THE ANDES

Eucalyptus is highly adapted to the arid conditions of the upper Andes. One concern, however, is that eucalyptus desiccates landscapes even further because it transpires relatively large quantities of water. None of the native species, however, appear to be able to grow as fast and tall as eucalyptus.

VENEZUELA

COLOMBIA

ECUADOR

PERU

VILCANOTA

BOLIVIA

BRAZIL

◀ CORDILLERA VILCABAMBA

The snowline of Ucayali headwaters in Peru begins at approximately 13,100–14,750 ft (4,000–4,500 m). Even during the stormiest months snow covers a relatively small percentage of the Andes. Andean snowmelt has no significant influence on river levels in the lowlands of the Amazon. The glacial stream shown here arises in the Cordillera Vilcanota near the Veronica peaks.

◀ ALPINE STREAMS

The temperature of this Ucayali headwater stream at 12,450 ft (3,800 m) in the Cordillera de Carabaya near the Hualla Hualla peak was 8°C in May. The trees are eucalyptus, which have been planted for timber and firewood.

◀ ALPINE LAKES

The Andes are studded with alpine lakes, many of which are filled by snowmelt. All alpine lakes in the Ucayali watershed are relatively small.

The Pacaya-Samiria National Reserve does have a valuable economic resource—petroleum. Current agreements restrict drilling to a small part of the reserve. A small pipeline carries crude oil from wells to barges on the Marañón River. Barges then carry the oil across the river to the beginning of the North Peruvian pipeline. Oil revenues are not used directly to foster development of the Pacaya-Samiria National Reserve. However, the Institute of Peruvian Amazonian Investigations carries out some research in the reserve that is largely financed by petroleum companies.

The Santiago-Comaina Reserved Zone occupies a large area between the Marañón and Morana Rivers and the crest of the Cordillera del Condor. The North Peruvian pipeline crosses the southeastern corner of the Santiago-Comaina Reserved Zone. The Cordillera del Condor is a mountainous region that Peru and Ecuador have fought three wars over for ownership. A peace treaty ended the dispute in 1998. Part of the treaty obligates both countries to set up protected areas in the Cordillera del Condor.

Although the political dispute appears to be resolved, little has been done to promote conservation of the Cordillera del Condor region. Abandoned land mines from the wars still exist, and few scientists may be interested in confronting this danger.

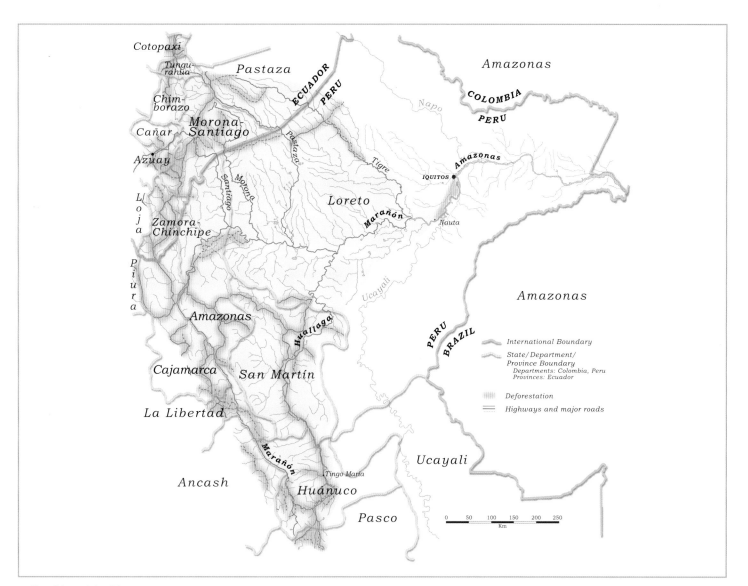

🔺 THE MARAÑÓN VALLEY

Occupying 138,200 square miles (358,000 km²), the Marañón Valley is the seventh largest tributary basin in the Amazon. It is approximately 850 miles (1,400 km) long, making it the 11th longest tributary of the Amazon River. Approximately 80 percent of the Marañón Basin is in Peru; the other 20 percent is in Ecuador. The Marañón Basin includes nine departments in Peru and eight provinces (equivalent to Peruvian departments) in Ecuador. The large department of Loreto in Amazonian Peru occupies more area of the Marañón Basin than do all the provinces of Ecuador combined. The Marañón River is called the Amazonas after its confluence with the Ucayali.

THE MARAÑÓN VALLEY

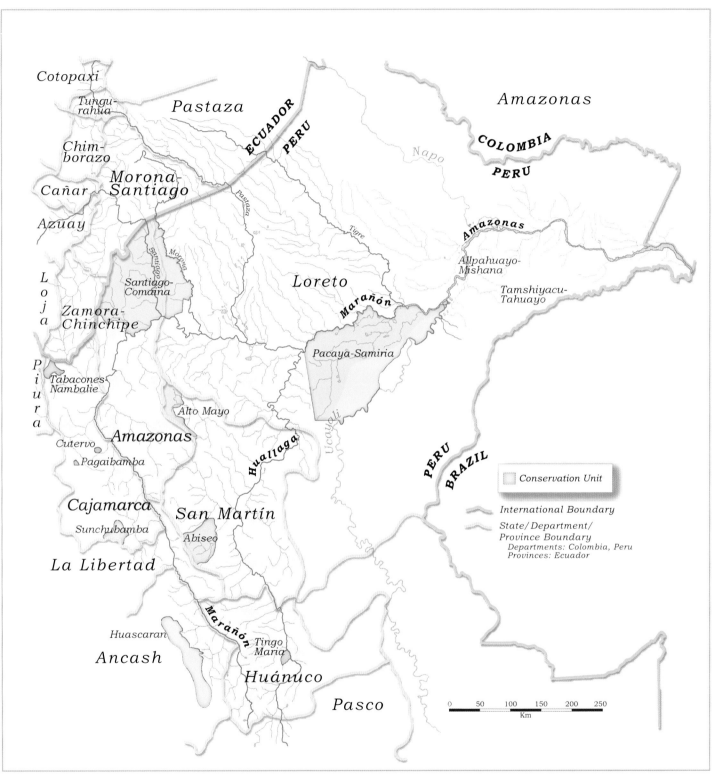

▲ **CONSERVATION UNITS AND INDIGENOUS AREAS OF THE MARAÑÓN VALLEY**

The Pacaya-Samiria National Reserve between the Marañón and Ucayali is the largest protected area in the Marañón Valley and is also Peru's largest national park. The Santiago-Comaina Reserved Zone is still being studied to determine its protection status. National parks in the Marañón Valley, such as Abiseo and Huascarán, include small headwater rivers at high elevations. Part of the Cordillera Azul between the Huallaga and Ucayali River is being studied for protection status and has been proposed as the Cordillera Azul Biabo National Park.

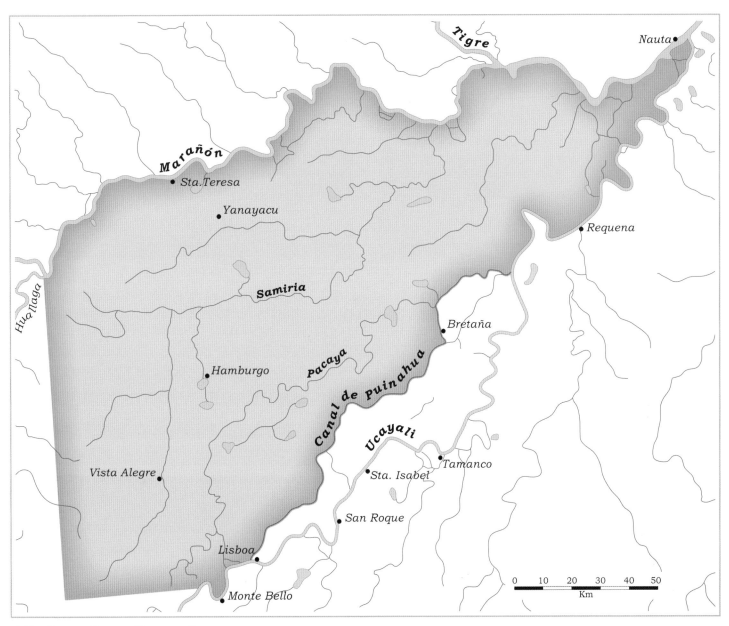

Nauta

Tigre

Marañón

• *Sta. Teresa*

• *Yanayacu*

• *Requena*

Huallaga

Samiria

• *Brétaña*

Pacaya

• *Hamburgo*

Canal de Puinahua

Ucayali

• *Tamanco*

• *Sta. Isabel*

• *Vista Alegre*

• *San Roque*

Lisboa

• *Monte Bello*

| 0 | 10 | 20 | 30 | 40 | 50 |

Km

▲ THE PACAYA-SAMIRIA NATIONAL RESERVE

Pacaya-Samiria occupies approximately 8,300 square miles (21,500 km²) between the Marañón and Ucayali Rivers. Nearly all of the reserve is subject to flooding. Most of the national reserve is in the Marañón drainage. Pacaya-Samiria is the largest protected floodplain in the Amazon Basin. The reserve has been selectively logged but there has been no large-scale deforestation. Although the reserve is sparsely populated, there are perhaps 100,000 people living in villages and towns mostly along the Ucayali and Marañón Rivers.

▶ THE LOWER MARAÑÓN

The Marañón is a highly turbid river. The main channel of the lower section of the River in the department of Loreto reaches 1.2–1.9 miles (2–3 km) in width. There has been relatively little deforestation along the Marañón, and most agricultural plots are small.

▲ **YANAYACU IN PACAYA-SAMIRIA NATIONAL RESERVE**
Rivers such as the Yanayacu, whose headwaters arise within the Pacaya-Samiria National Reserve, are relatively turbid. During the floods Pacaya-Samiria is invaded by overflow from the Marañón and Ucayali.

▲ **WATER, FOREST, AND FLOATING MEADOWS**
The location of the Pacaya-Samiria National Reserve at the confluence of the Ucayali and Marañón makes it an important nurseries region for fish, especially for some migratory species whose young are born in river channels and then carried downstream by currents before entering floodplains. Pacaya-Samiria probably serves as a major nursery for both the Ucayali and the Marañón. The rich mix of channels, lakes, floating meadows, and flooded forests makes Pacaya-Samiria one of the most important fish reserves in the Amazon Basin.

▲ **BABY AROWHANAS**
Arowhanas are mouth-brooders, that is, the male retains the newborn in his mouth until the yolk sacs are absorbed and the fry are large enough to fend for themselves. In most of the Amazon, fishermen catching species for the aquarium trade kill brooding male arowhanas to remove the young. Pacaya-Samiria fishermen have stopped killing the brooding males and retain them in nets while carefully removing the brood. The adults are then returned to the river.

▲ **THE ORNAMENTAL FISH TRADE**
Peru is a major exporter of aquarium fish from the Amazon. Ornamental fish captured in the Pacaya-Samiria National Reserve are transported to Iquitos and then flown to the United States, Europe, and Japan.

◀ FISHERIES IN THE PACAYA-SAMIRIA NATIONAL RESERVE

Fish is an important resource for residents of Pacaya-Samiria. Overfishing has generally not been a problem because fishing boats lack refrigeration and major urban centers are 10–15 hours away by motorized canoe.

▶ A HELPING HAND FOR TURTLES

After birth the newborn turtles are kept in captivity and fed for one to two weeks before release into the rivers and lakes of Pacaya-Samiria. It will be highly instructive to know to what extent sandbox incubators can increase turtle populations to the extent that they can be exploited on a sustainable basis for food.

▼ GUARD HOUSES IN PACAYA-SAMIRIA

The Pacaya-Samiria National Reserve is experimenting with guard stations manned by local residents that protect resources in their areas from outside intruders.

▲ THE PALM PROBLEM

Palm swamps dominated by aguaje (*Mauritia flexuosa*) occupy approximately one-third of the Pacaya-Samiria National Reserve. Aguaje fruits are popular in Amazonian Peru, and Pacaya-Samiria's palm swamps represent one source of income. The palms were being felled to remove fruit. This practice has apparently stopped and climbers are experimenting with various techniques, such as the scaling-scaffolding shown here, to harvest the fruit faster.

CHAPTER TWELVE

THE NORTHWESTERN TRIBUTARIES REGION

Where the Equatorial Amazon and the Andes Meet

All of the Amazon River's large northern tributaries have headwaters that traverse the equator, and the mouth of the Amazon meets the Atlantic slightly north of the equator. The equatorial influence is most pronounced, however, in the rivers of the northwestern Amazon. A large part of the northwestern Amazon is a relatively high precipitation region where average annual totals exceed approximately 120 in. (3,000 mm).

The largest tributary basin in the northwestern Amazon is that of the Caquetá-Japurá. The Caquetá-Japurá River is approximately 1,750 miles (2,800 km) long. It is the fourth longest tributary of the Amazon River. About two-thirds of the tributary is in Colombia, where it is known as the Caquetá. The other one-third is in Brazil, where it is called the Japurá. The Caquetá-Japurá Basin occupies approximately 11,200 square miles (289,000 km²), or just over 4 percent of the Amazon Basin. Eighty percent of the Basin is in Colombia. It is the ninth largest tributary basin in the Amazon and encompasses seven Colombian departments and one Brazilian state. Most of the basin is in the Colombian departments of Caquetá

and Amazonas and the state of Amazonas in Brazil.

The headwaters of the Japurá are nearly 3,100 miles (5,000 km) from the Amazon River mouth. The headwaters of the Caquetá River arise in the Cordillera Oriental of Colombia, which is less than 60 miles (100 km) from the upper Magdalena Valley and is only about 150 miles (250 km) south of Bogotá. Annual precipitation ranges from about 90 in. (2,300 mm) near the mouth of the Japurá to more than 120 in. (3,000 mm) in the middle and upper Caquetá Valley. Near the foothills annual average rainfall can exceed 200 in. (5,000 mm).

The northwestern drainage of the Caquetá Basin includes not only the high Cordillera Oriental but also an extensive eastern foothill region that is generally below 1,640 ft (500 m). The middle Caquetá—usually defined as the area between Araracuara and the Brazilian border—is noted for its large number of rocky outcroppings and cataracts. Deep gorges with high vertical walls, such as the Cañón de Araracuara, also exist here. For most of its length, the Caquetá River meanders around broad curves, and there are some extensive floodplains. The lower 125 miles (200 km) of the

◄ **WHERE THE CAQUETÁ-JAPURÁ MEETS THE AMAZON.**

The enormous floodplain delta region where the Caquetá-Japurá meets the Amazon. All of the forest shown in this photo is inundated for approximately six months annually.

▲ THE CAQUETÁ-JAPURÁ VALLEY

The Caquetá-Japurá Valley encompasses approximately 10,800 square miles (280,000 km²), most of which is in Colombia. The 1,750-mile-long (2,800 km) Caquetá-Japurá is the fifth longest tributary in the Amazon Basin. In Colombia the tributary is called the Caquetá, whereas in Brazil it is known as the Japurá. The Caquetá-Japurá is a muddy river, but one of its largest tributaries, the Apaporis, is a blackwater river. There are numerous cataracts in the middle section of the Caquetá (for example near Araracuara) that are not navigable. There are seven Colombian departments and one Brazilian state in the Caquetá-Japurá Basin. Much of the Caquetá Basin is under guerilla or drug-baron control and not generally accessible to outside researchers. Researchers from Colombia's Tropenbos Foundation in Bogotá, however, have been able to study in the area and have provided valuable insights about the ecology of the troubled region.

Japurá River join with the Solimões River floodplain to form one of the largest wetlands in the Amazon. The lower Japurá demarcates the eastern border of the Mamirauá Sustainable Development Reserve in Brazil.

The Caquetá-Japurá is a muddy river with numerous blackwater and clearwater tributaries that arise largely in the lowlands. The Apaporis River, whose confluence with the Caquetá is at the Colombian-Brazilian border, is the largest blackwater tributary. It is famous for its strikingly beautiful waterfalls and rapids. Annual river-level fluctuation has been measured for a few years at Araracuara on the middle Caquetá and averages approximately 29.5 ft (9 m). Near gorges, however, annual river-level fluctuations reaching 56 ft (17 m) have been reported. The annual river-level fluctuation of the lower Japurá is largely controlled by the Solimões River and averages approximately 33 ft (10 m).

Indigenous groups dominate the sparse population of most of the Caquetá-Japurá. Florencia, with more than 100,000 residents, is the most populous city in the valley. It is the capital of the department of Caquetá. Araracuara, with approximately 30,000 residents, is the largest city in the middle Caquetá Valley. There is daily air service between Araracuara and Bogotá.

Most of the colonization within the Caquetá-Japurá Valley has been in the foothill region along the road between Mocoa and Florencia. This is also a major coca-growing region. Other colonized areas include Araracuara, Puerto Santander, and La Pedrera, in the middle Caquetá. The major roads into the Caquetá Valley are restricted to the foothill region.

▲ **CONSERVATION UNITS AND INDIGENOUS AREAS OF THE CAQUETÁ-JAPURÁ VALLEY**

Indigenous groups who exercise control over local resources inhabit most of the middle and lower Caquetá-Japurá. The most important designated areas for protection in Colombia are Chiribiquete National Park along the blackwater Araporis and Cahuinari National Park along the lower Caquetá. In Brazil the Mamirauá Sustainable Development Reserve includes the right bank of the mouth region of the Japurá. The Mamirauá Sustainable Development Reserve is functionally a part of the lower Caquetá-Japurá river system, as well as the middle Solimões.

THE CAQUETÁ-JAPURÁ VALLEY

Bogotá is connected to Chiribiquete National Park in the department of Caquetá by a road that crosses the Colombian departments of Meta and Guaviare. Commercial fishermen in the middle Caquetá region target catfish, which cargo planes transport to Bogotá. The Tefé fleet—based in the middle Solimões region in Brazil—fish the lower Japurá River. The floodplains of the lower Japurá and the adjoining Solimões have been extensively logged. Brazilian gold miners have explored the region near the Brazilian-Colombian border for alluvial-gold deposits. Apparently too little ore was found to spur a rush to the area.

Colombian guerrilla forces or drug traffickers have controlled the upper and middle Caquetá Valley since the 1980s. The Caquetá Valley is the world's largest cocaine-processing region. As mentioned previously, indigenous groups granted land rights from the Colombian government inhabit most of the middle and lower Caquetá Valley. The federal government established two large protected areas in the region: Chiribiquete National Park in the Andean foothill region and Cahuinari National Park near the Brazilian border.

The Putumayo-Içá is the only river in the Amazon Basin that drains territory in Colombia, Ecuador, Peru, and Brazil. No other Amazon River tribu-

CAQUETÁ, COLOMBIA

▲ **HARPOON FISHERMEN OF THE CAQUETÁ**
Migratory catfish originating in Brazil move upstream through the Araracuara rapids of the middle Caquetá in Colombia to reach Andean foothill spawning habitats.

▲ **MIDDLE CAQUETÁ**
The Caquetá at Araracuara in Colombia.

tary passes through four countries. The Negro and Madeira Rivers each pass through three countries. The Putumayo River demarcates most of the Peruvian-Colombian border. The river's lower 150 miles (250 km) are in Brazil, where it is known as the Içá. Near the Brazilian border, Colombia has exclusive claim to a 30-mile-long (50 km) stretch of the Putumayo in the southern panhandle area. This gives the country access to the Amazon River between Peru and Brazil.

The Putumayo-Içá River is approximately 1,000 miles (1,600 km) long. It is the tenth longest tributary of the Amazon River. The river's narrow basin encompasses 57,100 square miles (148,000 km²), or approximately 2.2 percent of the Amazon Basin. It is the 11th largest basin in the Amazon. The Putumayo-Içá Valley is located within the large Colombian departments of Putumayo and Amazonas and the Peruvian department of Loreto. The river's headwaters are in the Ecuadorian province of Napo. The Içá River is entirely within the Brazilian state of Amazonas.

The Putumayo-Içá Valley is one of the most isolated valleys in the Amazon Basin. Few scientific studies have been done in the valley. The headwaters of the Putumayo-Içá arise at nearly 13,100 ft (4,000 m) in the Colombian Andes. The sediment concentrations in the river are high enough to make it a muddy river; however, they are only about one-third the level of the sediment concentrations in the adjacent Amazon River. No sizeable tributaries empty into the Putumayo-Içá. The river primarily drains an area in Peru north of the Napo and Amazonas rivers.

▲ **THE ARARACOARA GORGE OF THE MIDDLE CAQUETÁ (COLOMBIA)**

The middle Caquetá flows across an outlying extension of the Andes and is studded with numerous cataracts and gorges, the Araracoara Gorge being the most famous because of its narrow passage.

There are no major cataracts on the Putumayo-Içá, and it is navigable for most of its length. The river meanders extensively and has a relatively large floodplain, whose area has not yet been calculated. It appears to be four to five times the size of that along the Içá, which has been estimated at 965 square miles (2,500 km²). Annually, most of the Putumayo-Içá Valley receives more than 120 in. (3,000 mm) of rain.

The Putumayo-Içá Valley is sparsely populated. Numerous indigenous groups, such as the Tikuna in Brazil, live along the banks of the main river. Drug traffickers and guerrilla groups have caused problems there. The most developed area of the valley is in the foothill region, centered on the Orito oil fields. The trans-Andino pipeline transports crude oil from the fields to Tumaco on the Colombian coast. In addition, a secondary pipeline from Ecuador connects to the trans-Andino pipeline at Orito. Rebels have repeatedly bombed the pipeline during Colombia's ongoing civil war, but it is not known how much oil has been spilled due to the bombings or what impacts the spills have had on aquatic ecosystems. Because the petroleum business is privatized in Colombia, oil exploration and drilling in the Orito region is expected to intensify.

Only Colombia has designated any protected areas within the Putumayo-Içá Valley. La Playa National Park occupies approximately 1,600 square miles (4,220 km²) of mostly upland forest near the Colombian-Ecuadorian border. Amacayacu National Park covers approximately 1,135 square miles (2,935 km²). It is in the panhandle (sometimes called the *trapezium* by Colombians) north of the Amazonas. The small rivers within the park flow into the Putumayo and Amazonas Rivers in Colombia and into the Içá in Brazil. Nearly one-half of the Putumayo Valley on the Colombian side is part of the Predio Putumayo Indigenous Reserve.

The Napo Basin is the smallest of the Amazon's tributary basins that

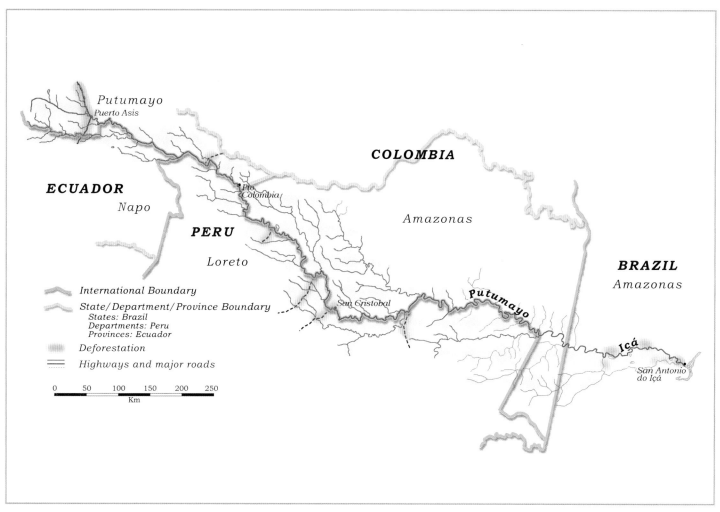

▲ THE PUTUMAYO-IÇÁ VALLEY

The Putumayo-Içá is shared by Colombia, Ecuador, Peru, and Brazil and is the only tributary of the Amazon River that drains territory in more than three countries. Most of the Putumayo delineates borders between Colombia and Peru or between Colombia and Ecuador.

occupy at least 38,600 square miles (100,000 km²). Encompassing approximately 42,500 square miles (110,000 km²), or 1.6 percent of the Amazon Basin, the Napo Basin is the 13th largest tributary area of the Amazon River. Of the Amazon's large tributaries, the 550-mile-long (885 km) Napo River exceeds only the Trombetas in eastern Brazil in length. Approximately 60 percent of the Napo Basin is in Ecuador; the other 40 percent is in Peru. The Napo Basin accounts for most of the drainage area of the Amazon River within Ecuador. The region of the Napo Valley located in Peru is

entirely within the department of Loreto. The Ecuadorian section of the valley is divided among four provinces, with more than one-half in the large province of Napo.

The headwaters of the Napo River arise within 60–120 miles (100–200 km) of Quito, Ecuador's capital in the high Andes. Andean headwaters of the Napo above approximately 1,300 ft (400 m) run clear except during heavy rainstorms. In the lowlands the Napo is a muddy and highly meandering river with a large floodplain. The Curaray, a blackwater river with sections in Ecuador and Peru, is the only large

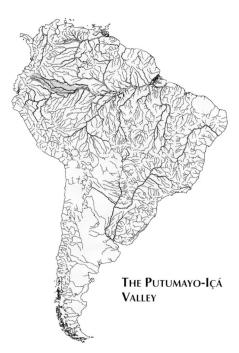

THE PUTUMAYO-IÇÁ VALLEY

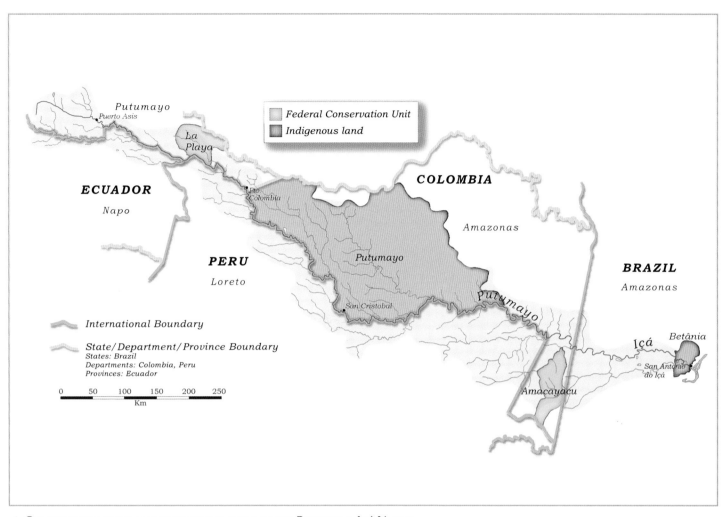

▲ CONSERVATION UNITS AND INDIGENOUS AREAS OF THE PUTUMAYO-IÇÁ VALLEY

Only Colombia has designated protected areas in the Putumayo-Içá Valley. La Playa National Park and Amacayacu National park are at distant ends of the Putumayo in Colombia.

tributary of the Napo. There are also numerous small blackwater tributaries in the Napo Basin from the foothills to the mouth region.

Annual precipitation totals in the Napo Basin vary from approximately 100 to 200 in. (2,500–5,000 mm). The highest totals are on the Andean slopes. Annual river-level fluctuations along the Napo have not been measured. The average annual river-level fluctuation of the lower Napo in Peru is approximately 27.9 ft (8.5 m), which is similar to that of the Amazonas near Iquitos. Floodplains along the Napo are inundated from about

December through May each year.

Although the Napo Valley occupies only a small part of the Amazon Basin, the media and environmental groups have spotlighted it because of the large petroleum reserves known to exist in the "Oriente," as the eastern Amazon region is called in Ecuador. Roads built by the oil company Texaco-Gulf in the late 1960s and 1970s opened the Oriente to both extensive oil exploration and agricultural colonization. The main highway runs from Quito to Lago Agrio, where the trans-Ecuadorian pipeline joins the trans-Andino pipeline to send crude oil to coastal refineries. A

highway from Ambato, south of Quito, enters the southern Napo Basin. Ecuadorian roads in the Oriente now cross most of the headwaters of the Napo River and extend well beyond the foothills.

Since the 1970s the road network in the Oriente has attracted large numbers of agricultural colonists from the highlands. Perhaps 100,000 people from the highlands have now settled in the Oriente. Most farming is restricted to the uplands, where bananas, manioc, coffee, cacao, maize, and vegetables are grown. Cattle ranching is expanding rapidly, and large pastures are widespread

▲ THE NAPO VALLEY

The Napo Basin occupies approximately 44,400 square miles (115,000 km²) in Ecuador and Peru and is the smallest of the Amazon's large tributaries with drainage areas of at least 38,600 square miles (100,000 km²). The 550-mile-long (885 km) muddy Napo enters the Amazonas approximately 50 miles (80 km) downstream of Iquitos. Napo headwaters are nearly 2,750 miles (4,400 km) from the mouth of the Amazon River. Most of Ecuador's share of the Amazon Basin is in the Napo drainage. The entire Napo Basin in Peru is in the department of Loreto, while the Ecuadorian share lies within four provinces (equivalent to Peruvian departments).

throughout the upper Napo Valley. The pastures, unlike those in most of the Amazon Basin, do not dry out because of the appreciable amounts of rainfall throughout the year in most of the Oriente. The most extensively deforested region in the Oriente is between the Aguarico and Napo Rivers.

Most environmental concern in the upper Napo Valley has focused on the petroleum pipeline in the Oriente. It runs approximately 150 miles (250 km) southward from the Ecuador-Colombian border to the southern Napo Basin. Pipelines—usually above ground—cross all of the major rivers in the upper Napo Basin. Due to the

unstable geology of the upper Napo Valley and the extensive deforestation in some areas, swollen rivers, extensive runoff, and landslides can cause pipelines to rupture.

At higher elevations the main pipeline is vulnerable to volcanic activity and earthquakes. In 1987, for example, a major earthquake shattered a portion of the pipeline and large quantities of crude oil reportedly flowed into the Aguarico and Napo Rivers. No large-scale downstream impacts, however, were recorded. Secondary pipelines that cross the Napo have also been ruptured and have caused local fish kills and destroyed floodplain

crops. Environmental and indigenous groups have accused Petroecuador (Ecuador's government-run petroleum company) and Texaco of causing extensive oil pollution of the headwaters of the Napo River. Both companies are being sued. Most of Ecuador's known petroleum reserves lie within the upper Napo Basin. Ecuador relies heavily on petroleum revenues, which account for more than one-half of its gross national product.

Ecuador has two relatively large protected areas in the Napo Basin. Roads built by petroleum companies enter into both areas. Yasuni National Park is just south of the Napo near the

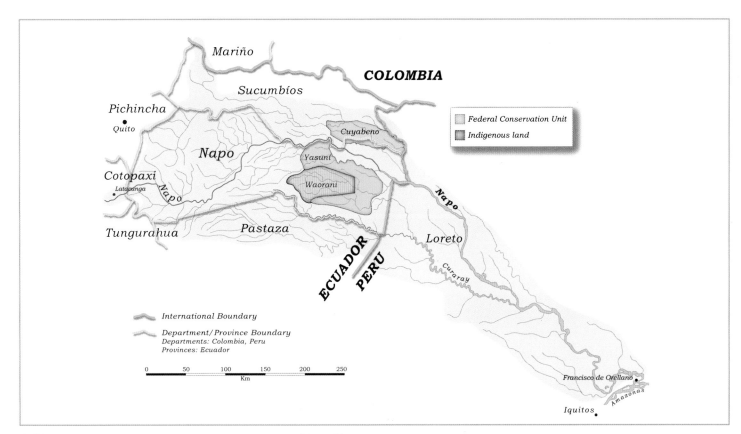

▲ **CONSERVATION UNITS AND INDIGENOUS AREA OF THE NAPO VALLEY**

There are only two large protected areas in the Napo Valley. Most of the Cuyabeno National Wildlife Reserve is subject to seasonal flooding whereas the Yasuni National Park is mostly upland forest. Oil companies operate near the parks and a pipeline runs through Cuyabeno. There has been heavy colonization and deforestation along the roads constructed by petroleum companies.

Peruvian border and encompasses approximately 2,500 square miles (6,500 km²) of mostly upland forest. Two indigenous groups, the Waorani and the Quichua, inhabit much of the park. Colonists have recently moved into the park and have deforested large areas to grow crops. Hunting and fishing have also increased in the park to supply a local market at Coca.

The Cuyabeno Wildlife Production Reserve encompasses about 965 square miles (2,500 km²) near the Colombian border along the Aguarico River, a tributary of the Amazon. Cuyabeno receives 135–155 in. (3,500–4,000 mm) of rain annually, and most of the reserve is subject to seasonal flooding. In general Cuyabeno can be considered as a large wetland area. Four indigenous groups—the Siona-Secoya, the Quichua, the Cofane, and the Shuar—inhabit the reserve along with colonists who have recently arrived.

Government and conservation groups have implemented indigenous- and community-based multiple-use programs to manage the reserve. Ecotourism has become popular at Cuyabeno due to its rainforest and tropical rivers. The Ecuadorian government recently issued a decree blocking future oil mining, exploration, logging, and colonization in the Yasuni and Cuyabeno protected areas, but Peru has yet to establish any large protected areas in the Napo Basin.

THE NAPO VALLEY

CHAPTER THIRTEEN

THE NEGRO AND THE TROMBETAS
Black and Clear Waters from Ancient Lands

Most of the Amazon River's northern drainage in Brazil lies on the Guiana Shield, an ancient and highly eroded geologic region, most of which is less than 1,300 ft (400 m) in elevation. The Negro and Trombetas Rivers are the only large tributaries of the Amazon River that drain the Guiana Shield. The Negro is a giant blackwater river, whereas the Trombetas is a clearwater river.

The Negro Basin covers nearly 270,300 square miles (700,000 km²)—an area larger than the size of France. The basin is the third largest in the Amazon. The Negro Valley encompasses slightly more than 10 percent of the Amazon drainage. The Negro River is approximately 1,550 miles (2,500 km) long. Its Colombian headwaters are nearly 2,300 miles (3,700 km) from the Amazon River mouth. More than 90 percent of the Negro Basin is in Brazil; the rest lies mostly in Venezuela and Colombia, with less than 1 percent in neighboring Guyana. Most of the basin in Brazil lies in the states of Amazonas and Roraima. In Colombia, it lies in the departments of Vaupés and Guainía, and in Venezuela, in the federal territory of Amazonas. The Ministerial District Number 6 of Guyana

has a small headwater area of the Negro near the Brazilian border.

The Negro drains three principal regions: the northern tributaries of the river arise mostly on the southern Guiana Shield in Brazil; the northwestern headwaters arise in the Andean foothills of Colombia; and most of the right-bank tributaries arise in the lowlands below 650 ft (200 m). Pico de Neblina, Brazil's highest mountain, rises to 9,890 ft (3,014 m) on the far western part of the Guiana Shield.

The mountainous divide separating the Orinoco and Negro Basins ranges from 6,550 to 8,850 ft (2,000–2,700 m) in elevation. The principal mountain ranges of the divide are the Serra Pacaraima and the Serra Parima. The ancient Guiana Shield is characterized by its numerous sandstone tablelands and isolated granite hills. The Negro's largest tributary, the Branco, drains a large part of the southern Guiana Shield. Most Guiana Shield tributaries have numerous cataracts in their upper sections. The middle section of the Negro flows across the Guiana Shield between about the Brazilian-Colombian-Venezuelan border and the mouth of

◀ **RIVER SANDS AND BLACK WATERS**

Black waters are born in sandy soils, and runoff transports both the tea-like waters and sandy sediments into the Negro. During the low-water period Negro channels can become choked with sands.

International Boundary

Department/State Ministerial District Boundary
Departments: Colombia
States: Brazil, Venezuela
Ministerial District: Guyana

Deforestation

Highways and major roads

▲ THE NEGRO VALLEY

The Negro Valley encompasses nearly 270,000 square miles (700,000 km²), an area larger than the size of France. Of the Amazon River's tributary basins, only the Madeira and Tocantins Valleys are larger than the Negro Valley. The blackwater Negro is approximately 1,550 miles (2,500 km) long and, although its Colombian headwaters do not reach the high Andes, they are still nearly 2,300 miles (3,700 km) from the Amazon River mouth. The 480-mile-long (775 km) Branco, the Negro's largest tributary, is a semiturbid river almost entirely in the state of Roraima. More than 90 percent of the Negro Basin is in the Brazilian states of Amazonas and Roraima; nearly 10 percent lies largely in Venezuela and Colombia. Less than 1 percent is in Guyana.

the Branco. Evidence of the Guiana Shield is easily seen in the rocky outcroppings and cataracts at various points along this reach.

The upper Negro River is linked to the Orinoco River in Venezuela by the Casiquiare Channel. The Negro River is formed after the confluence of the Guainía River and Casiquiare Channel ("Canal Casiquiare" in Spanish) in Venezuela. Headwater erosion in this region has partly diverted water flow in the Casiquiare Channel southwestward to the Negro.

The Negro's principal tributary in Colombia is the Vaupés, which is called the Uaupés after it enters Brazil. Several of the Negro's western tributaries in Brazil, such as the Urubaxi, arise near the confluence of the Japurá and Solimões Rivers. During the rainy season small streams connect the Negro and Japurá Basins. The headwaters of the Negro arise in the foothills below the Andes at less than 1,000 ft (300 m).

The amount of average annual precipitation in the Negro Basin ranges from 60 to 135 in. (1,600–3,500 mm). The most abundant rains fall each year in the northwestern drainage, extending from the Andean foothills to approximately the city of São Gabriel

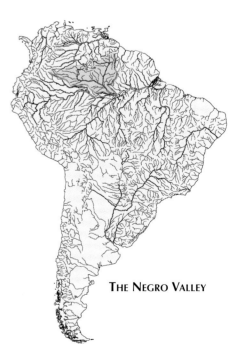

THE NEGRO VALLEY

NEGRO FEDERAL CONSERVATION UNITS

Jaú National Park is the largest national park in the Brazilian Amazon. Most of the other federal conservation units in the Negro Basin are a mix of indigenous areas with various protected designations. The Pico da Neblina National Park encompasses several tributaries of the upper Negro and also contains the highest point in Brazil.

NEGRO STATE CONSERVATION UNITS

The most protected and researched state conservation unit is the Anavilhanas Archipelago Ecological Station in the lower Negro. Included in this unit are more than 350 islands covered mostly with floodplain forest that is inundated for six to seven months each year.

NEGRO INDIGENOUS AREAS

Indigenous areas account for approximately 20 percent of the Negro Basin. The Yanomami occupy a large part of the headwaters of the Guiana Shield region. Colombia and Brazil have adjoining indigenous reserves in the northwestern Negro Basin. The new Manaus-Boa Vista highway passes through the Waimiri-Atroari Indigenous Area that includes left-bank tributaries of the lower Negro.

▲ THE LOWER NEGRO MOUTH-BAY

The mouth-bay of the lower Negro reaches depths of nearly 60 ft (100 m), making its bottom approximately 200–230 ft (60–70 m) below sea level. The deep and wide mouth-bay is thought to have been excavated during the last Ice Age when sea levels were lower than they are today and Amazonian rivers ran faster and cut deep into their beds. Unlike the Amazon River, the Negro transports little sediment. Subsequent to the last Ice Age, the blackwater tributary has not had time or the necessary material to fill its lower valley. The site shown here is opposite the port of Manaus.

▲ THE CONFLUENCE OF THE NEGRO AND AMAZON RIVER (SOLIMÕES)

The Negro is the largest blackwater river in the world, the sixth largest river in the world, and the Amazon's second largest tributary in terms of total annual discharge.

LOWER NEGRO

da Cachoeira along the Negro in Brazil. The equator passes nearly through São Gabriel da Cachoeira, 565 miles (910 km) upstream of the mouth of the Negro. The northwestern-drainage region gets a significant amount of rainfall every month, with the most rain falling from April through July. Northern Roraima gets the least amount of rain, where annual totals can be less than 60 in. (1,600 mm). Approximately 85 in. (2,200 mm) of rain falls yearly in the lower Negro region.

The main floods of the upper and middle Negro are between May and September. Water levels are usually highest in July and lowest from December through February. Water levels in the lower Negro up to approximately its confluence with the Branco River are controlled by the backwater effect of Amazon River. In contrast to the upper and middle Negro, the lower Negro is in flood from February through July and the flood peak is usually reached in June; the lowest water

months are September to December. Water levels in the middle and upper Negro are falling between December and February, whereas they are rising at that time in the lower river.

The average annual river-level fluctuation of the middle and upper Negro ranges from approximately 13 to 16.5 ft (4–5 m), whereas near the mouth—where measurements have been taken since 1902—it is 33 ft (10 m). Differences between the highest and lowest water levels within the middle and upper Negro range from 27.9 to 31.8 ft (8.5–9.7 m). In comparison, the difference between the highest and lowest water level in the lower Negro near Manaus is more than 53 ft (16 m). No data are available for the headwater region of the upper Negro in the Colombian foothills.

The most striking characteristic of the Negro River is its black water. It is the only large blackwater river in the Amazon Basin, accounting for approximately 13–14 percent of the total

MIDDLE NEGRO

△ THE SANDY TEAPOT

Negro black water can be thought of as a type of tea brewed in sandy soils. The tea leaves come from the stunted vegetation that grows in sandy soils. The black water works its way from groundwater to the streams that empty into the Negro.

△ CAMPINA FOREST AND BLACK WATER

Campina forests are often stunted vegetation islands surrounded by taller rainforest. It appears that black water will dominate smaller tributaries even if campina forests cover only one-third of the drainage area. The degree of blackness, that is, the total content of organic compounds, might be related to the relative area of campina forest in each drainage basin.

▷ THE STUNTED VEGETATION OF BLACKWATER PRODUCING AREAS

The stunted vegetation of the blackwater areas of the Negro is called *campina* or *campinarana*. There are too few nutrients in sandy soils to support tall rainforest.

△ BLACK WATER DRAINING A CAMPINA FOREST

Dark and clear organic acids derived from plant compounds are found in Negro waters. Little is yet known about the chemical composition of these compounds and their influence on aquatic life.

▲ BLACKWATER PURITY

Although dark in color the water in the Negro is nearly distilled because of its extremely low salt content. The Negro has the softest waters of any large river in the world. A combination of low nutrient content and high acidity greatly decrease the number of biting flies, such as mosquitoes, in Negro waters. Certain areas, however, have annoying black flies and sand flies.

VENEZUELA

COLOMBIA

ECUADOR

PERU

MIDDLE NEGRO

BOLIVIA

BRAZIL

annual discharge of the Amazon River. It is not only the Amazon's second largest river in terms of annual discharge, but it is also the world's largest blackwater river. In terms of annual discharge, the Negro is probably the sixth largest river in the world.

Blackwater rivers are extremely poor in nutrients and very acidic; they are the products of drainage areas where sandy soils dominate. Most of the Negro basin is covered with sandy soils and thus many of its tributaries are blackwater rivers. The Branco, the Negro's largest tributary, is an exception (Branco literally means "White River"). Although not as turbid as the Amazon River or the Madeira, the Branco is slightly muddy, especially during the high-water period. Other turbid tributaries of the Negro include the Padauari and several smaller rivers that arise on the Guiana Shield west of the Branco.

The Negro Basin covers an estimated 11, 600 square miles (30,000 km²) that are subject to seasonal inun-

dation, but the actual value is probably higher. The two largest areas that are seasonally inundated are the savannas in Roraima near Boa Vista and the enormous low-lying area north of the Negro between the Branco and Padauari Rivers. Dwarfed forest and palm swamps grow in much of the latter area, which is very sandy and stays flooded for about six months each year.

The largest floodplains in the Negro Basin are those along the right-bank tributaries. Extensive floodplains also can be found along a 185-mile-long (300 km) stretch of the main stream upriver from Barcelos. Two large archipelagoes, with more than 1,000 islands among them, exist in the lower and middle sections of the river. Almost all of the islands are completely inundated during the floods. Forests that are inundated for four to eight months per year dominate most of the floodplain area within the Negro Basin.

Most of the Negro Basin is sparsely populated. Sandy soils have discouraged

▲ NEGRO ARCHIPELAGOES

The Negro has more than 1,000 islands, most of which are in the middle and lower sections. Negro islands typically are covered mostly with floodable forest and have small internal lakes. Beaches can emerge during the low-water period at various points around the islands, but they are usually near the upstream and downstream points. Islands greatly increase the amount of shoreline habitat available for aquatic plants and animals that are adapted to live in environments receiving abundant sunlight.

▲ BLACKWATER FLOODED FORESTS

Herbaceous floating plants are relatively rare in the Negro except in the region below its confluence with the Branco that is influenced by turbid water of the tributary. Plankton production is controlled by the supply of nutrients. The effects of extremely low nutrient concentrations in the Negro on the food chain are counterbalanced by the large areas of flooded forests that provide aquatic animals with fruits, seeds, detritus, and other edible material. Nearly all of the forest shown in this photograph of the middle Negro is subject to seasonal flooding.

▲ JARÁ PALM FORESTS

Palms of the genus *Leopoldinia* often dominate floodable sandy areas along the Negro and its blackwater tributaries. Jará palms can remain healthy while underwater for most of the year.

Buriti (*Mauritia flexuosa*) forests are common throughout the Negro Basin in low-lying areas. The largest buriti forests are found north of the Negro between the Branco and Paduari. These palm forests are usually inundated for about six to seven months, although parts of them are flooded for as long as 10–11 months each year.

large-scale agricultural colonization along the blackwater rivers. Indigenous peoples inhabit much of the Guiana Shield region and upper drainage in Colombia, the largest group being the Yanomami in the northern tributaries of the Guiana Shield.

The Manaus-Boa Vista highway, which was recently paved, traverses the eastern drainage of the Negro Basin and enters Venezuela. Colonization along the highway is extensive except within the Waimiri-Atroari Indigenous Area in the lower Negro Basin. There are two main roads in the upper basin. One road runs from São Gabriel da Cachoeira to Cucuí at the Brazilian-Venezuelan border, bypassing cataracts on the Negro River that are difficult for boats to navigate. The other road, which starts at Villavicencio in the Andean foothills, crosses the Vaupe's headwaters in Colombia.

The most extensively colonized area in the Negro Valley is in the Brazilian state of Roraima. The city of Boa Vista has become the hub of this

area. Boa Vista's extensive road network has attracted large numbers of colonists from southern and northeastern Brazil. The Boa Vista-Bomfim highway reaches the Guyana border on the Tacutu (Takutu) River. Guyana is building a road from Georgetown to Lethem, opposite Bomfim on the Brazilian side. When this highway is finished, Roraima will have major highways to Venezuela and Guyana, further spurring colonization and development in the Branco Basin.

Roraima is one of the most deforested states in the Amazon Basin. An intense and hot dry season, along with extensive savannas, makes the task of controlling and extinguishing fires all but impossible. It is estimated that about one-third of the area of Roraima has been burned. Fires set in the savannas quickly spread to forested areas, which can burn easily because of the relatively dry rainforest growing throughout much of Roraima.

Most deforestation in Roraima has been for cattle ranching. Crop farming,

however, is expanding rapidly, both in the uplands and on the floodplains. The rich soils of some of the upper valleys are also attracting crop farmers. Rice is the principal crop grown on floodplains, whereas rice, maize, manioc, and soybeans dominate upland farming. Riparian forests between the Branco River and the savannas have largely been cut in areas where rice is grown.

Deforestation in Roraima appears to have led to increased erosion, which has increased sediment runoff into the Branco River. Consequently the River has high levels of turbidity. Most of the sediments in the lower Negro River are from the Branco River, including those that form the more than 350 islands of the Anavilhanas Archipelago in the lower Negro. Branco waters descend the Negro along the main stream's left margin. The turbidity in the Negro from the sediment load discharged by the Branco appears confined to the high-water period and is evident in the river for approximately 125 miles

(200 km) downstream of its confluence with the Branco. It is turbid mostly along its left bank.

The floodplains along the Negro and Branco Rivers have been extensively logged for a few species. The most commercially valuable species logged is virola (*Virola surinamensis*). Loggers have also cut most of the large kapok trees (*Ceiba pentrandra*) along the Branco River. (Kapok is not found along blackwater rivers.) Upland logging is concentrated near urban centers—especially Manaus and Boa Vista. Jauari palms (*Astrocaryum jauari*) have been extensively harvested along the middle Negro River for palm hearts, though the species is not threatened from over-harvesting. Gold miners have often invaded the Negro Valley. Local authorities have expelled most miners that have entered the Valley above Barcelos. Some dredge mining, however, has taken place in the cataract region above São Gabriel da Cachoeira. Most gold mining in the Negro Valley is done on or near Yanomami lands in Roraima, although some spills over into Venezuela. The lower Negro is also being dredged for gravel to supply the construction business in Manaus. Sandstone outcroppings along the banks of the Negro are excavated during the low-water period for construction rock.

The main economic activity within the blackwater areas of the Negro Valley is the aquarium trade. The most commercially valuable exported species is the cardinal tetra (*Paracheirodon axelrodi*). It is found only in the Negro and in a few small headwater tributaries of adjoining basins. In the past two decades, people have been moving

UPPER NEGRO

▶ **THE GUIANA SHIELD EXPOSED**
Cataracts are the clearest signs of the presence of the Guiana Shield in the Negro Valley. Cataracts are especially common in the upper Negro of Brazil because the Guiana Shield underlies most of this region. The cataract shown here is the Cachoeira do Aracu of the Daraá River, a left-bank blackwater tributary of the middle Negro. Cataract rocks are often overgrown with aquatic plants of the family Podostemaceae.

▲ **OUTLYING GUIANA SHIELD REMNANTS**
Isolated hills along the middle Negro are reminders of the presence of the ancient Guiana Shield.

▲ **MARAUIÁ CATARACTS**
The Marauiá, a left-bank tributary of the middle Negro, has headwaters in the Serra Tapirapeco on the Guiana Shield. Most of this tributary, as with many others in this region, are heavily studded with cataracts. Vines used to make baskets and furniture are one of the forest resources extracted from the middle Negro region.

▲ **THE CARDINAL NEON**

More than 100 species of ornamental fish are captured in the Negro Basin. By far the most important species captured captured annually is the cardinal neon (*Paracheirodon axelrodi*). The red and blue iridescence of cardinal neons and colors of several other beautiful species in the Negro appear to serve some adaptive purpose for living in black water.

▲ **BLACKWATER FISHING FOR ORNAMENTAL SPECIES**

The aquarium trade is one of the most important economic activities of the blackwater areas of the Negro Basin. Black waters have the most beautiful fish species in the Amazon.

▲ **THE AQUARIUM TRADE**

The Negro is the most heavily exploited river in the Amazon for aquarium fish. Fishermen at this site in the middle Negro region are holding ornamental species in nets awaiting transport to Manaus.

farther up tributaries of the Guiana Shield looking for fish to supply the aquarium trade. They are especially in search of species of *Corydoras*, one of the most popular ornamental-fish groups in the world. Ornamental fish caught in the Negro are transported by boat to Manaus and then flown to Miami. Large-scale commercial fisheries for food species are restricted mostly to the lower Negro and capture migratory schools moving in and out of the river during dispersal and spawning runs. On the Branco River near Boa Vista, commercial fishermen seasonally target migratory catfish.

Large parts of the areas designated for protection in the Negro Valley are made up of land belonging to Brazilian indigenous groups and national park land. The Yanomami occupy most of the headwater region of the northern tributaries of the Negro along the southern Guiana Shield. Various other indigenous groups live in the large northwestern upper Negro region in Brazil, Colombia, and Venezuela.

The largest national park in the Brazilian Amazon is Jaú National Park, which encompasses 8,800 square miles (22,700 km²) and takes in all of the blackwater Jaú Basin on the right bank of the lower Negro. Aquarium-trade fishermen exploit rivers within the park. Local residents have deforested some areas. Attempts are being made to integrate the aquarium trade into the management of Jaú National Park.

The Pico de Neblina National Park includes isolated headwaters of the Guiana Shield and also Pico de Neblina, Brazil's highest mountain. The Anavilhanas Archipelago Ecological Station is located in the lower Negro region and includes nearly 350 islands, which are mostly covered with forest subjected to six to seven months of annual flooding. The station also

BRANCO

▲ **BRANCO AT THE BEM QUERER RAPIDS**
The Branco, the Negro's largest tributary, is a slightly turbid river. The muddy waters of the Branco, however, have relatively little impact on the Negro's color or chemistry except along the left bank just downriver from the mouth of the tributary.

▲ **FOOTHILL TRIBUTARIES OF UPPER BRANCO**
Some Guiana Shield foothill tributaries of the upper Branco carry relatively heavy sediment loads, even during the dry season, as shown here.

▲ **TACUTU AT BRAZIL-GUYANA BORDER**
The Tacutu delineates part of the Brazilian-Guyana border, and is a muddy river typical in the color and chemistry of upper Branco tributaries. Brazil is on the left and Guyana is on the right in this photo.

includes areas along the left bank of the Negro with upland forest. Another important state protected area is the Maracá Ecological Station in Roraima, along the Uraricoeira, the largest tributary of the Branco River.

Over the past two decades, the Negro Valley has become a favorite stop for ecotourists visiting the central Amazon and the free trade zone in Manaus. Sport fishing for peacock bass has expanded throughout the Negro Valley and, in some areas, has caused conflict with local residents.

The Trombetas is the second smallest of the Amazon's tributary basins that are at least 38,600 square miles (100,000 km²). The Napo Basin in Ecuador is the smallest. The Trombetas River is approximately 450 miles (750 km) long and drains 51,700 square miles (134,000 km²), or 1.9 percent of the Amazon Basin. The headwaters of the Trombetas arise near the Guyana-Suriname border in the Serra Acaraí (also called "Acarí") and the Serra de

Tumucumaque. They are ancient hilly regions on the eastern Guiana Shield and are no higher than 2,300–2,950 ft (700–900 m). Almost the entire Trombetas Basin is in the Brazilian state of Pará. The headwater area of a small western tributary lies within the states of Roraima and Amazonas, accounting for approximately 1 percent of the area of the Trombetas Basin.

Most of the Trombetas Basin is on the Guiana Shield. Despite its intense dry season, most of the Basin is largely covered by rainforest. The amount of annual rainfall ranges from approximately 85 in. (2,200 mm) near the Trombetas River mouth to less than approximately 60 in. (1,600 mm) in the headwaters area.

The Trombetas River is a clear-water river, although the lower 12 miles (20 km) can be turbid when water from the Amazon River invades it. Within the Trombetas Basin there are also small, blackwater tributaries. The Amazon River largely controls

⧫ FLOODED SAVANNAS IN RORAIMA

The savanna regions of Roraima are subject to flooding from overflow of the Branco and local rainfall. Buriti palms (*Mauritia flexuosa*) colonize low-lying areas that remain swampy for most of the year.

⧫ DRY SEASON ON THE RORAIMA SAVANNAS

The Roraima savanna region undergoes an intense dry season for about four to six months each year. The previously inundated savannas become parched, and wetlands all but disappear except near streams, most of which are shaded by palms, as seen in the background at this site.

seasonal water levels in the lower Trombetas River. The river is in flood from March to August; the low-water period is from September to February. The dry season is intense in the middle and upper Trombetas Basin—many tributaries nearly become dry. The Trombetas River and its major tributaries are studded with cataracts, and riverbeds are often rocky. The first major cataract is near Cachoeira Porteira at the confluence of the Trombetas and Mapuera Rivers, approximately 160 miles (260 km) from the mouth of the Trombetas. This is also the site proposed for a dam.

The lower Trombetas region has been heavily colonized for cattle ranching. Its floodplains have been extensively deforested. *Quilombos*, or settlements that African slaves who escaped built in nineteenth century, exist in the region. The lower Trombetas River is extensively fished to supply the Oriximiná and Santarém markets.

Bauxite is the most commercially valuable resource in the Trombetas Basin. It is mined near Porto Trombetas, a rapidly growing city with plane service to Manaus and Belém. No roads, however, connect Porto Trombetas with other cities. A 12-mile-long (20 km) conveyor belt carries bauxite to a riverside dock, where it is loaded onto barges and ships and transported to the Barcarena plant near Belém for processing. The Norte Mining Company, whose partners include Reynolds and Alcoa, has replanted mined sites with a variety of native tree species. There have been no signs of any major river pollution near Porto Trombetas. Developing the Porto Trombetas area, however, has led to deforestation for cattle ranching.

Most of the Trombetas Basin is still isolated, and no major roads cross it. Cataracts prevent boat travel deep into its interior. Large parts of the basin are designated as indigenous areas. The Trombetas Biological Reserve in the lower course includes a large lake (Lago Erepecuru) and a 90-mile-long (150 km) left-bank stretch of the Trombetas that has important turtle nesting beaches. Opposite this stretch, on the right bank, is Saracá-Taguera National Forest. Porto Trombetas is at the northern boundary of the forest.

THE UPPER BRANCO

◀ **RICE ON THE BRANCO FLOODPLAIN**
The floodplains of the upper Branco are being converted for agriculture, with rice being the most important crop. The remaining clump of trees shown in this photograph is representative of the type of vegetation that was present before deforestation.

◀ **AGRICULTURAL COLONIZATION**
Agricultural colonization in Roraima has reached the hills of the Guiana Shield in the upper Branco Valley. The Branco's tributaries that are muddy drain through lowland areas of thick alluvial sediments. These soils have recently attracted farmers from southern Brazil and other areas outside of the Amazon Basin.

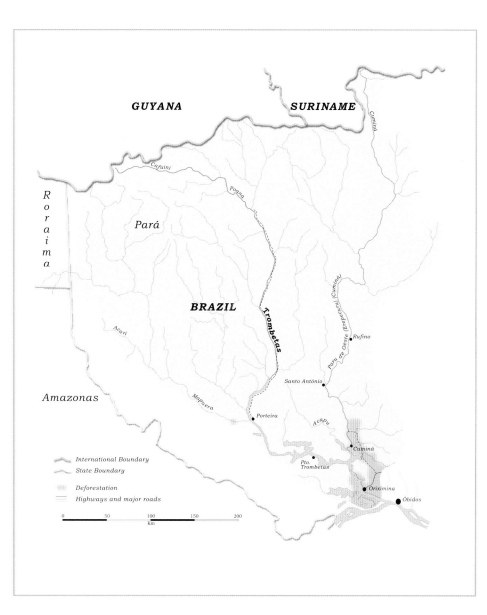

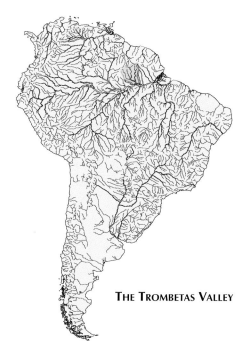

THE TROMBETAS VALLEY

The Trombetas Valley drains approximately 51,700 square miles (134,000 km²) or slightly less than 2 percent of the Amazon Basin. The Valley is almost entirely in the state of Pará. The 470-mile-long (760 km) clearwater river arises on the Guiana Shield in the Serra Acaraí and the Serra de Tumucumaque near the Guyana-Suriname border with Brazil. Bauxite mining, followed by gold and diamond mining are important to the economy of the area.

THE TROMBETAS VALLEY

TROMBETAS FLOODPLAIN LAKE

The lower Trombetas has a relatively large floodplain studded with numerous lakes. Colonization in this region has been extensive, and most of the floodplain forest has been extensively modified. At the lake site shown here, the floodplain forest is still relatively natural.

TROMBETAS

▲ THE UPPER TROMBETAS

The middle and upper Trombetas flows over the exposed Guiana Shield and is studded with cataracts and rocky outcroppings. An intense dry season in this region reduces average river depth to less than 3 ft (1 m).

Federal Conservation Unit

Indigenous land

GUYANA   SURINAME

Meha

Poana

Tumucumaque

Cuminá

Marapí

R o r a i m a

Pará   **BRAZIL**

Trombetas/Mapuera

Acari

Trombetas

Paru de Oeste (Erepecuru) (Cuminá)

Urucuriana

Zo'é

Rufino •

Nhamundá/Mapuera

Mapuera

Amazonas

Porteira • **Rebio do Rio Trombetas**

Pto. Trombetas •   Cuminá •

Saracataguera

International Boundary

State Boundary

Almeida •   Oriximiná •

Obidos •

0   50   100

Km

Amazonas

▲ TROMBETAS AT CACHOEIRA PORTEIRA

There have been proposals to build a dam at the Cachoeira Porteira rapids on the lower Trombetas. In 2002, however, there are no active plans to build the dam.

◄ CONSERVATION UNITS AND INDIGENOUS AREAS OF THE TROMBETAS VALLEY

Indigenous areas encompass about one-quarter of the Trombetas Basin. Headwater areas are difficult to reach because of cataracts, and there are no major roads across the Trombetas Basin. The only sizable designated protected areas are in the lower part of the Trombetas Valley. The Trombetas Biological Reserve is known for its turtle nesting beaches.

CHAPTER FOURTEEN

CONCLUSION
Everyone Lives Downstream

Rivers are ecological reflections of the lands they drain and, in recent history, of the activities of the human populations that live along them. Amazonian rivers have probably always been viewed on a relatively small scale. Indigenous peoples had neither a need nor methodology to understand the ecology of a large river over its entire length because their functional worlds revolved around relatively small areas.

Because of their huge basins and frequent transnational geography, Amazonian rivers are still usually viewed locally when their management is being planned. Yet the rapid changes now taking place in upland and lowland Amazonian environments make it imperative that all impacts are conceptualized and understood for their possible far-reaching consequences downstream and upstream.

Fortunately the Amazon is very large, and there is time to avoid many of the mistakes made in North America and Europe, where historically, river-basin management was ignored. Some Amazonian river valleys, such as the Tocantins of Brazil, will probably largely become human artifacts within

the next few decades. Others, such as the Negro Valley, offer more hope for long-term conservation planning because human settlement is relatively sparse. Most of the large river valleys of the Amazon will increasingly become a mixture of natural and human-modified landscapes. Finding the right balance between these two will largely determine the extent to which biodiversity in the valleys is preserved. It is naïve to believe that pristine river valleys will survive the onslaught of economic development.

Amazonian rivers thus far have escaped major industrial pollution, although real threats are present. Oil wells and pipelines in Colombia, Ecuador, and Peru, for example, have been vulnerable to earthquakes or terrorists. Any major oil spill could have devastating impacts downstream on rivers and their floodplains. Oil tankers and barges also present threats. To date the numerous oil spills from pipelines, tankers, and barges have been contained. Urbanization, gold mining, floodplain agriculture, and greatly increased boat traffic have resulted in river pollution. The Amazon River, however, appears to have escaped serious ecological

◀ **RIVER AND RAINFOREST AS ONE**
Flooded forest where the Amazon and Tapajós meet.

consequences because its huge volumes of water and sediments dilute contaminants.

Adequate surveys of urban pollutants in the rivers, however, have not been conducted: it is not known what is being dumped into the rivers. Amazonian antipollution policy is just beginning to take shape and is in a phase that might be called "wait and see." Near the mouth of the Amazon River, for example, large quantities of plastics and other human refuse are beginning to accumulate. One can assume that most of this refuse becomes buried in offshore sediments.

Mercury used in gold mining and excavated sediments continue to contaminate some rivers, such as the Beni in Peru and the Madre de Dios in Bolivia. Currently upland and floodplain deforestation pose the primary threats to Amazonian rivers. Crop farmers and livestock ranchers are deforesting headwater valleys in the Andean foothills and areas in the Brazilian and Guiana uplands. These activities are impacting, or will impact in the near future, hydrologic cycles. Floodplains are increasingly being used for large-scale agriculture, resulting in the loss of flooded forests, floating meadows, and the rich biodiversity associated with them. Commercial fishing and logging have now expanded into most of the Amazon Basin. An extensive road network, which will continue to grow and link Amazonian countries, will spur the growth of mining, agriculture, commercial fishing, and other economic activities.

Humans everywhere have settled near rivers and probably have done so since the emergence of *Homo sapiens*.

When the Europeans invaded the Amazon in the sixteenth century, the indigenous population lived mostly along the rivers. Today most of the Amazon's cities and towns are at the edges of large rivers; thus most people are located within a few kilometers of the Amazon River or one of its tributaries. Approximately 15 million people now live along Amazonian rivers. The population density in the Amazon has reached the point that human impacts are no longer merely local. In short, people are now downstream of one another throughout the entire Amazon Basin.

The Treaty of Tordesillas in 1494 divided ownership of territory in the New World between Spain and Portugal. Portugal eventually pushed the boundary westward, which put most of the Amazon Basin within the area that became Brazil. Unwittingly, as it were, Brazil—the largest country on the continent—would end up largely downstream of the Spanish-speaking countries to the west.

Until recently in human history, Brazil being downstream from its western neighbors meant very little ecologically because human impacts in the western Amazon Basin were relatively minor compared with the large-scale environmental changes of the past few decades. Now, however, environmental modifications, such as deforestation in headwater areas and river pollution from gold mining in Bolivia, Peru, Ecuador, and Colombia, are threatening ecosystems in the Amazon Basin in Brazil. Given the size of the Amazon River and its large Andean tributaries, Brazil is undoubtedly the most downstream country in the world.

Other than the Andes, the major

headwater regions of the Amazon Basin are the Brazilian and Guiana Shields, of which more than 99 percent are contained in Brazil. Of the three main headwater regions, the Brazilian Shield has been the most heavily modified by humans. More than one-half of the Tocantins Valley, for example, has been significantly modified by upland deforestation. The Tocantins River will soon have three large dams. Will what happened in the Tocantins Valley also take place in other large river valleys in the Amazon? If the answer is yes, to what extent will biodiversity be destroyed on large, regional scales?

The Brazilian government has suggested that the "magic" amount of rainforest that should not be developed is only 10 percent. This suggestion is not convincing to most scientists who study the region's biodiversity. We also believe that river basins should not be ignored in the debate on how much of the rainforest should be protected.

Conservation planners have yet to integrate Amazonian rivers and rainforests because most approaches target localized areas. Commercial fishing in the Amazon Basin demonstrates the need for regional rather than local planning, because the most lucrative commercial fish species migrate extensively. Migratory species depend on the maintenance of large areas, including floodplains and upland forests; they provide us with a real measure of the ecological unity of the Amazon River and its large tributaries.

Although Amazonian countries are separated from one another by political boundaries, the fish that cross these boundaries unite the countries ecologically. Ironically some of the most important food fishes in the Amazon Basin spawn in the Andean foothills, but their nurseries are primarily in Brazil. Andean countries need to be concerned about the overexploitation of these migratory fish in Brazilian waters. Likewise, Brazil needs to be concerned about the impacts on migratory fish from the destruction of their spawning habitats in the Andean foothills in Colombia, Ecuador, Peru, and Bolivia.

River-basin management makes sense ecologically, and, in many cases, economically. North American and European countries belatedly learned this after allowing pollution, headwater deforestation, floodplain modification, and impoundments to degrade most of their rivers. It is unrealistic to believe that any Amazonian country, or any country in the world, will entertain serious thoughts of protecting the entire watershed of a large river. Human activities will necessarily modify uplands, rivers, and wetlands and, in the case of the Amazon Basin, have been doing so for at least several thousand years.

The wet savannas of the Llanos de Mojos region of eastern Bolivia—one of the largest wetlands in the Amazon Basin—were extensively modified before the European Conquest. The wet savannas of Marajó Island, located near the mouth of the Amazon River, were also heavily modified by indigenous peoples, especially by the use of fire. Nevertheless, there is no credible evidence that the upper watersheds or the floodplains of large rivers that are dominated naturally by rainforest were as heavily modified at any one time in history as they are today. Scientists

claim that 10–15 percent of the Amazon Basin is currently deforested, the largest area ever deforested in the past 10,000 years. Indigenous groups have undoubtedly modified floodplains along the Amazon River, but not to the extent of what is occurring today between the Negro and Xingu Rivers, where nearly all of the natural forest has been destroyed or extensively disturbed.

The Amazonian-biodiversity debate has attracted worldwide attention. The media has familiarized the public relatively well with Amazonian rainforests and their importance as storehouses of unparalleled biodiversity. Professional conservation organizations have used various plant and animal (usually vertebrate) groups to define areas of the rainforest that are rich in biodiversity and thus in need of urgent protection. Amazonian countries, however, have seldom used biodiversity to define protected areas. Fortunately, rainforests, which are rich in biodiversity to begin with, grow in most Amazonian parks and reserves.

A promising outgrowth of the biodiversity approach has been the conservation-corridor concept. The concept calls for efforts to link already protected areas by officially protecting the areas that separate them, especially when they are relatively close to each other. By linking protected areas together, a conservation corridor is created.

Although several conservation corridors have been proposed, only two seem to have any chance of becoming established. The proposed *Southwestern Amazon Corridor* would include Manu National Park, the Los Amigos Concession and the Tambopata-Candamo Reserved Zone in Peru and Madidi

National Park and Isiboro-Secure National Park in Bolivia. If all of these conservation units become fully functional, then an Andean foothill and pre-Andean rainforest area approximately the size of France would be largely protected. The Southwestern Amazon Corridor would help benefit aquatic species by protecting the headwaters of the Amazon River's largest tributary, the Madeira.

The *Central Amazon Corridor,* encompassing 8,700 square miles (22,500 km²), links the Amazon (Solimões) and Negro Rivers. On the Amazon River side, the corridor includes the Mamirauá Sustainable Development Reserve and the adjoining Amanã Sustainable Development Reserve. On the Negro River side, the corridor includes Jaú National Park, which encompasses the Jaú Basin. Jaú is the largest of Brazil's national parks in the Amazon. The Central Amazon Corridor would protect the single largest floodplain area in the Brazilian Amazon. It would also protect a blackwater tributary of the Negro.

The Mamirauá Sustainable Development Reserve is an important fish reproduction and nurseries region in the western Amazon. Mamirauá, however, is located in a vulnerable geographical position because it could be impacted by degradation upstream in the upper Amazon River in Peru, Ecuador, and Colombia or in the Caquetá-Japurá River in Colombia and Brazil. Successfully protecting Mamirauá requires dealing with potential impacts coming from upstream of the reserve.

Another innovative approach has been to identify biodiversity hotspots and concentrate scientific and conservation resources in these areas. Hotspots are considered areas with high levels of biodiversity that potentially face immediate threats from human activities. Within the Amazon Basin, parts of the tropical Andes and the Brazilian scrub-savanna region known as the *cerrado* have been defined as hotspots. The cerrado is found mostly within the upper sections of the Tocantins, Xingu, and Tapajós Valleys. Brazil's rapidly expanding agricultural frontier is extensively modifying the cerrado.

The tropical Andes are a hotspot because the significant biodiversity in the montane forests there is threatened by recent colonization by Andean peoples moving to lower elevations. Deforestation of eastern Andean slopes is increasing in all of the Andean countries.

Rivers have not been considered for hotspot designation. Within the Amazon Basin, however, they need to be considered. For example, the tropical Andes provide important spawning habitats for migratory fish and watershed functions for an even larger number of fish species and other aquatic life found farther downstream. Similar to their terrestrial counterparts, the aquatic animals of the Brazilian cerrado are among the most highly threatened in the Amazon Basin. The hotspot approach would be strengthened in this area if it included cerrado watersheds for the protection of aquatic organisms, including migratory fishes. When government agencies and conservation organizations devise protection strategies that separate rivers and uplands, the importance of watershed manage-

ment to the well-being of both terrestrial and aquatic ecosystems is overlooked.

Social scientists working on conservation issues in the Amazon Basin have been heavily influenced by an approach that is generally referred to as "community management." Community management has been used throughout the world for various social programs in both urban and rural settings. In the Amazon Basin, community management usually operates under the basic premise that people who have inhabited an area for a few generations, even if they are not indigenous to the area, should have rights to local resources. People empowered with these rights, according to the philosophy of community management, should develop sustainable economies. The logic is that once empowered, local communities will protect the environment because it will be in their economic interests to do so. Community management in the Amazon Basin is being used in national- or state-protected areas, indigenous lands, and in areas outside parks and reserves where people with informal land have claimed usufruct rights.

All of the protected areas in the Amazon Basin have people living within them, and few government or conservation groups now believe, as most did several decades ago, that they should or could be removed. The two largest floodplain areas where community management has been implemented are the Pacaya-Samiria National Reserve in Peru and the Mamirauá Sustainable Development Reserve in Brazil. The peripheries of both reserves are well populated

and scattered villages exist within their limits.

Managers at the reserves have not been able to control floodplain logging. Most of Pacaya-Samiria has been logged, and few harvestable trees remain. Mamirauá is still being logged and will probably continue to be exploited until harvestable trees of first-class timber species are gone.

Community management of fisheries is being experimented with in both Pacaya-Samiria and Mamirauá. Commercial fisheries have been spotlighted as the best prospect for the long-term management of a sustainable resource inside a protected floodplain area, although additional economic programs, such as ecotourism, are needed to discourage uncontrolled logging and overexploitation of game and fish. As mentioned previously, however, most commercial fishermen in the Amazon target migratory species, which suggests that local management alone, will not be sufficient to conserve this resource.

Community management in floodplain or wetland areas that are not in national parks, reserves, or other areas with protection status in the Amazon Basin has been spearheaded by academics, especially cultural anthropologists and cultural geographers. They have taken on the role of community managers in much the fashion that evangelical Christians organize small communities and proselytize them. Community management in the Amazon, in fact, dates to the seventeenth century, when Jesuits organized disrupted Indian groups into communities to promote Catholicism and encourage economic development.

Currently, whereas Catholics and evangelicals focus on spiritual matters and almost any kind of economic development, cultural anthropologists, cultural geograhers, and other academics now emphasize local empowerment and sustainable development. Community-management projects appeal to various conservation organizations, foundations, and foreign-government agencies because the projects are usually inexpensive to carry out. The impacts academic community managers will have is unclear, and in the end they must compete with Catholic and evangelical community organizers, who are usually better organized and financed in the long run.

The most effective community-management programs outside of parks or reserves will probably be in indigenous areas, where language and culture unite local groups in areas that have been inhabited for generations. Many of these indigenous groups live in headwaters areas. Where they live outside of parks or reserves, however, there appears to be a trend toward adopting commercial logging and mining, once access to national economies has been established. This trend will probably continue because South American governments have never been able to prevent commercial and religious contact with indigenous peoples.

Successful conservation in the Amazon will not unfold overnight. Political and religious aspirations to improve social conditions must be accompanied by realistic insights on ecosystem functions, biodiversity, and inevitable cultural changes. Perhaps the main problem that governments, developers, academics, and local groups face when attempting to understand conservation needs is that the mass of information that has become available in the past three decades is seldom framed in ecological reality. In this book we have attempted to frame the Amazon Basin as an ecological whole. It is our hope that this approach allows the Amazon's valleys, rivers, and rainforests to be more easily visualized as a functioning whole.

El Dorado, or the gilded one, was the legendary treasure sought by early South American explorers. Ironically the greatest freshwater migratory fish in the world is also called dorado. This incredible species reminds us of the immensity of the Amazonian ecological theater. Amazonian life evolved in accordance with the scale of river basins. May the dorado become the ecological treasure whose brilliance illuminates the need to conserve ecosystem functions, from the Atlantic to the Andes via the great valleys of the Amazon.

▲ **FORESTS OF THE WATER.**
The flooded forest and water lilies shown here illustrate the beauty and complexity of aquatic habitats in the world's greatest river system.

BIBLIOGRAPHY

Adis, J. 1984. Seasonal igapó-forests of central Amazonian blackwater rivers and their terrestrial arthropod fauna. In H. Sioli (ed.), *The Amazon: Limnology and Landscape Ecology of a Mighty River and Its Basin,* pp. 245–268. Dr. W. Junk, Dordrecht, The Netherlands.

———. 2000. Terrestrial arthropods in soils from inundation forests and deforested floodplains of white water rivers in central Amazonia. In W. J. Junk, J. J. Ohly, M. T. F. Piedade, and M. G. M. Soares (eds.), *The Central Amazon Floodplain: Actual Use and Options for a Sustainable Management,* pp. 463–476. Backhuys, Leiden, The Netherlands.

Adis, J., and M. O. A. Ribeiro. 1989. Impact of deforestation on soil invertebrates from central Amazonian inundation forests and their survival strategies to long-term flooding. *Water Quality Bulletin* 14:88–98 + 140.

Albernaz, A. L. K. M., and J. M. Ayres. 1999. Selective logging along the middle Solimões River. In C. Padoch, J. M. Ayres, M. Pinedo-Vasquez, and A. Henderson (eds.), *Advances in Economic Botany,* Vol. 13, pp. 135–151. New York Botanical Garden Press, New York.

Alsdorf, D. E., J. M. Melack, T. Dunne, L. A. K. Mertes, L. L. Hess, and L. C. Smith. 2000. Interferometric radar measurements of water level changes on the Amazon flood plain. *Nature* 404:174–177.

Anderson, A. B. 1990. *Alternatives to Deforestation: Steps Toward Sustainable Use of the Amazon Rainforest.* Columbia University Press, New York.

———. 1990. Extraction and forest management by rural inhabitants in the Amazon estuary. In A. Anderson (ed.), *Alternatives to Deforestation: Steps Toward Sustainable Use of the Amazon Rainforest,* pp. 3–23. Columbia University Press, New York.

Anderson, A. B., and M. A. G. Jardim. 1989. Costs and benefits of floodplain forest management by rural inhabitants in the Amazon estuary: a case study of açaí palm production. *Fragile Lands in Latin America: The Search for Sustainable Uses,* pp. 114–132. Westview Press, Boulder, Colorado.

Anderson, A. B., A. Gely, and J. Strudwick. 1985. Um sistema agroflorestal na várzea do estuário Amazônico (Ilha das Onças, Município de Barcarena, Estado do Pará). *Acta Amazônica* 15:195–224.

Anderson, A. B., P. Magee, A. Gély, and M. A. G. Jardim. 1995. Forest management patterns in the floodplain of the Amazon estuary. *Conservation Biology* 9:47–61.

Anderson, A. B., I. Mousasticoshvily, and D. S. Macedo. 1999. Logging of *Virola surinamensis* in the Amazonian floodplain: impacts and alternatives. In C. Padoch, J. M. Ayres, M. Pinedo-Vasquez, and A. Henderson (eds.), *Advances in Economic Botany,* Vol. 13, pp. 119–133. New York Botanical Garden Press, New York.

Anderson, S. D., F. L. T. Marques, and M. F. M. Nogueira. 1999. The usefulness of traditional technology for rural development: the case of tidal energy near the mouth of the Amazon. In C. Padoch, J. M. Ayres, M. Pinedo-Vasquez, and A. Henderson (eds.), *Advances in Economic Botany,* Vol. 13, pp. 329–344. New York Botanical Garden Press, New York.

Araujo-Lima, C. A. R. M., and M. Goulding. 1997. *So Fruitful a Fish: Ecology, Conservation, and Aquaculture of the Amazon's Tambaqui.* Columbia University Press, New York.

Araujo-Lima, C. A. R. M., L. P. S. Portugal, and E. J. G. Ferreira. 1986. Fish-macrophyte relationship in the Anavilhanas Archipelago, a black water system in the central Amazon. *Journal of Fish Biology* 29:1–12.

Araujo-Lima, C. A. R. M., M. Goulding, B. Forsberg, R. Victoria, and L. Martinelli. 1998. The economic value of the Amazonian flooded forest from a fisheries perspective. *Verhandlungen der Internationalen Vereiningung für Theoretische und Angewandte Limnologie* 26:2177–2179.

Ayres, D. L. 1994. A implantação de uma unidade de conservação em área de várzea: a experiência de Mamirauá. In M. A. D'Inção and I. M. Silveira (eds.), *Amazônia e a Crise da Modernação,* pp. 403–412. Museu Paraense Emilio Goeldi, Belém, Brazil.

Ayres, J. M. 1986. Uakaries and Amazonian Flooded Forest. Ph.D. Thesis. Cambridge University, Cambridge, England.

———. 1993. *As Matas de Várzea do Mamirauá.* Sociedade Civil Mamirauá, Brasília, Brazil.

Ayres, J. M., A. R. Alves, H. L. Queiroz, M. Marmontel, E. Moura, D. M. Lima, A. Azevedo, M. Reis, P. Santos, R. Silveira, and D. Masterson. 1999. Mamirauá: the conservation of biodiversity in an Amazonian flooded forest. In C. Padoch, J. M. Ayres, M. Pinedo-Vasquez, and A. Henderson (eds.), *Advances in Economic Botany,* Vol. 13, pp. 203–216. New York Botanical Garden Press, New York.

Barbo, R. I., E. J. G. Ferreira, and E. G. Castellón. 1997. *Homem, Ambiente e Ecologia no Estado de Roraima.* Instituto Nacional de Pesquisas da Amazônia, Manaus, Brazil.

Barros, A. C., C. Uhl. 1999. The economic and social significance of logging operations on the floodplains of the Amazon estuary and prospects for ecological sustainability. In C. Padoch, J. M. Ayres, M. Pinedo-Vasquez, and A. Henderson (eds.), *Advances in Economic Botany,* Vol. 13, pp. 153–168. New York Botanical Garden Press, New York.

Barthem, R. B. 1985. Ocorrência, distribuição e biologia dos peixes da Baía de Marajó, estuário Amazônico. *Boletim do Museu Paraense Emilio Goeldi, Zoologia* 2:49–69.

———. 1997. *Os Bagres Balizadores: Ecologia, Migração e Conservação de Peixes Amazônicos.* Sociedade Civil Mamirauá/CNPq, Tefé, Brazil.

———. 1999. Várzea fisheries in the middle Rio Solimões. In C. Padoch, J. M. Ayres, M. Pinedo-Vasquez, and A. Henderson (eds.), *Advances in Economic Botany,* Vol. 13, pp. 7–28. New York Botanical Garden Press, New York.

Barthem, R., and M. Goulding. 1997. *The Catfish Connection.* Columbia University Press, New York.

Barthem, R. B., M. Ribeiro, and M. Petrere. 1991. Life strategies of some long-distance migratory catfish in relation to hydroelectric dams in the Amazon basin. *Biological Conservation* 55:339–345.

Barthem, R. B., H. Guerra, and M. Valderrama. 1995. *Diagnóstico de Los Recursos Hidrobiológicos de la Amazonia.* Tratado de Cooperación Amazonica, Lima, Peru.

Bates, H. W. 1863. *The Naturalist on the River Amazon: A Record of Adventures, Habits of Animals, Sketches of Brazilian and Indian Life, and Aspects of Nature Under the Equator, During Eleven Years of Travel.* J. Murray, London.

Batista, V. S., C. E. C. Freitas, A. J. I. Silva, and D. Freire-Brasil. 2000. The fishing activity of the river people in the floodplain of the central Amazon. In W. J. Junk, J. J. Ohly, M. T. F. Piedade, and M. G. M. Soares (eds.), *The Central Amazon Floodplain: Actual Use and Options for a Sustainable Management,* pp. 417–432. Backhuys, Leiden, The Netherlands.

Bayley, P. B. 1989. Aquatic environments in the Amazon basin, with an analysis of carbon sources, fish production, and yield. *Canadian Special Publications in Fisheries and Aquatic Science* 106:399–408.

Bayley, P. B., and M. Petrere. 1989. Amazon fisheries: assessment methods, current status and management options, *Proceedings of the International Large River Symposium. Canadian Special Publications, Fisheries and Aquatic Science,* Vol. 106, pp. 385–398.

Bayley, P. B., and R. E. Sparks. 1989. The flood pulse concept in river-floodplain systems. *Fish and Aquatic Sciences* 106:110–127.

Bernoux, M., P. M. A. Graça, C. C. Cerri, P. M. Fearnside, B. J. Feigl, and M. C. Piccolo. 2001. Carbon storage in biomass and soils. In M. E. McClain, R. L. Victoria, and J. E. Richey (eds.), *The Biogeochemistry of the Amazon Basin,* pp. 165–184. Oxford University Press, New York.

Bigarella, J. J., and A. M. M. Ferreira. 1985. Amazonian geology and the Pleistocene and the Cenozoic environments and paleoclimates. In G. T. Prance and T. E. Lovejoy (eds.), *Key Environments: Amazonia,* pp. 49–71. Peragmon Press, Oxford, England.

Bodmer, R. E., P. E. Puertas, J. E. Garcia, D. R. Dias, and C. Reyes. 1999. Game animals, palms and people of the flooded forests: management considerations for the Pacaya-Samiria National Reserve, Peru. In C. Padoch, J. M. Ayres, M. Pinedo-Vasquez, and A. Henderson (eds.), *Advances in Economic Botany,* Vol. 13, pp. 217–231. New York Botanical Garden Press, New York.

Browder, J. O., and B. J. Godfrey. 1997. *Rainforest Cities: Urbanization, Development, and Globalization of the Brazilian Amazon.* Columbia University Press, New York.

Brown, F., K. Kainer, and E. Amaral. 2001. Extractive reserves and participatory research as factors in the biogeochemistry of the Amazon Basin. In M. E. McClain, R. L. Victoria, and J. E. Richey (eds.), *The Biogeochemistry of the Amazon Basin,* pp. 122–138. Oxford University Press, New York.

Bueno, C. R., K. Yuyama, H. Noda, D. F. Silva Filho, F. M. Machado, and W. O. Paiva. 2000. Non-conventional crops: a feasible alternative for Amazonian floodplains. In W. J. Junk, J. J. Ohly, M. T. F. Piedade, and M. G. M. Soares (eds.), *The Central Amazon Floodplain: Actual Use and Options for a Sustainable Management,* pp. 171–190. Backhuys, Leiden, The Netherlands.

Campbell, D. G. 1992. A comparison of the phytosociology and dynamics of three floodplain (várzea) forests of known ages, rio Juruá, western Brazilian Amazon. *Botanical Journal of the Linnaean Society* 108:213–237.

Carvalho, J. L., and B. Merona. 1986. Estudos sobre dois peixes migratórios do baixo Tocantins, antes do fechamento da barragem de Tucuruí. *Amazoniana* 9:595–607.

Chao, N. L., P. Petry, G. Prang, L. Sonnenschien, and M. Tlusty. 2001. *Conservation and Management of Ornamental Fish Resources of the Rio Negro Basin, Amazonia, Brazil (Projeto Piaba).* Editora da Universidade do Amazonas, Manaus, Brazil.

Chernela, J. M. 1993. *The Wanano Indians of the Brazilian Amazon.* University of Texas Press, Austin, Texas.

Chibnik, M. 1994. *Risky Rivers: The Economics and Politics of Floodplain Farming in Amazonia.* University of Arizona Press, Tucson, Arizona.

Clark, K., and C. Uhl. 1987. Farming, fishing, and fire in the history of the upper Rio Negro region of Venezuela. *Human Ecology* 15:1–26.

Cleary, D. 1990. *Anatomy of the Amazon Gold Rush*. Macmillan, New York.

Coomes, O. T. 1992. Blackwater rivers, adaptation, and environmental heterogeneity in Amazonia. *American Anthropologist* 94:698–701.

———. 1998. Traditional peasant agriculture along a blackwater river of the Peruvian Amazon. *Revista Geografica* 124:33–54.

Cordoba, E. A. 2000. Bagres de la Amazonia Colombiana: *Un Recurso sin Fronteras.* Instituto Amazonico de Investigaciones Científicas, Ministerio del Medio Ambiente, Bogotá, Colombia.

Crampton, W. G. R. 1999. The impact of the ornamental fish trade on the discus *Symphysodon aequifasciatus*: a case study from the floodplain forests of Estacão Ecológica Mamirauá. In C. Padoch, J. M. Ayres, M. Pinedo-Vasquez, and A. Henderson (eds.), *Advances in Economic Botany,* Vol. 13, pp. 29–44. New York Botanical Garden Press, New York.

Cuevas, E. 2001. Soil versus biological controls on nutrient cyclying in terra firma forests. In M. E. McClain, R. L. Victoria, and J. E. Richey (eds.), *The Biogeochemistry of the Amazon Basin,* pp. 53–67. Oxford University Press, New York.

Daly, D. C., and G. T. Prance. 1989. *Brazilian Amazon*. New York Botanical Garden Press, New York.

DeMaster, D. J., and R. C. Aller. 2001. Biogeochemical processes on the Amazon shelf: changes in dissolved and particulate fluxes during river/ocean mixing. In M. E. McClain, R. L. Victoria, and J. E. Richey (eds.), *The Biogeochemistry of the Amazon Basin,* pp. 328–357. Oxford University Press, New York.

Denevan, W. M. 1966. *The Aboriginal Cultural Geography of the Llanos de Mojos of Bolivia*. University of California Press, Berkeley, California.

———. 2001. *Cultivated Landscapes of Native Amazonia and the Andes*. Oxford University Press, New York.

Devol, A. H., and J. I. Hedges. 2001. Organic matter and nutrients in the mainstem Amazon river. In M. E. McClain, R. L. Victoria, and J. E. Richey (eds.), *The Biogeochemistry of the Amazon Basin,* pp. 275–306. Oxford University Press, New York.

Dias-Filho, M. B., E. A. Davidson, and C. J. R. D. Carvalho. 2001. Linking biogeochemical cycles to cattle pasture management and sustainability in the Amazon Basin. In M. E. McClain, R. L. Victoria, and J. E. Richey (eds.), *The Biogeochemistry of the Amazon Basin,* pp. 84–105. Oxford University Press, New York.

Dickinson, R. E. 1987. The Geophysiology of Amazonia. Vegetation and Climate Interactions. John Wiley & Sons, New York.

Dickinson, R. E., and H. Virji. 1987. Climate change in the humid tropics, especially Amazonia, over the last twenty thousand years. In R. E. Dickinson (ed.), *The Geophysiology of Amazonia: Vegetation and Climate Interactions,* pp. 91–106. John Wiley & Sons, New York.

Durand, E., and D. McCaffrey. 1999. The Pacaya-Samiria project: enhancing conservation and improving livelihoods in Amazonian Peru. In C. Padoch, J. M. Ayres, M. Pinedo-Vasquez, and A. Henderson (eds.), *Advances in Economic Botany,* Vol. 13, pp. 233–246. New York Botanical Garden Press, New York.

Eden, M. J. 1994. Environment, politics and Amazonian deforestation. *Land Use Policy* 11:55–66.

Etter, A. 1992. Caracterización ecológica general de la intervención humana en la Amazonía colombiana. In G. Andrade, A. Hurtado, and R. Tozza (eds.), *Amazonia Colombiana*. Comisión Nacional de Investigaciónes Amazonicas, Bogotá, Colombia.

Fearnside, P. M. 1990. Balbina: lições trágicas da Amazônia. *Ciência Hoje* 11:34–43.

Ferreira, E. J. G., and J. A. S. Zuanon. 1998. *Peixes Comerciais do Médio Amazonas: Regiao de Santarém, Pará.* Ministerio do Meio Ambiente, Edicoes IBAMA, Brasilia, Brazil.

Ferreira, E. J. G., G. M. Santos, E. L. M. Leão, and L. A. Oliveira. 1993. *Bases Científicas para Estratégicas de Preservação e Desenvolvimento da Amazônia,* Vol. 2. Instituto Nacional de Pesquisas da Amazônia, Manaus, Brazil.

Fisch, G. 1990. Climatic aspects of the Amazonian tropical forest. *Acta Amazônica* 20:39–48.

Fisch, G., J. A. Marengo, and C. A. Nobre. 1998. Uma Revisão geral sobre o clima da Amazônia. *Acta Amazônica* 28:101–126.

Fittkau, E. J. 1964. Remarks on limnology of central-Amazon rain-forest streams. *Verhandlungen der Internationalen Vereiningung für Theoretische und Angewandte Limnologie* 15:1092–1096.

———. 1970. Limnological conditions in the headwater region of the Xingu River Brasil. *Tropical Ecology* 11:20–25.

Forsberg, B. R., A. H. Devol, J. E. Richey, L. A. Martinelli, R. L. Victoria, and H. Santos. 1988. Factors controlling nutrient concentrations in Amazon floodplain lakes. *Limnology and Oceanography* 33:41–56.

Forsberg, B. R., J. M. Godoy, and R. L. Victoria. 1989. Development and erosion in the Brazilian Amazon: a geochronological case study. *Geojournal* 19:402–405.

Foster, R. B. 1990. Long-term change in forest communities of the rio Manu floodplain. In A. H. Gentry (ed.), *Four Neotropical Rainforests,* pp. 565–572. Yale University Press, New Haven, Connecticut.

Frailey, C. D., E. L. Lavina, A. Rancy, and J. P. d. S. Filho. 1988. A proposed Pleistocene/Holocene lake in the Amazon Basin and its significance to Amazon geology and biogeography. *Acta Amazônica* 18:199–143.

Freire, E. M. S. 1991. *As Várzeas Amazônicas—Características e Possibilidades de Uso.* Embrapa, Belém, Brazil.

Freitas, M. L. D. 1998. *Amazonia: Heaven of a New World.* Editora Campus, Rio de Janeiro.

Furch, K. 1997. Chemistry of várzea and igapó soils and nutrient inventory of their floodplain forests. In W. J. Junk (ed.), *The Central Amazon Floodplain: Ecology of a Pulsing System,* pp. 47–67. Springer, Berlin.

Furch, K., and W. J. Junk. 1997. Physiochemical conditions in floodplains. In W. J. Junk (ed.), *The Central Amazon Floodplain: Ecology of a Pulsing System,* pp. 69–108. Springer, Berlin.

Furtado, L. G. 1987. *Curralistas e Redeiros de Maruda: Pescadores do Litoral do Pará.* Ministério da Ciência e Tecnologia, Belém, Brazil.

———. 1993. *Pescadores do Rio Amazonas: Um Estudo Antropológo da Pesca Ribeirinha Numa Área Amazônica.* Museu Paraense Emílio Goeldi, Belém, Brazil.

Gascon, C., R. Mesquita, N. Higuchi, B. J. Cabarle, G. S. Hartshorn, I. A. Bowles, R. E. Rice, R. A. Mittermeier, and G. A. B. d. Fonseca. 1998. Logging on in the rain forests. *Science* 4:1453.

Gentry, A. H., and J. Lopez-Parodi. 1980. Deforestation and increased flooding of the upper Amazon. *Science* 210:1354–1356.

Gentry, A. H., and J. Terborgh. 1990. Comparison and dynamics of the Cocha Cashu mature floodplain forest. In A. H. Gentry (ed.), *Four Neotropical Rainforests,* pp. 542–564. Yale University Press, New Haven, Connecticut.

Goulding, M. 1980. *The Fishes and the Forest: Explorations in Amazonian Natural History.* University of California Press, Berkeley, California.

———. 1981. *Man and Fisheries on an Amazon Frontier.* Dr. W. Junk, Dordrecht, The Netherlands.

———. 1988. Ecology and management of migratory food fishes of the Amazon Basin. In F. Almeda and C. M. Pringle (eds.), *Tropical Rainforests: Diversity and Conservation*, pp. 71–86. California Academy of Sciences, San Francisco, California.

———. 1989. *Amazon: The Flooded Forest*. The British Broadcasting Company, London.

———. 1994. Amazon rivers and their biodiversity. In S. Monteiro and L. Kaz (eds.), *Amazonia: Flora and Fauna,* pp. 85–94. Edicoes Alumbramento, Rio de Janeiro.

———. 1999. Fish and fisheries: introduction. In C. Padoch, J. M. Ayres, M. Pinedo-Vasquez, and A. Henderson (eds.), *Advances in Economic Botany*, Vol. 13, pp. 1–6. New York Botanical Garden Press, New York.

Goulding, M., M. L. Carvalho, and E. J. G. Ferreira. 1988. *Rio Negro: Rich Life in Poor Water: Amazonian Diversity and Foodchain Ecology as Seen Through Fish Communities*. SPB Academic Publishing bv, The Hague.

Goulding, M., N. J. H. Smith, and D. Mahar. 1996. *Floods of Fortune: Ecology and Economy Along the Amazon*. Columbia Unversity Press, New York.

Grabert, H. 1967. Sobre o desaguamento natural do sistema fluvial do rio Madeira desde a construção do Andes. In H. Lent (ed.) *Atas do Simpósio Sobre a Biota Amazônica,* Vol. 1, pp. 209–214.

Gutjahr, E. 2000. Prospects for arable farming in the floodplains of the central Amazon. In W. J. Junk, J. J. Ohly, M. T. F. Piedade, and M. G. M. Soares (eds.), *The Central Amazon Floodplain: Actual Use and Options for a Sustainable Management,* pp. 141–170. Backhuys, Leiden, The Netherlands.

Hasse, S. 1996. *O Brasil da Soja: Abrindo Fronteiras*, Semeando Cidades. L & PM Editores, Porto Alegre, Brasil.

Hiraoka, M. 1985. Cash cropping, wage labor and urban migration in the Peruvian Amazon. *Studies in Third World Societies* 32:199–242.

———. 1985. Changing floodplain livelihood patterns in the Peruvian Amazon. *Tsukuba Studies in Human Geography* 9:243–275.

———. 1985. Floodplain farming in the Peruvian Amazon. *Geographical Review of Japan* 58:1–23.

———. 1989. Agricultural systems on the floodplains of the Peruvian Amazon. In M. Hiraoka (ed.), *Fragile Lands of Latin America: Strategies for Sustainable Development,* pp. 75–101. Westview Press, Boulder, Colorado.

———. 1992. Caboclo and ribereno resource management in Amazonia: a review. In K. H. Redford and C. Padoch (eds.), *Conservation of Neotropical Forests: Working from Traditional Resource Use,* pp. 134–157. Columbia University Press, New York.

———. 1999. Forest biomass and wood consumption in the lower course of the Amazon: a case study of the Urubueua Island. *Acta Amazônica* 29:79–95.

———. 1999. Mirití (Mauritia flexuosa) palms and their uses and management among the Ribeirinhos of the Amazon estuary. In C. Padoch, J. M. Ayres, M. Pinedo-Vasquez, and A. Henderson (eds.), *Advances in Economic Botany,* Vol. 13, pp. 169–186. New York Botanical Garden Press, New York.

Hoorn, C., J. Guerrero, G. A. Sarmiento, and M. A. Lorente. 1995. Andean tectonics as a cause for changing drainage patterns in Miocene northern South America. *Geology* 23:237–240.

Hoppe, A. 1992. Mining in the Amazonian rainforests. *Nature* 355:593–594.

Hund, M., and J. J. Ohly. 2000. Permanent crop cultivation on central Amazonian floodplains. In W. J. Junk, J. J. Ohly, M. T. F. Piedade, and M. G. M. Soares (eds.), *The Central Amazon Floodplain: Actual Use and Options for a Sustainable Management,* pp. 191–214. Backhuys, Leiden, The Netherlands.

Institut Français de la Recherche Scientifique pour le Développement en Coopération. 1988. *Conditions Ecologiques et Economiques de la Production d'Une Ile de Várzea: L'Ile Du Careiro.* Institut Français de la Recherche Scientifique pour le Développement en Coopération, Paris.

Irion, G., and J. Adis. 1979. Evolução de florestas amazônicas inundadas, de igapó—um exemplo do rio Tarumã-Mirim. *Acta Amazônica* 9:299–303.

Irion, G., J. Adis, and W. J. Junk. 1983. Sedimentological studies of the Ilha de Marchantaria in the Solimões/Amazon river near Manaus. *Amazoniana* 8:1–18.

Irion, G., W. J. Junk, and J. A. S. N. Mello. 1997. The large central Amazonian river floodplains near Manaus: geological, climatological, hydrological, and geomorphological aspects. In W. J. Junk (ed.), *The Central Amazon Floodplain: Ecology of a Pulsing System,* pp. 23–46. Springer, Berlin.

Irmler, U. 1977. Inundation-forest types in the vicinity of Manaus. *Biogeographica* 8:17–29.

Jordon, C. F. 2001. The interface between economics and nutrient cycling in Amazon land development. In M. E. McClain, R. L. Victoria, and J. E. Richey (eds.), *The Biogeochemistry of the Amazon Basin,* pp. 156–164. Oxford University Press, New York.

Junk, W. J. 1982. Amazonian floodplains: their ecology, present and potential use. *Revue d'Hydrobiologie Tropicale* 15:285–301.

———. 1986. Aquatic plants of the Amazon system. In B. R. Davies and K. F. Walker (eds.), *The Ecology of River Systems,* pp. 319–337. Dr. W. Junk, Dordrecht, The Netherlands.

———. 1989. Flood tolerance and tree distribution in central Amazonian floodplains. In L. B. Holm-Nielsen, I. C. Nielsen, and H. Balslev (eds.), *Tropical Forests: Botanical Dynamics, Speciation and Diversity,* pp. 47–64. Academic Press, San Diego, California.

———. 1993. Wetlands of tropical South America. In D. F. Whigham (ed.), *Wetlands of the World,* pp. 679–739. Kluwer, Dordrecht, The Netherlands.

———. 1997. *The Central Amazon Floodplain: Ecology of a Pulsing System.* Springer, Berlin.

———. 1997. General aspects of floodplain ecology with special reference to Amazonian floodplains. In W. J. Junk (ed.), *The Central Amazon Floodplain: Ecology of a Pulsing System,* pp. 3–20. Springer, Berlin.

———. 2000. The central Amazon floodplain: concepts for the sustainable use of its resources. In W. J. Junk, J. J. Ohly, M. T. F. Piedade, and M. G. M. Soares (eds.), *The Central Amazon Floodplain: Actual Use and Options for a Sustainable Management,* pp. 75–94. Backhuys, Leiden, The Netherlands.

Junk, W. J., and C. Howard-Williams. 1984. Ecology of aquatic macrophytes in Amazonia. In H. Sioli (ed.), *The Amazon: Limnology and Landscape Ecology of a Mighty River and Its Basin,* pp. 269–293. Dr. W. Junk, Dordrecht, The Netherlands.

Junk, W. J., and H.-J. Krambeck. 2000. Climate and hydrology. In W. J. Junk, J. J. Ohly, M. T. F. Piedade, and M. G. M. Soares (eds.), *The Central Amazon Floodplain: Actual Use and Options for a Sustainable Management,* pp. 95–108. Backhuys, Leiden, The Netherlands.

Junk, W. J., and J. A. S. N. Mello. 1987. Impactos ecológicos das represas hidrelétricas na bacia Amazônica brasileira. In G. Kohlhepp and A. Schrader (eds.), *Homem e Natureza na Amazônia,* pp. 367–407. Geographisches Institut, Tubingen, Germany.

Junk, W. J., and M. T. F. Piedade. 1997. Plant life in the floodplain with special reference to herbaceous plants. In W. J. Junk (ed.), *The Central Amazon Floodplain: Ecology of a Pulsing System,* pp. 147–185. Springer, Berlin.

Junk, W. J., J. J. Ohly, M. T. F. Piedade, and M. G. M. Soares. 2000. Actual use and options for the sustainable management of the central Amazon floodplain: discussion and conclusions. In W. J. Junk, J. J. Ohly, M. T. F. Piedade, and M. G. M. Soares (eds.), *The Central Amazon Floodplain: Actual Use and Options for a Sustainable Management,* pp. 535–580. Backhuys, Leiden, The Netherlands.

———. 2000. *The Central Amazon Floodplain: Actual Use and Options for a Sustainable Management.* Backhuys, Leiden, The Netherlands.

Kahn, F., and A. Henderson. 1999. An overview of the palms in the várzea in the Amazon region. In C. Padoch, J. M. Ayres, M. Pinedo-Vasquez, and A. Henderson (eds.), *Advances in Economic Botany,* Vol. 13, pp. 187–193. New York Botanical Garden Press, New York.

Kalliola, R., and S. F. Paitán. 1998. *Geoecología y Desarrollo Amazónico: Estudio Integrado en La Zona de Iquitos, Perú.* Turun Yliopiston Julkaisuja, Turku, Finland.

———. 1998. Presentación del estudio. In R. Kalliola and S. F. Paitán (eds.), *Geoecología y Dessarrollo Amazónico: Estudio Integrado en La Zona de Iquitos, Perú,* pp. 11–16. Turun Yliopiston Julkaisuja, Turku, Finland.

Kalliola, R., M. Puhakka, and W. Danjoy. 1993. *Amazonia Peruana: Vegetación Humeda Tropical en El Llano Subandino.* Universidad de Turku, Turku, Finland.

Kalliola, R., P. Jokinen, and E. Tuukki. 1999. Fluvial dynamics and sustainable development in the upper Rio Amazonas, Peru. In C. Padoch, J. M. Ayres, M. Pinedo-Vasquez, and A. Henderson (eds.), *Advances in Economic Botany,* Vol. 13, pp. 271–282. New York Botanical Garden Press, New York.

Kauffman, S., G. P. Arce, and R. M. Pozo. 1998. Suelos aluviales recientes de la zona Iquitos-Nauta. In R. Kalliola and S. F. Paitán (eds.), *Geoecología y Dessarrollo Amazónico: Estudio Integrado en La Zona de Iquitos, Perú,* pp. 231–252. Turun Yliopiston Julkaisuja, Turku, Finland.

Klammer, G. 1984. The relief of extra-andean Amazon basin. In H. Sioli (ed.), *The Amazon: Limnology and Landscape Ecology of a Mighty River and Its Basin,* pp. 47–84. Dr. W. Junk, Dordrecht, The Netherlands.

Lima, C. A. R. M. A., M. T. Piedade, and F. A. R. Barbosa. 1998. Water as a major resource of the Amazon. In M. L. D. Davies de Freitas (ed.), *Amazonia: Heaven of a New World,* pp. 55–70. Editora Campus, Rio de Janeiro.

Lima, D. M. 1999. Equity, sustainable development, and biodiversity preservation: some questions about ecological partnerships in the Brazilian Amazon. In C. Padoch, J. M. Ayres, M. Pinedo-Vasquez, and A. Henderson (eds.), *Advances in Economic Botany,* Vol. 13, pp. 247–263. New York Botanical Garden Press, New York.

Lima, R. M. B., and M. Saragoussi. 2000. Floodplain home gardens on the central Amazon in Brazil. In W. J. Junk, J. J. Ohly, M. T. F. Piedade, and M. G. M. Soares (eds.), *The Central Amazon Floodplain: Actual Use and Options for a Sustainable Management,* pp. 243–268. Backhuys, Leiden, The Netherlands.

Lima, R. R., and M. M. Tourinho. 1994. *Várzeas da Amazônia Brasileira: Principais Características e Possibilidades Agropecuárias.* Faculdade de Ciências Agrárias do Pará, Belém, Brazil.

———. 1994. *Várzeas da Costa Amapaense Principais Características e Possibilidades Agropecuárias.* Faculdade de Ciências Agrárias do Pará, Belém, Brazil.

————. 1995. *Várzeas do Nordeste Paraense e Pré-Amazônia Maranhense: Características e Possibilidades Agropecuárias.* Faculdade de Ciências Agrárias do Pará, Belém, Brazil.

————. 1996. *Várzeas do Rio Pará: Principais Características e Possibilidades Agropecuárias.* Faculdade de Ciências Agrárias do Pará, Belém, Brazil.

Linna, A., G. Irion, S. Kauffman, F. Wesselingh, and R. Kalliola. 1998. Heterogeneidad edáfica de la zona de Iquitos: origen y comprensión de sus propiedades. In R. Kalliola and S. F. Paitán (eds.), *Geoecología y Dessarrollo Amazónico: Estudio Integrado en La Zona de Iquitos, Perú,* pp. 461–480. Turun Yliopiston Julkaisuja, Turku, Finland.

Lisboa, P. L. B. 1997. *Caxiuanã.* Museu Paraense Emílio Goeldi, Belém, Brazil.

Lovejoy, N. R., E. Bermingham, and A. P. Martin. 1998. Marine incursion into South America. *Nature* 396:421–422.

MacQuarrie, K. 2001. *Donde los Andes Encuentran al Amazonas.* Francis O. Patthey & Sons, Barcelona, Spain.

Mallas, J., and N. Benedicto. 1986. Mercury and gold mining in the Brazilian Amazon. *Ambio* 15:248–249.

Mamirauá, S. C. 1996. *Mamirauá Management Plan.* Sociedade Civil Mamirauá, Manaus, Brazil.

Marengo, J. 1992. Interannual variability of surface climate in the Amazon Basin. *International Journal of Climatology* 12:853–863.

————. 1995. Variation and change in South America streamflow. *Climatic Change* 31:99–117.

Marengo, J., J. Tomasella, and C. Uvo. 1998. Long-term streamflow and rainfall fluctuations in tropical South America: Amazônia, Eastern Brazil and Northwest Peru. *Journal of Geophysical Research* 103:1775–1783.

Marengo, J. A. 1998. Climatología de la zona de Iquitos, Peru. In R. Kalliola and S. F. Paitán (eds.), *Geoecología y Dessarrollo Amazónico: Estudio Integrado en La Zona de Iquitos, Perú,* pp. 35–58. Turun Yliopiston Julkaisuja, Turku, Finland.

Marengo, J. A., and C. A. Nobre. 2001. General characteristics and variability of climate in the Amazon Basin and its links to the global climate system. In M. E. McClain, R. L. Victoria, and J. E. Richey (eds.), *The Biogeochemistry of the Amazon Basin,* pp. 17–41. Oxford University Press, New York.

Martinelli, L. A. 1988. Mercury contamination in the Amazon: a gold rush consequence. *Ambio* 17:252–254.

Martinelli, L. A., J. R. Ferreira, and B. R. Forsberg. 1988. Gold rush produces mercury contamination in Amazon. *Cultural Survival Quarterly* 13:32–34.

Martinelli, L. A., R. L. Victoria, and J. E. Richey. 1989. Suspended sediment load in the Amazon basin: an overview. *Geo* 19:381–389.

Maurice-Bourgoin, L., I. Quiroga, J. L. Guyot, and O. Malm. 1999. Mercury pollution in the upper Beni River, Amazonian Basin, Bolivia. *Ambio* 28:302–306.

Maurice-Bourgoin, L., I. Quiroga, J. Chincheros, and P. Courau. 2000. Mercury distribution in waters and fishes of the upper Madeira rivers and mercury exposure in riparian Amazonian populations. *The Science and Total Environment* 260:73–86.

McClain, M. 2001. The relevance of biogeochemistry to Amazon development and conservation. In M. E. McClain, R. L. Victoria, and J. E. Richey (eds.), *The Biogeochemistry of the Amazon Basin,* pp. 3–16. Oxford University Press, New York.

McClain, M., and H. Elsenbeer. 2001. Terrestrial inputs to Amazon streams and internal biogeochemical processing. In M. E. McClain, R. L. Victoria, and J. E. Richey (eds.), *The Biogeochemistry of the Amazon Basin,* pp. 185–208. Oxford University Press, New York.

McClain, M. E., R. L. Victoria, and J. E. Richey. 2001. *The Biogeochemistry of the Amazon Basin*. Oxford University Press, New York.

McGrath, D., F. Castro, E. Câmara, and C. Futemma. 1999. Community management of floodplain lakes and the sustainable development of Amazonian fisheries. In C. Padoch, J. M. Ayres, M. Pinedo-Vasquez, and A. Henderson (eds.), *Advances in Economic Botany,* Vol. 13, pp. 59–82. New York Botanical Garden Press, New York.

McGrath, D. G., F. Castro, C. R. Futemma, B. D. Amaral, and J. A. Calabria. 1993. Manejo comunitário da pesca nos lagos de várzea do Baixo Amazonas. In L. G. Furtado, W. Leitão, and A. F. d. Mello (eds.), *Povos das Águas: Realidade e Perspectivas na Amazônia,* pp. 213–230. Museu Paraense Emílio Goeldi, Belém and Pará, Brazil.

Meade, R. H. 1984. Sediment storage in rivers and estuaries. *Eos—Transactions, American Geophysical Union* 65:216.

———. 1994. Suspended sediments of the modern Amazon and Orinoco rivers. *Quaternary International* 21:29–39.

Meade, R. H., T. Dunne, J. E. Richey, U. M. Santos, and E. Salati. 1985. Storage and remobilization of suspended sediment in the lower Amazon river of Brazil. *Science* 228:488–490.

Meade, R. H., J. M. Rayol, S. C. Conceição, and J. R. G. Natividade. 1991. Backwater effects in the Amazon River basin of Brazil. *Environmental Geology and Water Science* 18:105–114.

Melack, J. M. 1984. Amazon floodplain lakes: shape, fetch, and stratification. *Verhandlungen der Internationalen Vereiningung für Theoretische und Angewandte Limnologie* 22:1278–1282.

Melack, J. M., and B. R. Forsberg. 2001. Biogeochemistry of Amazon floodplain lakes and associated wetlands. In M. E. McClain, R. L. Victoria, and J. E. Richey (eds.), *The Biogeochemistry of the Amazon Basin,* pp. 235–274. Oxford University Press, New York.

Merona, B. 1990. Amazon fisheries: general characteristics based on two case-studies. *Interciência* 15:461–468.

Mertes, L. A. K. 1985. Floodplain Development and Sediment Transport in the Solimões-Amazon River, Brazil. Ph.D. Thesis. University of Washington, Seattle, Washington.

Miller, M. C., M. Kannan, and P. A. Colinvaux. 1984. Limnology and primary productivity of Andean and Amazonian tropical lakes of Ecuador. *Verhandlungen der Internationalen Vereiningung für Theoretische und Angewandte Limnologie* 22:1264–1270.

Molion, L. C. B. 1987. On the dynamic climatology of the Amazon basin and associated rain-producing mechanisms. In R. E. Dickinson (ed.), *The Geophysiology of Amazonia: Vegetation and Climate Interactions,* pp. 391–408. John Wiley & Sons, New York.

———. 1989. The Amazonian forests and climatic stability. *The Ecologist* 19:211–213.

Nelson, B. W. 1994. Natural forest disturbance and change in the Brazilian Amazon. *Remote Sensing Reviews* 10:105–125.

Nepstad, D., R. S. Moutinho, and D. Markewitz. 2001. The recovery of biomass, nutrient stocks and deep-soil functions in secondary forests. In M. E. McClain, R. L. Victoria, and J. E. Richey (eds.), *The Biogeochemistry of the Amazon Basin,* pp. 139–158. Oxford University Press, New York.

Nepstad, D., D. McGrath, A. Alencar, A. C. Barros, G. Carvalho, M. Santilli, and M. C. V. Diaz. 2002. Enhanced frontier governance in Amazonia. *Science* 25:629–631.

Noda, S. N., H. Noda, and H. P. Santos. 2000. Family farming systems in the floodplains of the state of Amazonas. In W. J. Junk, J. J. Ohly, M. T. F. Piedade, and M. G. M. Soares (eds.), *The Central Amazon Floodplain: Actual Use and Options for a Sustainable Management,* pp. 215–242. Backhuys, Leiden, The Netherlands.

Nogueira, F., and W. J. Junk. 2000. Mercury from goldmining in Amazon wetlands: contamination sites, intoxification levels and dispersion pathways. In W. J. Junk, J. J. Ohly, M. T. F. Piedade, and M. G. M. Soares (eds.), *The Central Amazon Floodplain: Actual Use and Options for a Sustainable Management*, pp. 477–504. Backhuys, Leiden, The Netherlands.

Nordin, C. F., and R. H. Meade. 1985. The Amazon and the Orinoco River. In *McGraw-Hill Encyclopedia of Science & Technology,* pp. 385–390. McGraw-Hill, New York.

Nordin, C. F., R. H. Meade, and W. F. Curtis. 1980. Size distribution of Amazon river bed sediment. *Nature* 286:52–53.

Oca, I. M. 1997. *Geografía y Recursos Naturales de Bolivia,* Third Edition. Edobol, La Paz, Bolivia.

Ohly, J. J. 1986. Water-buffalo husbandry in the central Amazon region. *Animal Research and Development* 24:23–40.

———. 2000. Artificial pastures on central Amazonian floodplains. In W. J. Junk, J. J. Ohly, M. T. F. Piedade, and M. G. M. Soares (eds.), *The Central Amazon Floodplain: Actual Use and Options for a Sustainable Management,* pp. 291–312. Backhuys, Leiden, The Netherlands.

———. 2000. Development of central Amazonia in the modern era. In W. J. Junk, J. J. Ohly, M. T. F. Piedade, and M. G. M. Soares (eds.), *The Central Amazon Floodplain: Actual Use and Options for a Sustainable Management,* pp. 27–74. Backhuys, Leiden, The Netherlands.

Ohly, J. J., and M. Hund. 2000. Floodplain animal husbandry in central Amazonia. In W. J. Junk, J. J. Ohly, M. T. F. Piedade, and M. G. M. Soares (eds.), *The Central Amazon Floodplain: Actual Use and Options for a Sustainable Management,* pp. 313–344. Backhuys, Leiden, The Netherlands.

Ohly, J. J., and W. J. Junk. 1999. Multiple use of central Amazon floodplains: combining ecological conditions, requirements for environmental protection, and socioeconomic needs. In C. Padoch, J. M. Ayres, M. Pinedo-Vasquez, and A. Henderson (eds.), *Advances in Economic Botany,* Vol. 13, pp. 283–299. New York Botanical Garden Press, New York.

Padoch, C. 1988. People of the floodplain and forest. In J. S. Denslow and C. Padoch (eds.), *People of the Tropical Rain Forest,* pp. 127–140. University of California Press, Berkeley, California.

Padoch, C., and M. Pinedo-Vasquez. 1999. Farming above the flood in the várzea of Amapá: some preliminary results of the Projeto Várzea. In C. Padoch, J. M. Ayres, M. Pinedo-Vasquez, and A. Henderson (eds.), *Advances in Economic Botany,* Vol. 13, pp. 345–354. New York Botanical Garden Press, New York.

Paitán, S. F. 1998. Agroforestería amazónica: una alternativa a la agricultura migratoria. In R. Kalliola and S. F. Paitán (eds.), *Geoecología y Dessarrollo Amazónico: Estudio Integrado en La Zona de Iquitos, Perú,* pp. 417–442. Turun Yliopiston Julkaisuja, Turku, Finland.

Paitán, S. F., E. G. Romero, and R. Kalliola. 1998. Características generales de la zona de Iquitos. In R. Kalliola and S. F. Paitán (eds.), *Geoecología y Dessarrollo Amazónico: Estudio Integrado en La Zona de Iquitos, Perú,* pp. 17–34. Turun Yliopiston Julkaisuja, Turku, Finland.

Parolin, P. 2000. Growth, productivity and use of trees in white water floodplains. In W. J. Junk, J. J. Ohly, M. T. F. Piedade, and M. G. M. Soares (eds.), *The Central Amazon Floodplain: Actual Use and Options for a Sustainable Management,* pp. 375–392. Backhuys, Leiden, The Netherlands.

Patton, J. L., and M. N. F. Silva. 1998. Rivers, refuges and ridges: geography of speciation of Amazonian mammals. In H. D. Berlocher (ed.), *Endless Forms: Species and Speciation.* Oxford University Press, Oxford.

Peidade, M. T. F., M. Worbes, and W. J. Junk. 2001. Geo-ecological controls on elemental fluxes in communities of higher plants in Amazonian floodplains. In M. E. McClain, R. L. Victoria, and J. E. Richey (eds.), *The Biogeochemistry of the Amazon Basin,* pp. 209–234. Oxford University Press, New York.

Peres, C. A., and B. Zimmerman. 2001. Perils in parks or parks in peril? Reconciling conservation in Amazonian reserves with and without use. *Conservation Biology* 15:793–797.

Petrere, M. 1985. Migraciónes de peces de água dulce en America Latina: algunos comentários. *Copescal Documento Ocasional* 1:1–31.

Pfeiffer, W. C. 1988. Mercury inputs into the Amazon region, Brazil. *Environmental Technology Letters* 9:325–330.

Pfeiffer, W. C., O. Malm, and C. M. M. Souza. 1991. Mercury pollution in the Madeira river ecosystem, Rondônia, Brazil. *Forest Ecology and Management* 38:239–245.

Piedade, M. T. F., and W. J. Junk. 2000. Natural grasslands and herbaceous plants in the Amazon floodplain and their use. In W. J. Junk, J. J. Ohly, M. T. F. Piedade, and M. G. M. Soares (eds.), *The Central Amazon Floodplain: Actual Use and Options for a Sustainable Management*, pp. 269–290. Backhuys, Leiden, The Netherlands.

Pinedo-Vasquez, M. 1999. Changes in soil formation and vegetation on silt bars and backslopes of levees following intensive production of rice and jute. In C. Padoch, J. M. Ayres, M. Pinedo-Vasquez, and A. Henderson (eds.), *Advances in Economic Botany,* Vol. 13, pp. 301–311. New York Botanical Garden Press, New York.

Pires, J. M., and H. M. Koury. 1959. Estudo de um trecho de mata de várzea proximo a Belém. *Boletim Técnico do Instituto Agrônimo do Norte* 36:3–44.

Pires, J. M., and G. T. Prance. 1985. The vegetation types of the Brazilian Amazon. In G. T. Prance and T. E. Lovejoy (eds.), *Key Environments: Amazonia,* pp. 109–145. Peragmon Press, Oxford, England.

Prance, G. T. 1978. The origin and evolution of the Amazonian flora. *Interciência* 3:207–222.

———. 1978. The phytogeographic subdivisions of Amazônia and their influence on the selection of biological reserves. In G. T. Prance and T. S. Elias (eds.), *Extinction Is Forever,* pp. 195–213. New York Botanical Garden Press, Millbrook, New York.

———. 1982. *Biological Diversification in the Tropics.* Columbia University Press, New York.

Prance, G. T., and T. E. Lovejoy. 1985. *Key Environments: Amazonia.* Peragmon Press, Oxford, England.

Putzer, H. 1984. The geological evolution of the Amazon basin and its mineral resources. In H. Sioli (ed.), *The Amazon: Limnology and Landscape Ecology of a Mighty River and Its Basin,* pp. 16–46. Dr. W. Junk, Dordrecht, The Netherlands.

Queiroz, H. L., and W. G. R. Crampton. 1999. *Estratégias para Manejo de Recursos Pesqueiros em Mamirauá.* Sociedade Civil Mamirauá/CNPq, Brasília, Brazil.

Raffles, H. A. 1999. Exploring the anthropogenic Amazon: estuarine landscape transformations in Amapá, Brazil. In C. Padoch, J. M. Ayres, M. Pinedo-Vasquez, and A. Henderson (eds.), *Advances in Economic Botany*, Vol. 13, pp. 355–370. New York Botanical Garden Press, New York.

Rai, H., and G. Hill. 1984. Primary production in the Amazonian aquatic ecosystem. In H. Sioli (ed.), *The Amazon: Limnology and Landscape Ecology of a Mighty River and Its Basin,* pp. 311–335. Dr. W. Junk, Dordrecht, The Netherlands.

Räsänen, M. E., J. Salo, and R. Kalliola. 1987. Fluvial perturbance in the western Amazon basin: regulation by long-term sub-Andean tectonics. *Science* 238:1398–1401.

Räsänen, M. E., A. M. Linna, J. C. R. Santos, and F. R. Negri. 1995. Late Miocene tidal deposits in the Amazonian foreland basin. *Science* 269:386–390.

Räsänen, M., A. Linna, G. Irion, L. R. Hermani, R. V. Huaman, and F. Weisselingh. 1998. Geología y geoformas de la zona de Iquitos. In R. Kalliola and S. F. Paitán (eds.), *Geoecología y Dessarrollo Amazónico: Estudio Integrado en La Zona de Iquitos, Perú,* pp. 59–138. Turun Yliopiston Julkaisuja, Turku, Finland.

Richey, J. E., and N. M. G. Ribero. 1987. Elemental cycling in the Amazon basin biogeochemistry: a riverine perspective, *The Geophysiology of Amazonia,* pp. 245–250. John Wiley & Sons, New York.

Richey, J. E., L. A. Mertes, and R. L. Victoria. 1989. Sources and routing of the Amazon river flood wave. *Global Biogeochemical Cycles* 3:191–204.

Richey, J. E., J. I. Hedges, A. H. Devol, P. D. Quay, R. Vitoria, L. A. Martinelli, and B. R. Forsberg. 1990. Biogeochemistry of carbon in the Amazon river. *Limnology and Oceanography* 35:352–371.

Richey, J. E., R. L. Victoria, and E. Salati. 1991. The biogeochemistry of a major river system: the Amazon case study. In E. T. Degens, S. Kempe, and J. E. Richey (eds.), *Biogeochemistry of Major World Rivers,* pp. 57–74. John Wiley & Sons, New York.

Richey, J. E., J. M. Melack, A. K. Aufdenkampe, V. M. Ballester, and L. L. Hess. 2002. Outgassing from Amazonian rivers and wetlands as a large tropical source of atmospheric CO_2. *Nature* 416:617–620.

Rodríguez Fernandez, C. A. 1999. *Arponeros de la Trampa del Sol (Sustentabilidad de la Pesca Comercial en el Medio río Caquetá).* Tropenbos, Bogotá, Colombia.

Rodríguez Fernandez, R. 1991. *Bagres, Malleros e Cuerderos en El Bajo Rio Caquetá.* Tropenbos, Bogotá, Colombia.

Roosevelt, A. C. 1991. *Mound Builders of the Amazon: Geophysical Archaeology on Marajó Island, Brazil.* Academic Press, San Diego, California.

———. 1999. Twelve thousand years of human-environment interaction in the Amazon floodplain. In C. Padoch, J. M. Ayres, M. Pinedo-Vasquez, and A. Henderson (eds.), *Advances in Economic Botany,* Vol. 13, pp. 371–392. New York Botanical Garden Press, New York.

Rudel, T. K., and B. Horowitz. 1993. *Tropical Deforestation: Small Farmers and Land Clearing in the Ecuadorian Amazon.* Columbia University Press, New York.

Ruffino, M. L. 1999. Fisheries development in the lower Amazon River. In C. Padoch, J. M. Ayres, M. Pinedo-Vasquez, and A. Henderson (eds.), *Advances in Economic Botany,* Vol. 13, pp. 101–111. New York Botanical Garden Press, New York.

Ruokalainen, K., and H. Tuomisto. 1998. Vegetación natural de la zona de Iquitos. In R. Kalliola and S. F. Paitán (eds.), *Geoecología y Dessarrollo Amazónico: Estudio Integrado en La Zona de Iquitos, Perú,* pp. 253–368. Turun Yliopiston Julkaisuja, Turku, Finland.

Salati, E. 1984. Amazon basin: a system in equilibrium. *Science* 225:129–225.

———. 1985. The climatology and hydrology of Amazonia. In G. T. Prance and T. E. Lovejoy (eds.), *Key Environments: Amazonia,* pp. 18–48. Peragmon Press, Oxford, England.

———. 1987. The forest and the hydrological cycle. In R. E. Dickinson (ed.), *The Geophysiology of Amazonia: Vegetation and Climate Interactions,* pp. 273–296. J. Wiley & Sons, New York.

Salati, E., and J. Marques. 1981. Climatology of the Amazon region. In H. Sioli (ed.), *The Amazon: Limnology and Landscape Ecology of a Mighty River and Its Basin,* Vol. 56, pp. 85–126. Dr. W. Junk, Dordrecht, The Netherlands.

Salati, E., J. Marques, and L. Molion. 1978. Origem e distribuição das chuvas na Amazônia. *Interciência* 3:200–205.

Salati, E., T. E. Lovejoy, and P. B. Vose. 1983. Precipitation and water recycling in tropical rainforests with special reference to the Amazon basin. *The Environmentalist* 3:67–71.

Salati, E., P. B. Vose, and T. E. Lovejoy. 1986. Amazon rainfall: potential effects on deforestation and plans for future research. In G. T. Prance (ed.) *Tropical Rain Forests and the World Atmosphere,* pp. 61–74. Westview Press, Boulder, Colorado.

Salati, E., R. L. Victoria, and L. A. Martinelli. 1989. Deforestation and its role in possible changes in the Brazilian Amazon. In R. DeFries and T. F. Malone (eds.), *Global Change and Our Common Future: Papers From a Forum,* pp. 159–171. National Academy of Sciences Press, Washington, D.C.

Salo, J., and J. T. Vásquez. 1998. Potencialidad de uso del recurso biodiversidad en Loreto. In R. Kalliola and S. F. Paitán (eds.), *Geoecología y Dessarrollo Amazónico: Estudio Integrado en La Zona de Iquitos, Perú,* pp. 493–514. Turun Yliopiston Julkaisuja, Turku, Finland.

Seyler, P. T., and G. R. Boaventura. 2001. Trace elements in the mainstem Amazon River. In M. E. McClain, R. L. Victoria, and J. E. Richey (eds.), *The Biogeochemistry of the Amazon Basin,* pp. 307–327. Oxford University Press, New York.

Sierra, R. 2000. Dynamics and patterns of deforestation in the western Amazon: the Napo deforestation front, 1986–1996. *Applied Geography* 20:1–16.

Sioli, H. 1984. The Amazon and its main affluents: hydrography, morphology of the river courses, and river types. In H. Sioli (ed.), *The Amazon: Limnology and Landscape Ecology of a Mighty River and Its Basin,* pp. 127–165. Dr. W. Junk, Dordrecht, The Netherlands.

———. 1984. *The Amazon: Limnology and Landscape Ecology of a Mighty River and Its Basin.* Dr. W. Junk, Dordrecht, The Netherlands.

Smith, N. J. H. 1981. *Man, Fishes and the Amazon.* Columbia University Press, New York.

———. 1985. The impact of cultural and ecological change on Amazonian fisheries. *Biological Conservation* 32:355–373.

———. 1999. *The Amazon River Forest: A Natural History of Plants, Animals, and People.* Oxford University Press, New York.

———. 1999. Land resource management: introduction. In C. Padoch, J. M. Ayres, M. Pinedo-Vasquez, and A. Henderson (eds.), *Advances in Economic Botany,* Vol. 13, pp. 325–328. New York Botanical Garden Press, New York.

———. 2002. *Sweet Sea.* University of Texas Press, Austin, Austin, Texas.

Smith, N. J. H., E. A. S. Serrão, P. T. Alvim, and I. C. Falesi. 1995. *Amazonia: Resiliency and Dynamism of the Land and Its People.* United Nations University Press, Tokyo, Japan.

Soares, M. G. M., and W. J. Junk. 2000. Commercial fishery and fish culture of the state of Amazonas: status and perspectives. In W. J. Junk, J. J. Ohly, M. T. F. Piedade, and M. G. M. Soares (eds.), *The Central Amazon Floodplain: Actual Use and Options for a Sustainable Management,* pp. 433–462. Backhuys, Leiden, The Netherlands.

Sternberg, H. O. R. 1975. *Amazon River of Brazil*. Springer Verlag, New York.

———. 1998. *A Água e o Homem na Várzea do Careiro*. Second Edition. Museu Praense Emilio Goeldi, Belém, Brazil.

Tello, S. 1997. Pesca y esfuerzo de pesca en la Reserva Nacional Pacaya-Samiria y area de influencia. In T. G. Fang, R. E. Bodmer, R. Aquino, and M. H. Valqui (eds.), *Manejo de Fauna Silvestre en la Amazonía,* pp. 229–235. Instituto de Ecología, La Paz, Bolivia.

Tovar Narváez, A., and P. Vásquez Ruesta. 1997. Evaluación ecológica de la Reserva Nacional Pacaya-Samiria (1992–1993). In T. G. Fang, R. E. Bodmer, R. Aquino, and M. H. Valqui (eds.), *Manejo de Fauna Silvestre en la Amazonía,* pp. 87–92. Instituto de Ecología, La Paz, Bolivia.

Tuomisto, H., and K. Ruokolainen. 1998. Uso de especies indicadadoras para determnar características del bosque y de la tierra. In R. Kalliola and S. F. Paitán (eds.), *Geoecología y Dessarrollo Amazónico: Estudio Integrado en La Zona de Iquitos, Perú,* pp. 481–492. Turun Yliopiston Julkaisuja, Turku, Finland.

Tuomisto, H., K. Ruokolainen, and J. Salo. 1992. Lago Amazonas: fact or fancy? *Acta Amazônica* 22:353–361.

Uhl, C., and I. C. G. Vieira. 1989. Ecological impacts of selective logging in the Brazilian Amazon: a case study from the Paragominas region of the state of Pará. *Biotropica* 21:98–106.

Uryu, Y., O. Malm, I. Thornton, I. Payne, and D. Cleary. 2001. Mercury contamination of fish and its implications for other wildlife of the Tapajós Basin, Brazilian Amazon. *Conservation Biology* 15:438–446.

Valle-Ferreira, L. 1997. Is there a difference between the white water floodplain forest (várzea) and back water floodplain forests (Igapó) in relation to number of species and density? *Revista Brasileira de Ecologia* 1:60–62.

Vieira, R. S. 2000. Legislation and the use of Amazonian floodplains. In W. J. Junk, J. J. Ohly, M. T. F. Piedade, and M. G. M. Soares (eds.), *The Central Amazon Floodplain: Actual Use and Options for a Sustainable Management,* pp. 505–534. Backhuys, Leiden, The Netherlands.

Waldhoff, D., and L. M. Alencar. 2000. Production and chemical composition of fruit from trees in floodplain forests of central Amazonia and their importance for fish production. In W. J. Junk, J. J. Ohly, M. T. F. Piedade, and M. G. M. Soares (eds.), *The Central Amazon Floodplain: Actual Use and Options for a Sustainable Management,* pp. 393–416. Backhuys, Leiden, The Netherlands.

Wallace, A. R. 1853. *Narrative of Travels on the Amazon and Rio Negro, With an Account of the Native Tribes, and Observations on the Climate, Geology, and Natural History of the Amazon Valley*. Reeve and Co., London.

Wilson, D. E., and A. Sandoval. 1996. *Manu: The Biodiversity of Southeastern Peru*. Smithsonian Institution Press, Washington, D.C.

Worbes, M., H. Klinge, and J. D. Revilla. 1992. On the dynamics, floristic subdivision and geographical distribution of várzea forests in central Amazonia. *Journal of Vegetation Science* 3:553–564.

PHOTOGRAPHY CREDITS

Oliver Coomes, 122(bottom)

Clark Erickson, 47(left), 156(bottom left), 156(bottom right)

Efrem Ferreira, 129, 224, 225(top), 225(bottom)

Mario Hiraoka, 121(bottom right), 123(top left), 123(top right), 123(bottom left), 123(bottom right), 187(right)

Michael Goulding, 14, 27, 31, 38, 39, 40, 42, 43(top), 43(bottom), 44, 47(right), 48(left), 48(right), 49(left), 49(right), 50(bottom), 51(top), 51(bottom), 54, 57, 58(top), 58(bottom left), 58(bottom right), 59, 61(left), 61(top right), 61(middle), 61(bottom), 62(top), 62(bottom), 64(top), 64(bottom), 66, 67, 68, 69(top), 70(left), 70(right), 71(top), 72, 73, 74, 77(left), 77(top right), 77(bottom), 78, 79(left), 79(right), 80, 81(top), 81(bottom), 82, 83(top), 83(bottom), 84(top left), 84(top right), 84(bottom), 85(left), 85(right), 86(top left), 86(top right), 86(bottom), 88(top), 88(bottom), 89(top), 89(bottom right), 90(top left), 90(bottom left), 90(top right), 90(bottom right), 91(top), 91(middle right), 92(top), 92(bottom), 93(right), 93(left), 94, 95(top), 95(bottom), 96(top), 96(bottom left), 96(bottom right), 97(top), 97(bottom left), 97(bottom right), 100(left), 100(right), 101, 103, 104(top), 104(middle), 104(bottom), 105, 106(top), 106(bottom), 107(top), 107(bottom left), 107(bottom right), 108(top), 108(bottom left), 108(bottom right), 109, 110(top left), 110(top right), 110(bottom left), 110(bottom right), 111(top), 111(bottom), 112(top), 112(bottom left), 112(bottom right), 113(top), 113(bottom left), 113(bottom right), 114, 115(top), 115(bottom right), 121(bottom left), 122(top), 128(top left), 128(top right), 128(bottom left), 128(bottom right), 130, 131(top), 131(bottom left), 131(bottom right), 132, 133(left), 133(right)134, 138, 139(top), 139(bottom left), 139(bottom right), 140(top), 140(middle), 140(bottom), 141, 144(top), 144(bottom), 145(top), 145(bottom), 146, 150(top), 150(bottom), 151(top), 151(middle), 151(bottom), 152, 153, 154, 155, 156(top), 158(top), 158(bottom), 159(left), 159(right), 160(top), 160(middle), 160(bottom), 161(top), 161(bottom), 162, 163(top), 163(bottom), 164(top), 164(bottom left), 164(bottom right), 165, 166(top), 166(bottom left), 166(bottom right), 167(top), 167(bottom left), 167(bottom right), 168(top), 168(middle), 168(bottom), 169(top), 169(bottom), 170(top), 170(bottom left), 170(bottom right), 171(top), 171(middle), 171(bottom), 176, 177, 180(top left), 180(bottom left), 180(right), 181(top), 181(middle), 181(bottom), 182, 186, 188(top), 188(bottom), 189(top), 189(bottom), 190, 191(top), 191(bottom), 192(top), 192(bottom left), 192(bottom right), 193(top), 193(middle), 193(bottom), 194(top), 194(middle), 194(bottom), 197, 198(top left), 198(top right), 198(bottom left), 198(bottom right), 199(top), 199(middle left), 199(middle right), 199(bottom), 210, 214(top), 215(top left), 215(bottom left), 215(top right), 215(bottom right), 216, 217(top), 217(bottom left), 217(bottom right), 218, 219(top), 219(bottom left), 219(bottom right), 220(top left), 220(top right), 220(bottom), 221(top), 221(middle), 221(bottom), 222(top), 222(bottom), 223(top), 223(bottom), 226, 231, 254-255, back cover

Loren McIntyre, 1, 2, 3, 4, 5, 6, 11, 23, 52, 98, 124, 172

Luiz Claudio Marigo, Cover, 2, 12, 46, 50(top), 69(bottom), 71(bottom), 115(bottom left), 116, 117(top), 117(bottom), 118(top), 118(bottom left), 118(bottom right), 119, 120(top), 120(bottom), 200, 214(bottom)

Heinz Plenge, 187(left)

Carlos Alberto Rodríguez, 204(left), 204(right), 205

Nigel Smith, 89(bottom left), 91(middle left), 91(bottom)

INDEX

FOLLOWING PAGES:
TIDAL FOREST OF AMAZON ESTUARY
Near the Atlantic the Amazon's floodplain forests are inundated twice daily by the tides, such as shown here along a small river in the state of Amapá, Brazil.